Captain America
The Extremists

MARVEL KNIGHTS

STORY
JOHN NEY RIEBER AND CHUCK AUSTEN

PENCILS
TREVOR HAIRSINE AND JAE LEE

INKS
JAE LEE AND DANNY MIKI
WITH ALLEN MARTINEZ

COLORS
DAVE STEWART AND JOSE VILLARRUBIA

LETTERS
DAVE SHARPE
WITH RICHARD STARKINGS AND COMICRAFT'S WES ABBOTT

COVER ART
JOHN CASSADAY

EDITOR
JOE QUESADA

ASSISTANT EDITOR
NICK LOWE

ASSOCIATE MANAGING EDITOR
KELLY LAMY

MANAGING EDITOR
NANCI DAKESIAN

EDITOR IN CHIEF
JOE QUESADA

PRESIDENT
BILL JEMAS

Captain America

THE EXTREMISTS

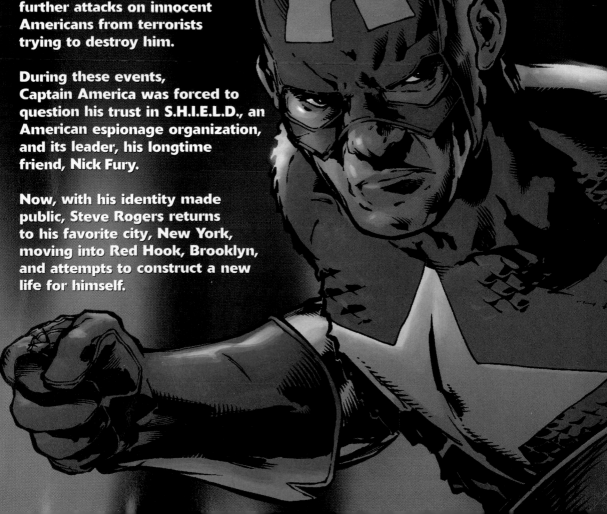

PREVIOUSLY IN CAPTAIN AMERICA ...

After defeating a band of terrorists in a small town in Kansas, Captain America revealed his secret identity to the world, in hopes of avoiding further attacks on innocent Americans from terrorists trying to destroy him.

During these events, Captain America was forced to question his trust in S.H.I.E.L.D., an American espionage organization, and its leader, his longtime friend, Nick Fury.

Now, with his identity made public, Steve Rogers returns to his favorite city, New York, moving into Red Hook, Brooklyn, and attempts to construct a new life for himself.

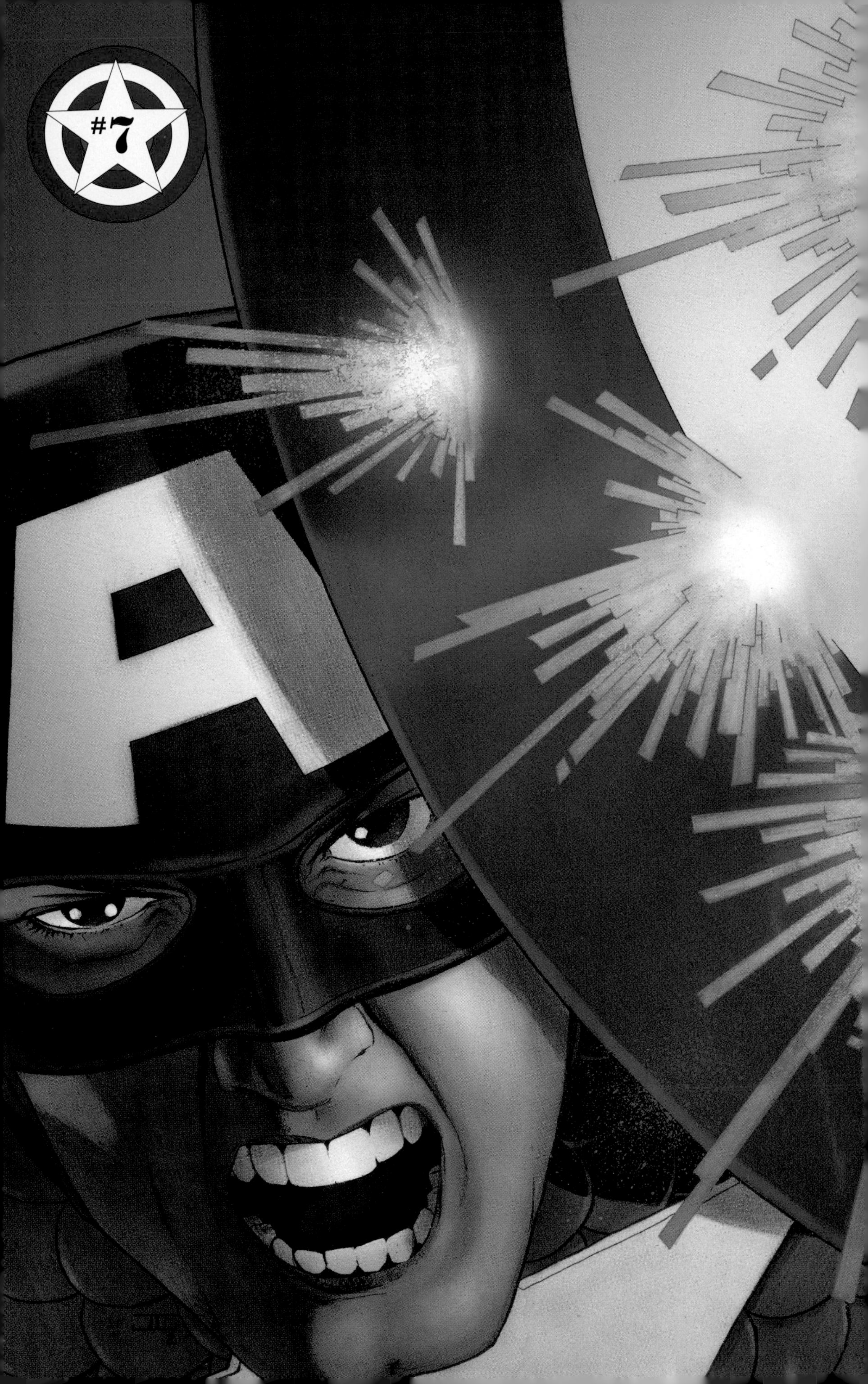
#7

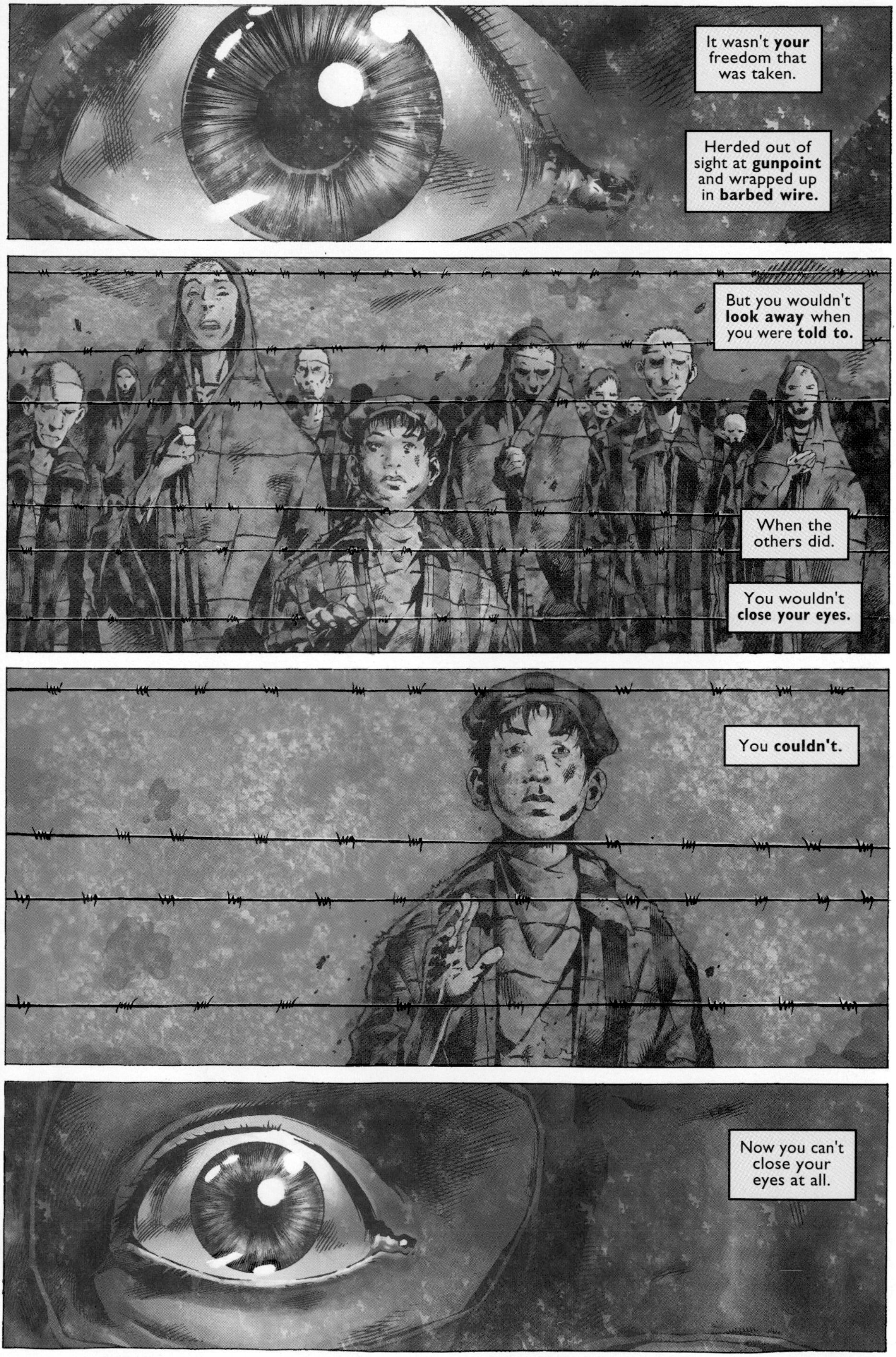
It wasn't your freedom that was taken.
Herded out of sight at gunpoint and wrapped up in barbed wire.
But you wouldn't look away when you were told to.
When the others did.
You wouldn't close your eyes.
You couldn't.
Now you can't close your eyes at all.

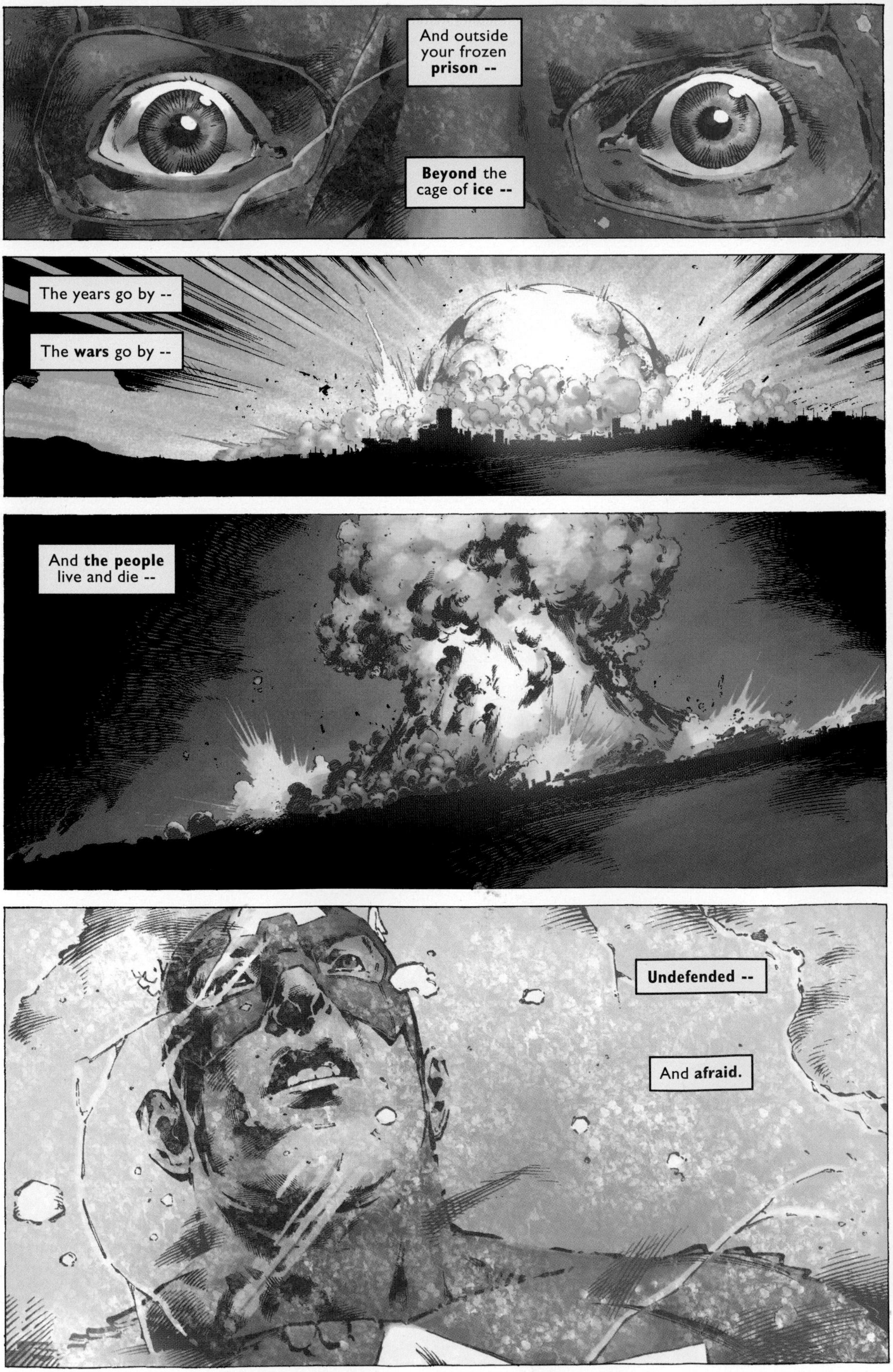
And outside your frozen **prison --**
Beyond the cage of **ice --**
The years go by --
The **wars** go by --
And **the people** live and die --
Undefended --
And **afraid.**

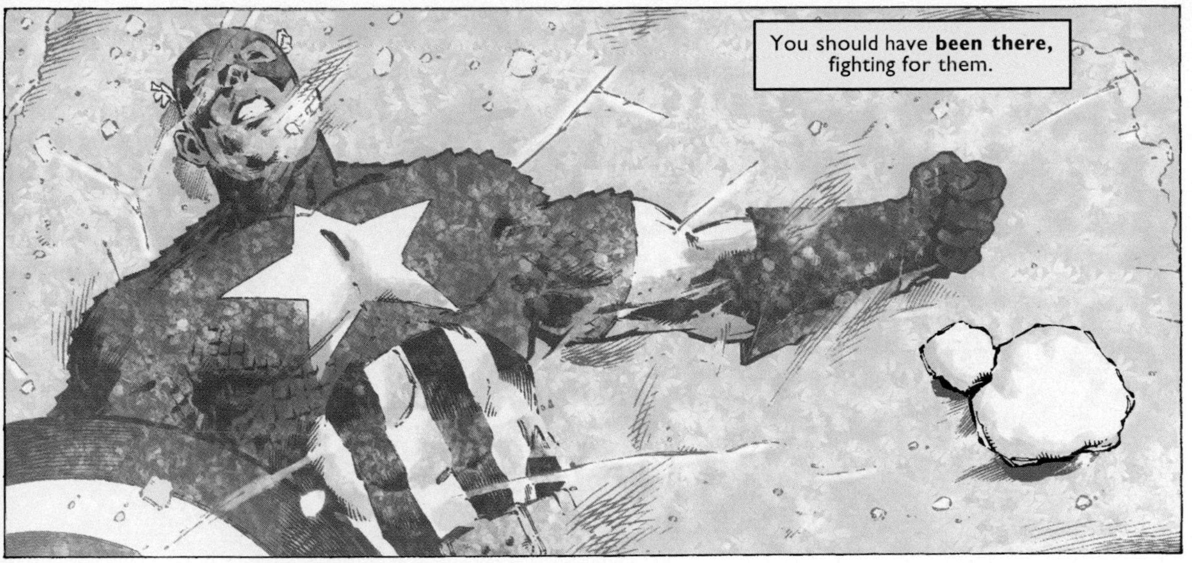
You should have **been there,** fighting for them.

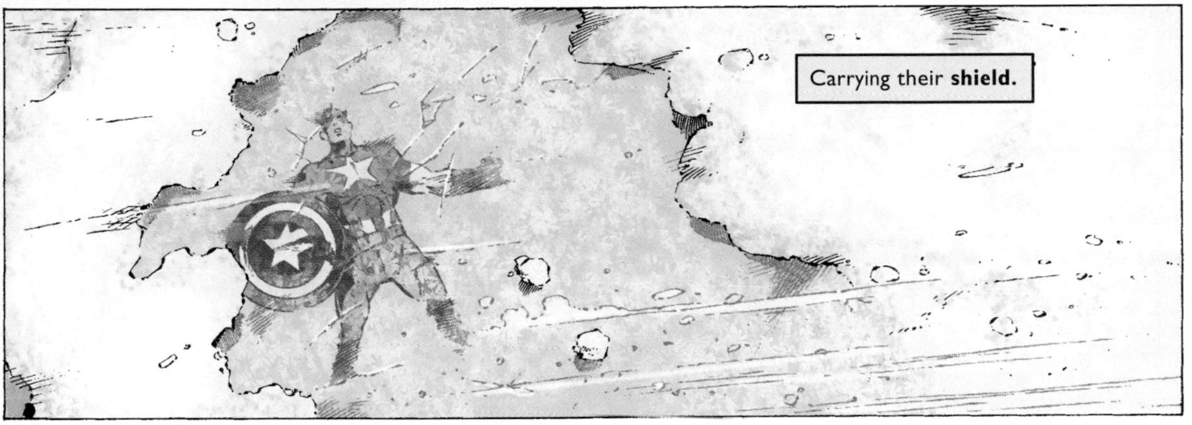
Carrying their **shield.**

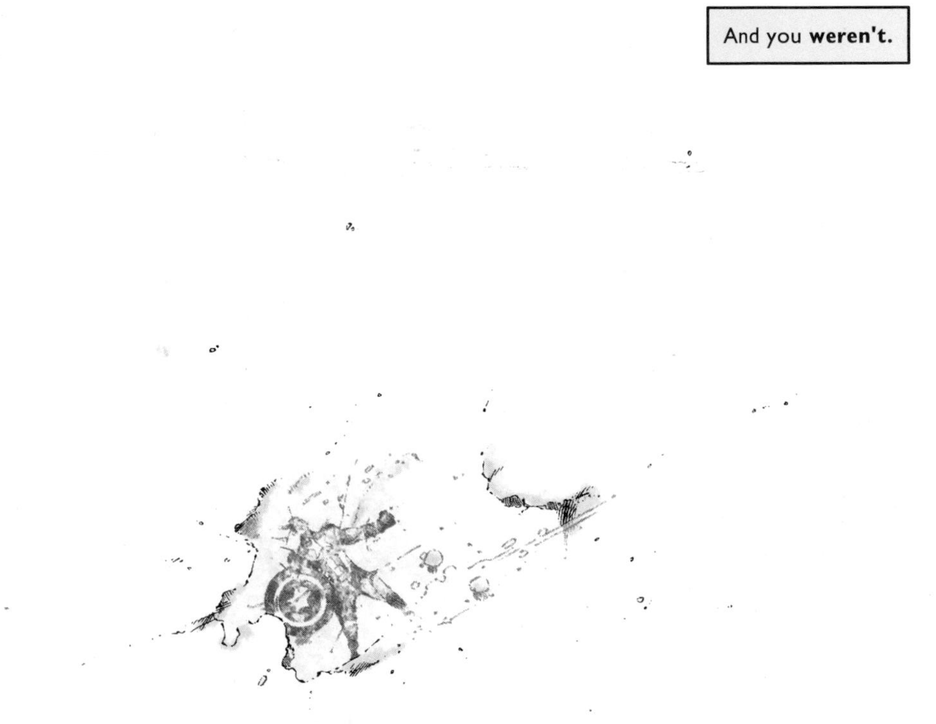
And you **weren't.**

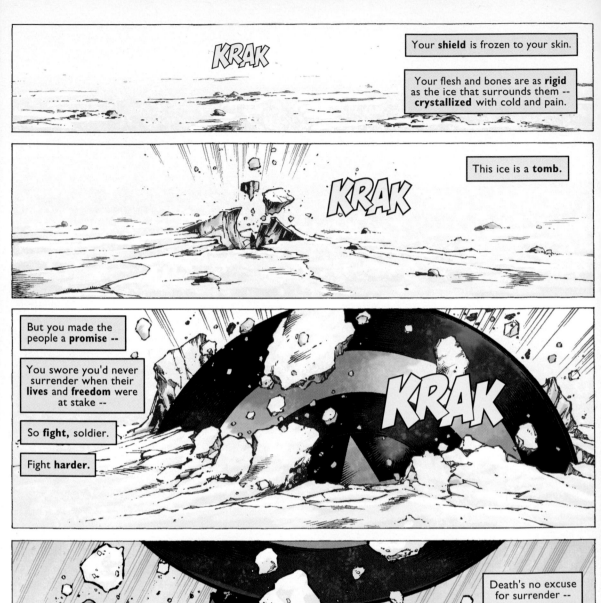

KRAK

Your **shield** is frozen to your skin.

Your flesh and bones are as **rigid** as the ice that surrounds them -- **crystallized** with cold and pain.

KRAK

This ice is a **tomb.**

But you made the people a **promise** --

You swore you'd never surrender when their **lives** and **freedom** were at stake --

So **fight,** soldier.

Fight **harder.**

KRAK

Death's no excuse for surrender --

When it's **freedom** you're fighting for.

KRAK

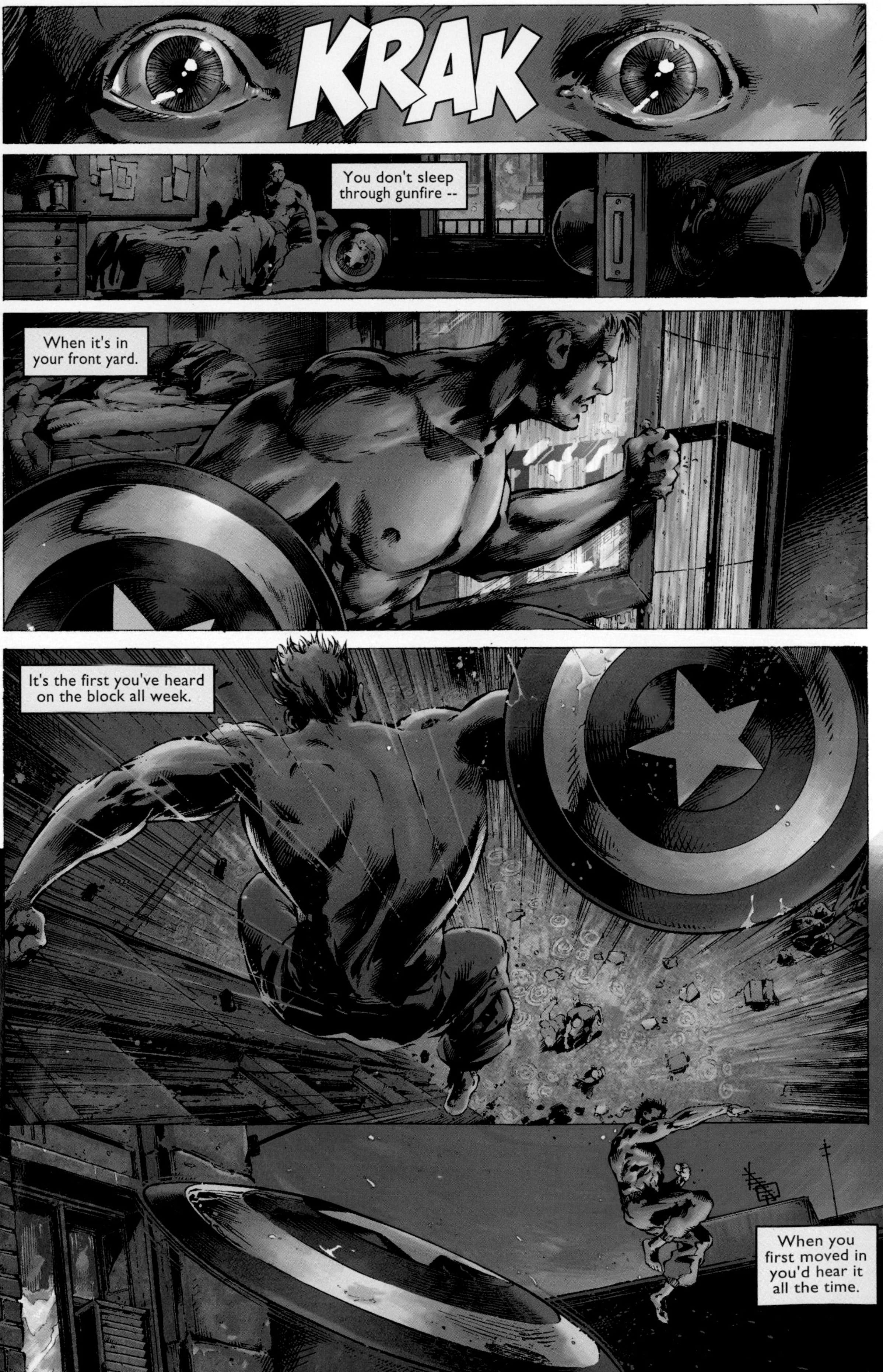
KRAK
You don't sleep through gunfire --
When it's in your front yard.
It's the first you've heard on the block all week.
When you first moved in you'd hear it all the time.

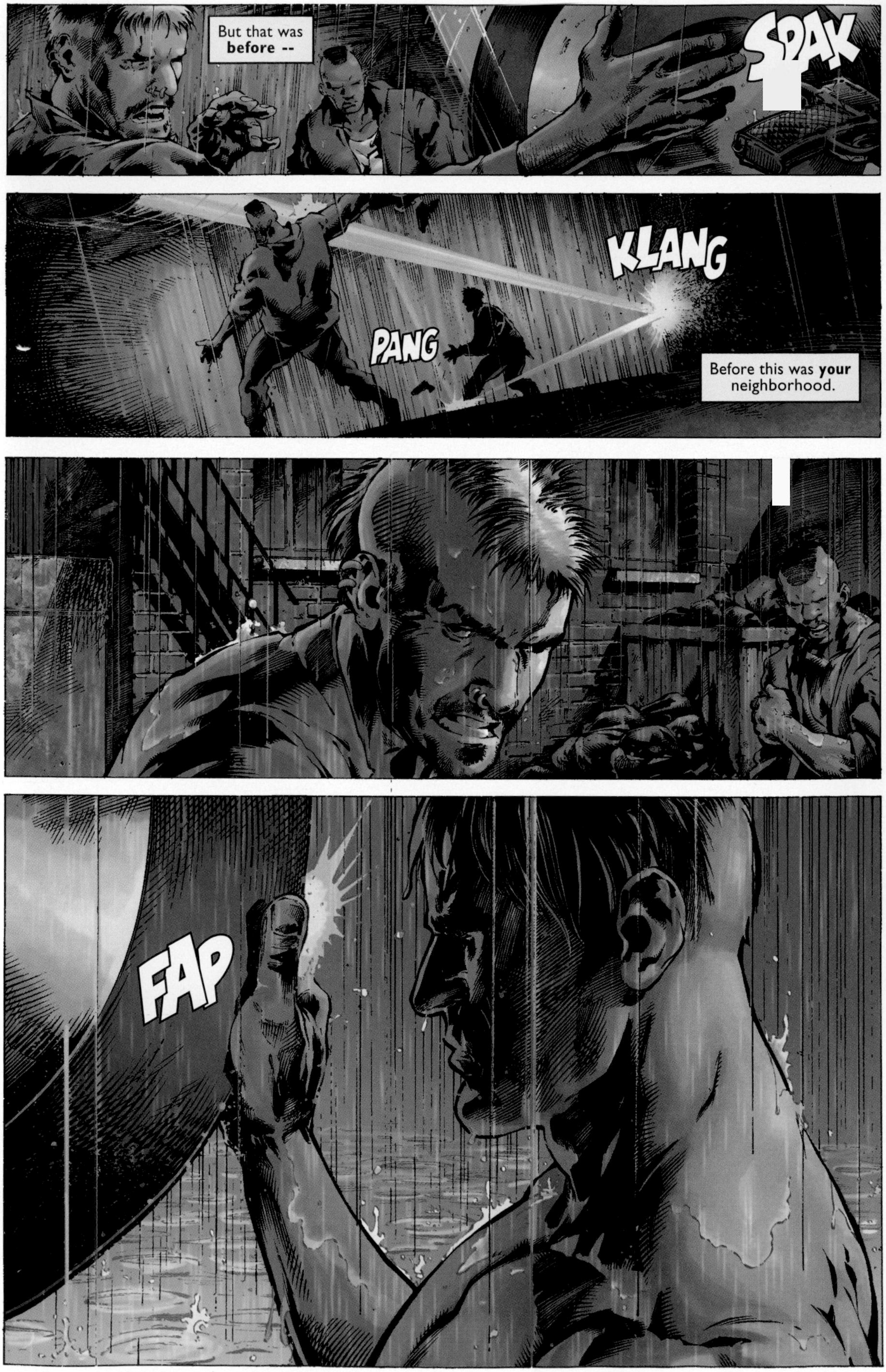
But that was before --
SPAK
KLANG
PANG
Before this was your neighborhood.
FAP

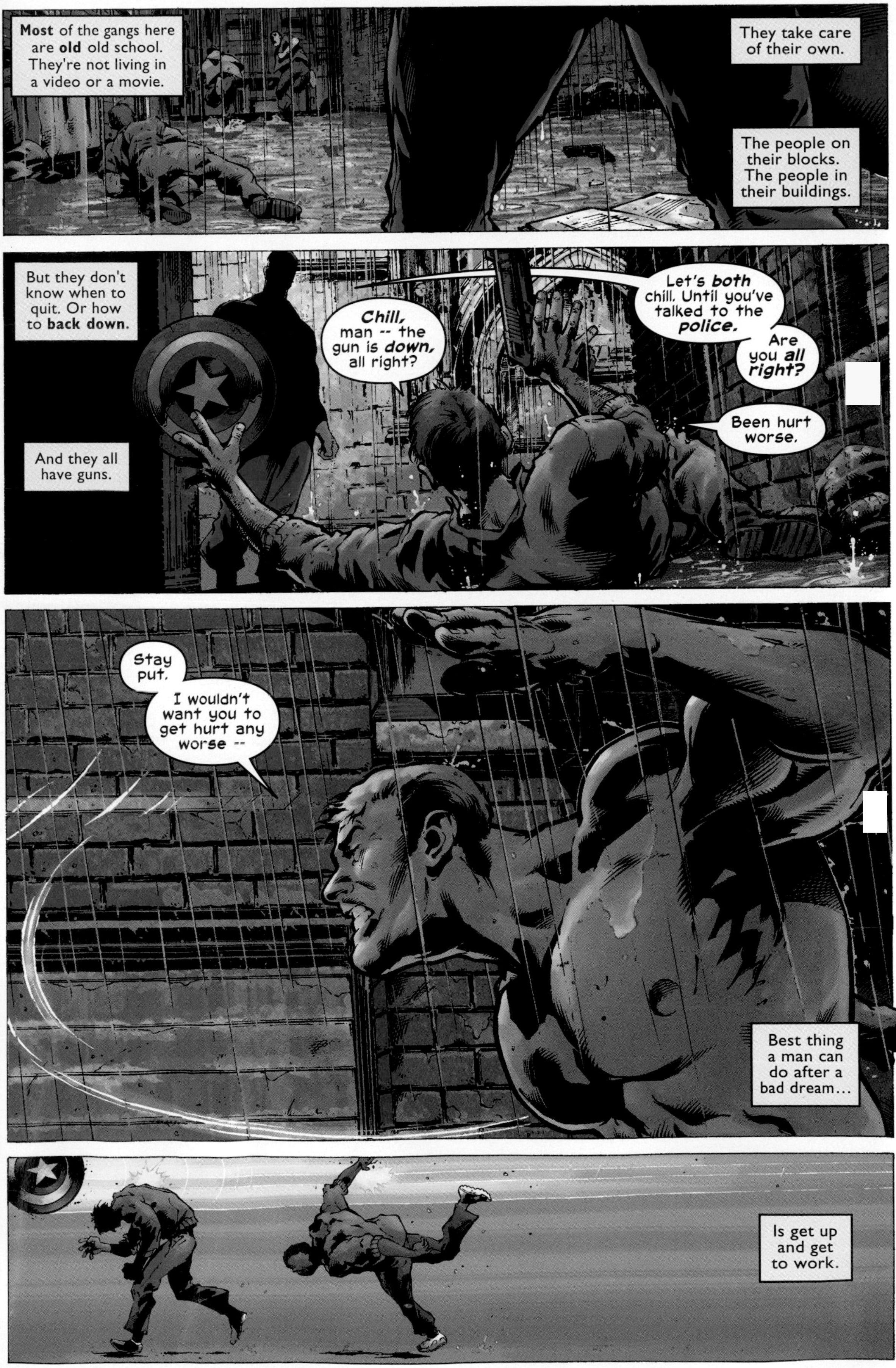

Most of the gangs here are old old school. They're not living in a video or a movie.
They take care of their own.
The people on their blocks. The people in their buildings.
But they don't know when to quit. Or how to back down.
And they all have guns.
Chill, man -- the gun is down, all right?
Let's both chill. Until you've talked to the police.
Are you all right?
Been hurt worse.
Stay put.
I wouldn't want you to get hurt any worse --
Best thing a man can do after a bad dream...
Is get up and get to work.

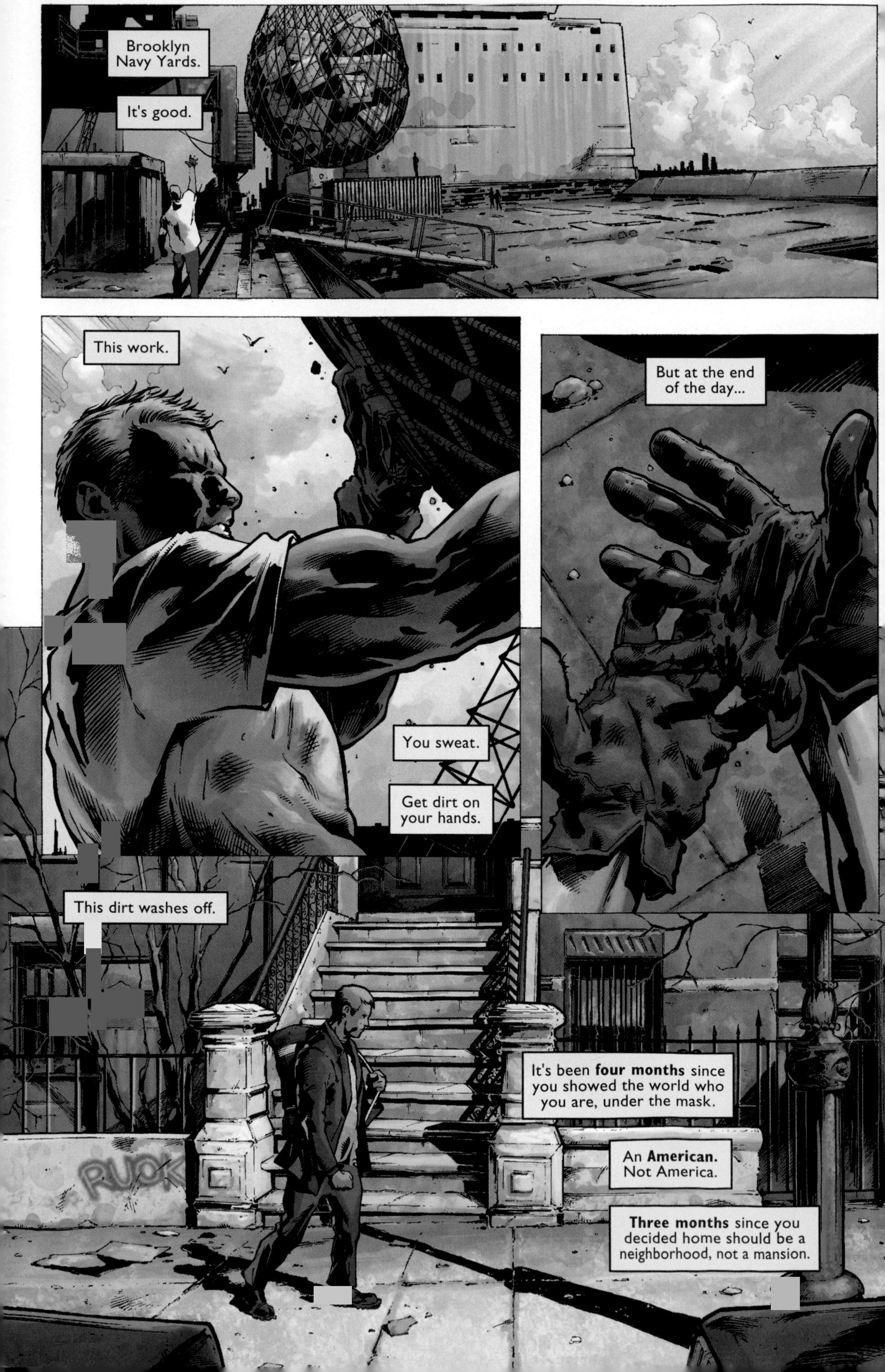

Brooklyn Navy Yards.
It's good.
This work.
You sweat.
Get dirt on your hands.
But at the end of the day...
This dirt washes off.
It's been **four months** since you showed the world who you are, under the mask.
An **American.** Not America.
Three months since you decided home should be a neighborhood, not a mansion.

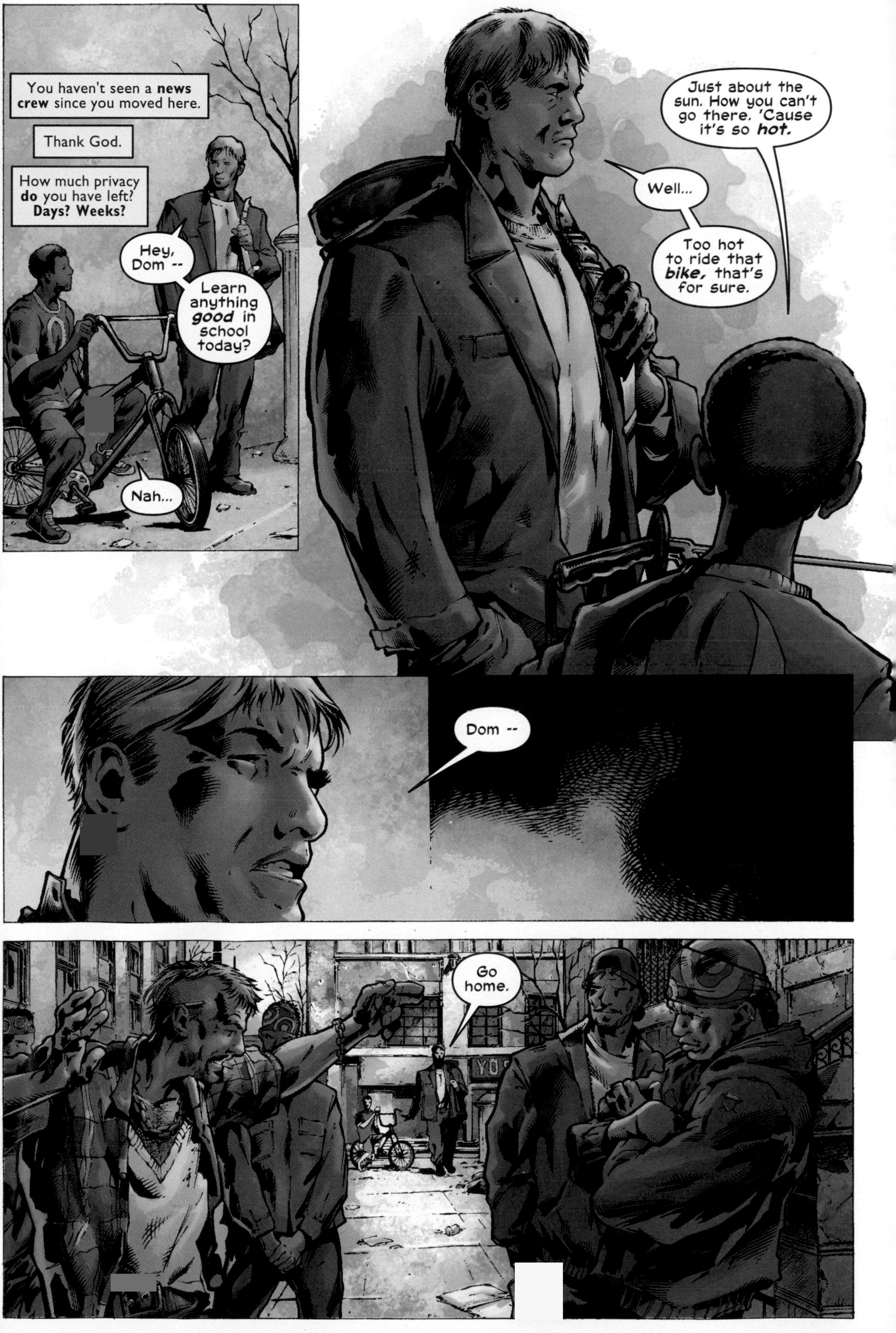
You haven't seen a **news crew** since you moved here.
Thank God.
How much privacy **do** you have left? **Days? Weeks?**
Hey, Dom --
Learn anything ***good*** in school today?
Nah...
Well...
Just about the sun. How you can't go there. 'Cause it's so ***hot.***
Too hot to ride that ***bike,*** that's for sure.
Dom --
Go home.

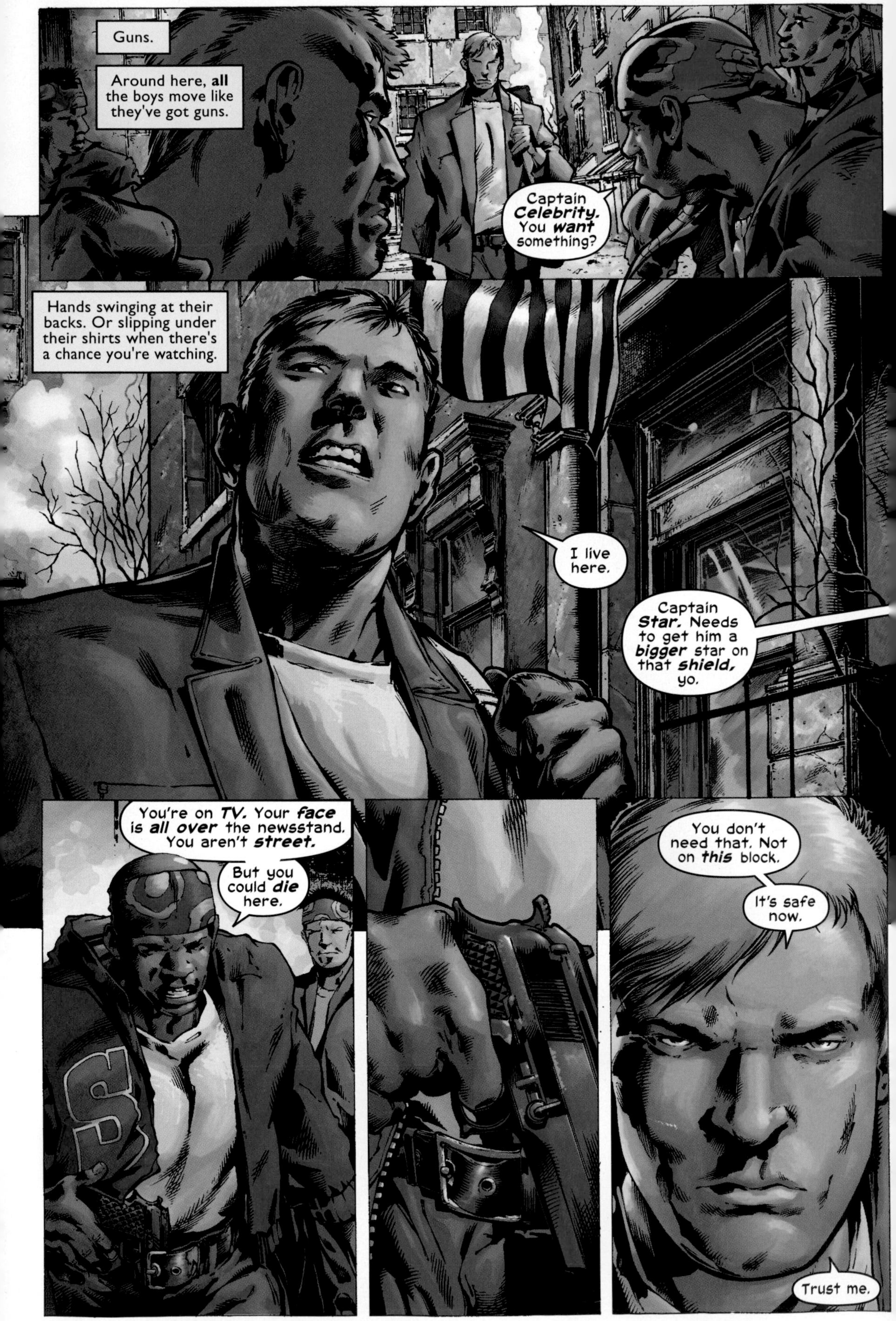
Guns.
Around here, **all** the boys move like they've got guns.
Captain ***Celebrity.*** You ***want*** something?
Hands swinging at their backs. Or slipping under their shirts when there's a chance you're watching.
I live here.
Captain ***Star.*** Needs to get him a ***bigger*** star on that ***shield,*** yo.
You're on ***TV.*** Your ***face*** is ***all over*** the newsstand. You aren't ***street.***
But you could ***die*** here.
You don't need that. Not on ***this*** block.
It's safe now.
Trust me.

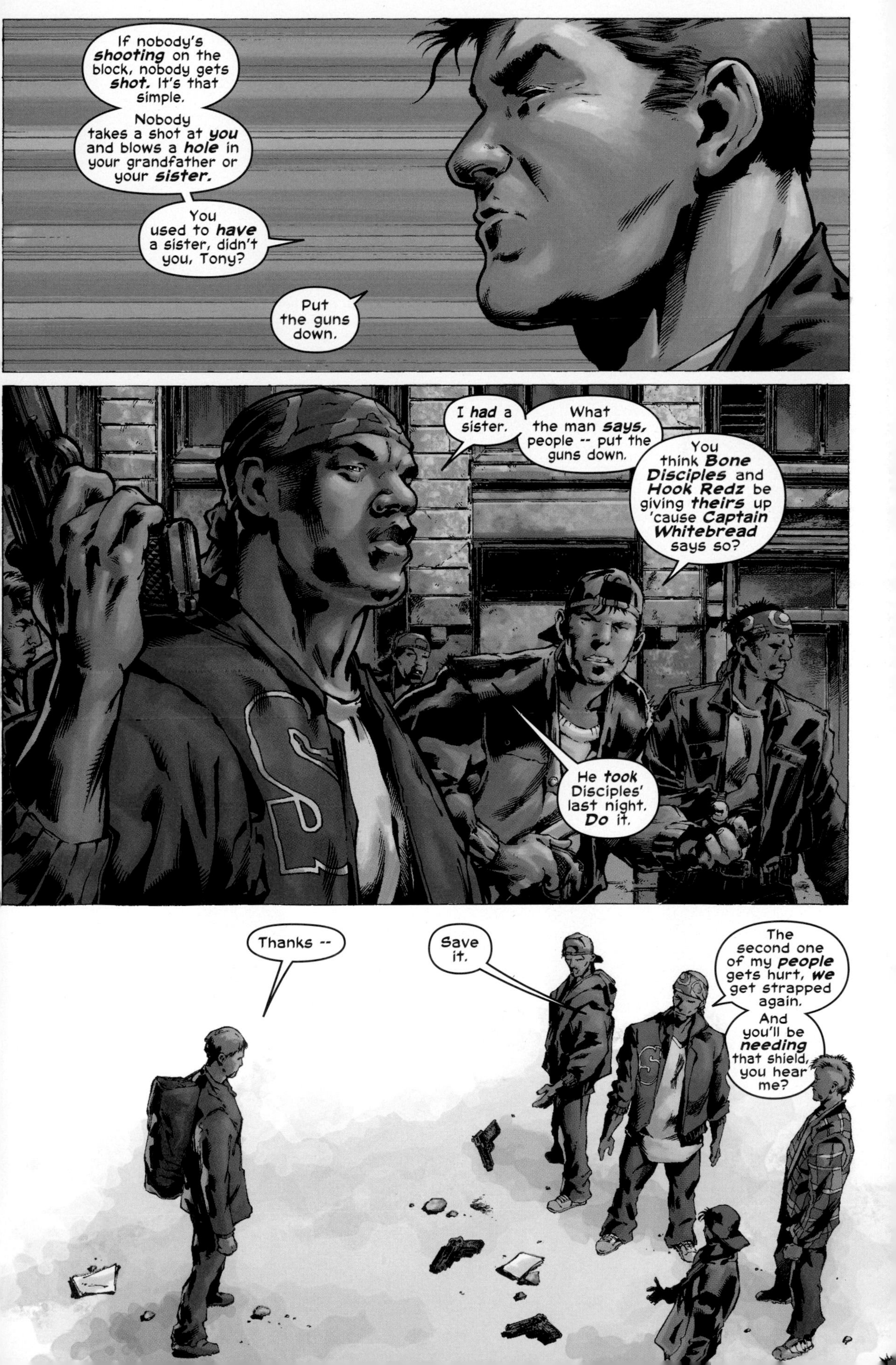

If nobody's shooting on the block, nobody gets shot. It's that simple.
Nobody takes a shot at you and blows a hole in your grandfather or your sister.
You used to have a sister, didn't you, Tony?
Put the guns down.
I had a sister.
What the man says, people -- put the guns down.
You think Bone Disciples and Hook Redz be giving theirs up 'cause Captain Whitebread says so?
He took Disciples' last night. Do it.
Thanks --
Save it.
The second one of my people gets hurt, we get strapped again.
And you'll be needing that shield, you hear me?

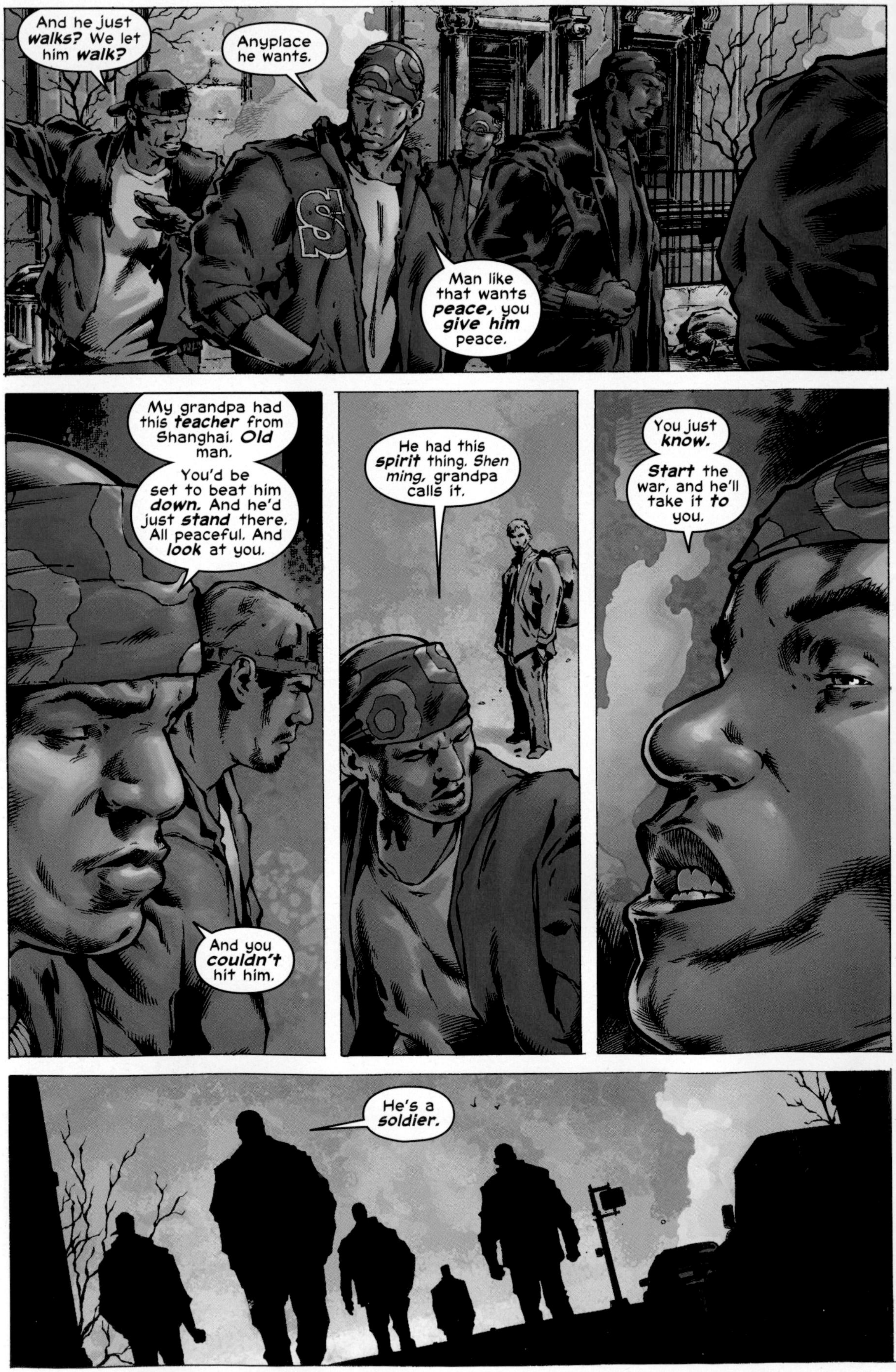
And he just walks? We let him walk?
Anyplace he wants.
Man like that wants peace, you give him peace.
My grandpa had this teacher from Shanghai. Old man.
You'd be set to beat him down. And he'd just stand there. All peaceful. And look at you.
And you couldn't hit him.
He had this spirit thing. Shen ming, grandpa calls it.
You just know.
Start the war, and he'll take it to you.
He's a soldier.

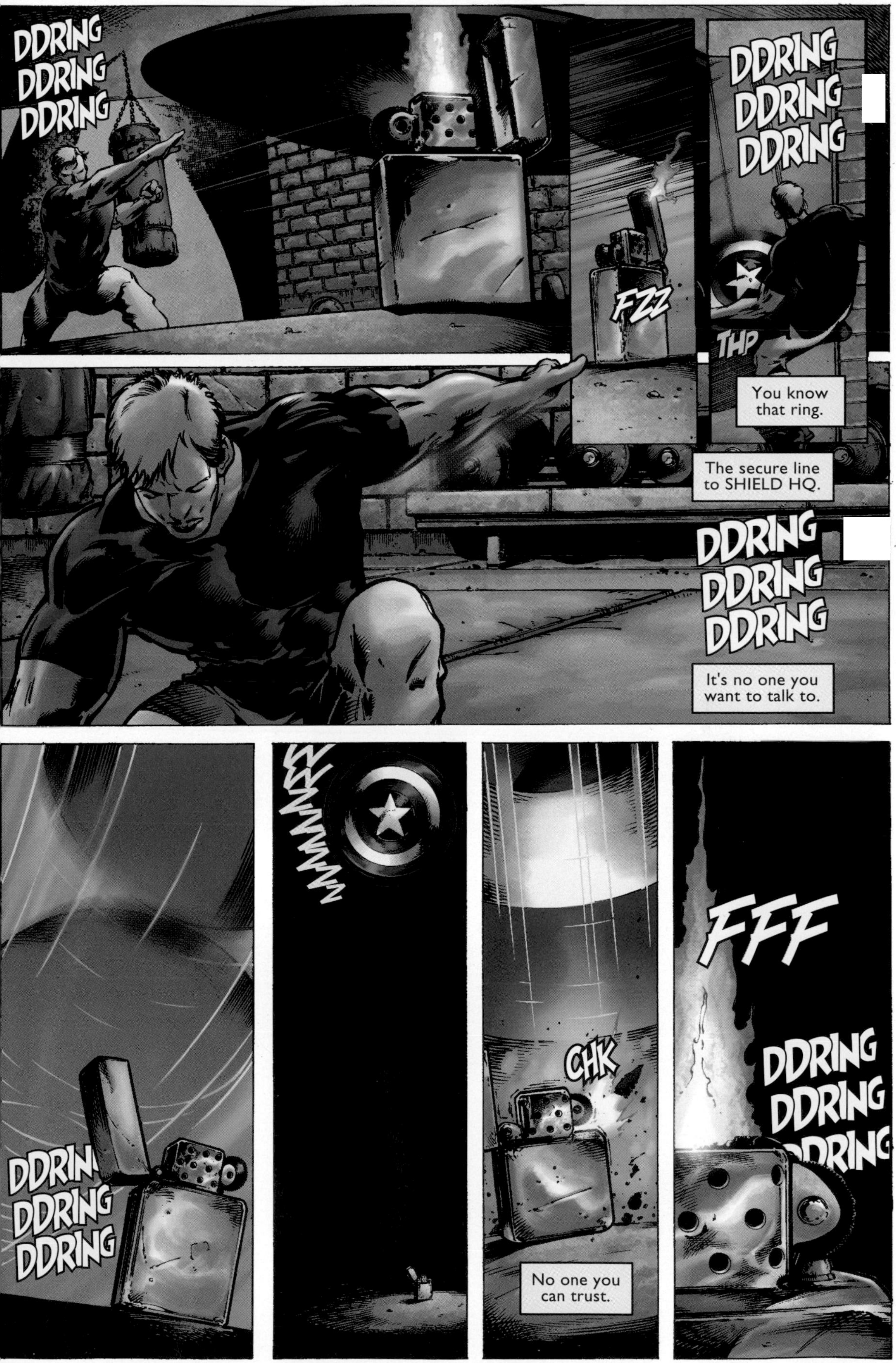
DDRING
DDRING
DDRING
FZZ
DDRING
DDRING
DDRING
THP
You know that ring.
The secure line to SHIELD HQ.
DDRING
DDRING
DDRING
It's no one you want to talk to.
DDRING
DDRING
CHK
No one you can trust.
FFF
DDRING
DDRING

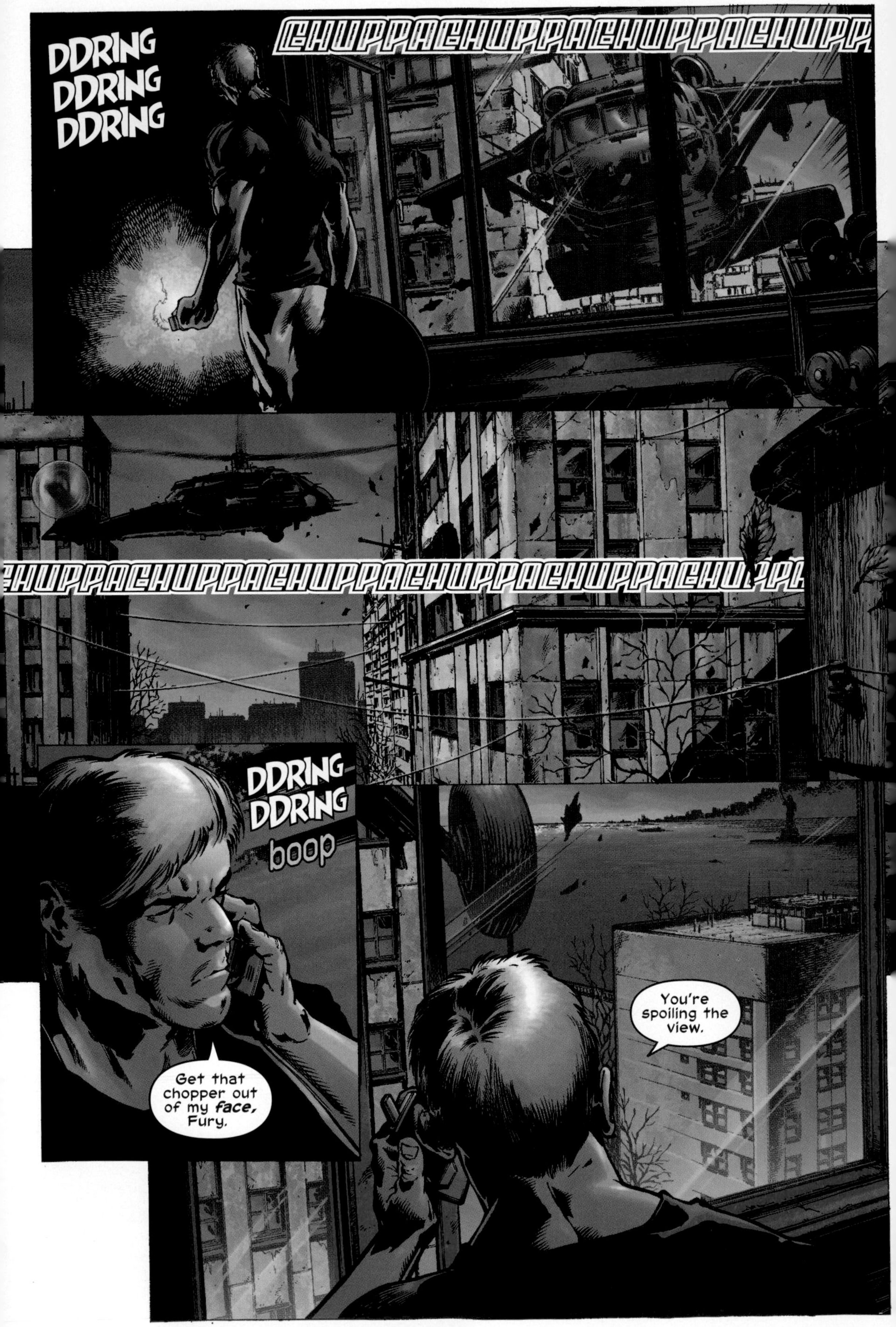
DDRING
DDRING
DDRING
CHUPPACHUPPACHUPPACHUPP
CHUPPACHUPPACHUPPACHUPPACHUPPACHUPP
DDRING
DDRING
boop
Get that chopper out of my *face,* Fury.
You're spoiling the view.

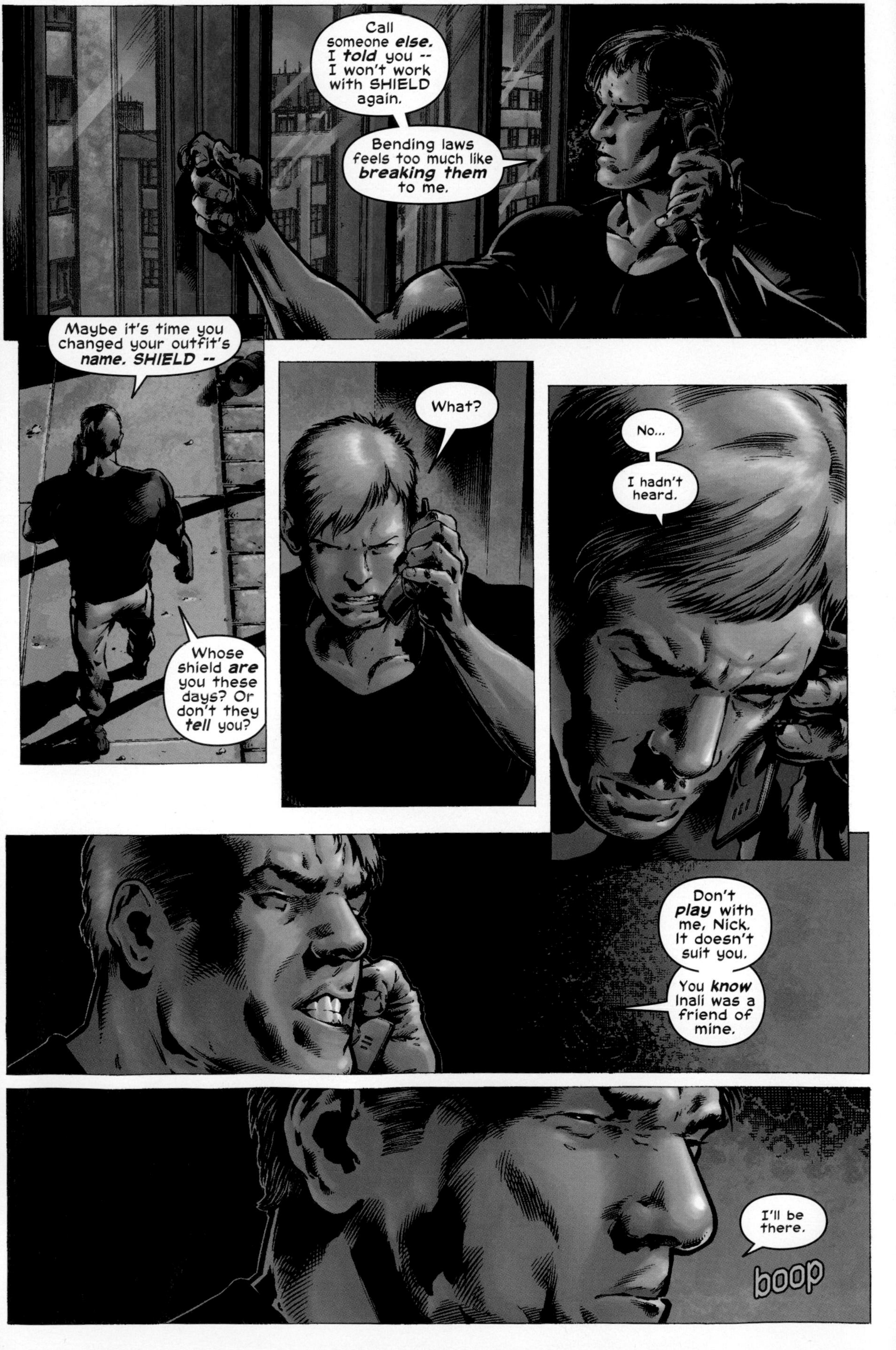

Call someone *else.* I *told* you -- I won't work with SHIELD again.
Bending laws feels too much like *breaking them* to me.
Maybe it's time you changed your outfit's *name. SHIELD --*
Whose shield *are* you these days? Or don't they *tell* you?
What?
No...
I hadn't heard.
Don't *play* with me, Nick. It doesn't suit you.
You *know* Inali was a friend of mine.
I'll be there.
boop

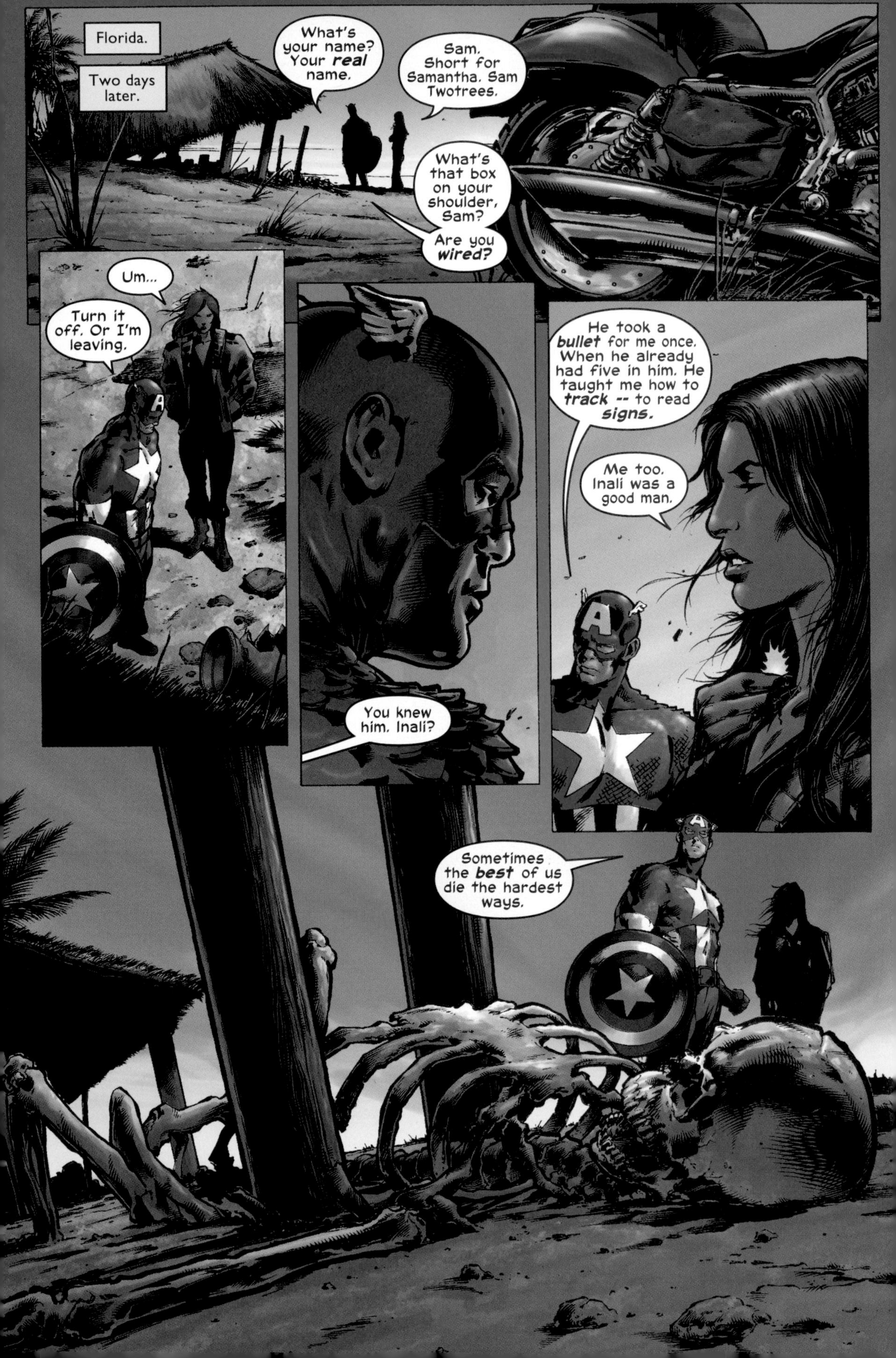
Florida.
Two days later.
What's your name? Your *real* name.
Sam. Short for Samantha. Sam Twotrees.
What's that box on your shoulder, Sam?
Are you *wired?*
Um...
Turn it off. Or I'm leaving.
You knew him. Inali?
He took a *bullet* for me once. When he already had five in him. He taught me how to *track* -- to read *signs.*
Me too. Inali was a good man.
Sometimes the *best* of us die the hardest ways.

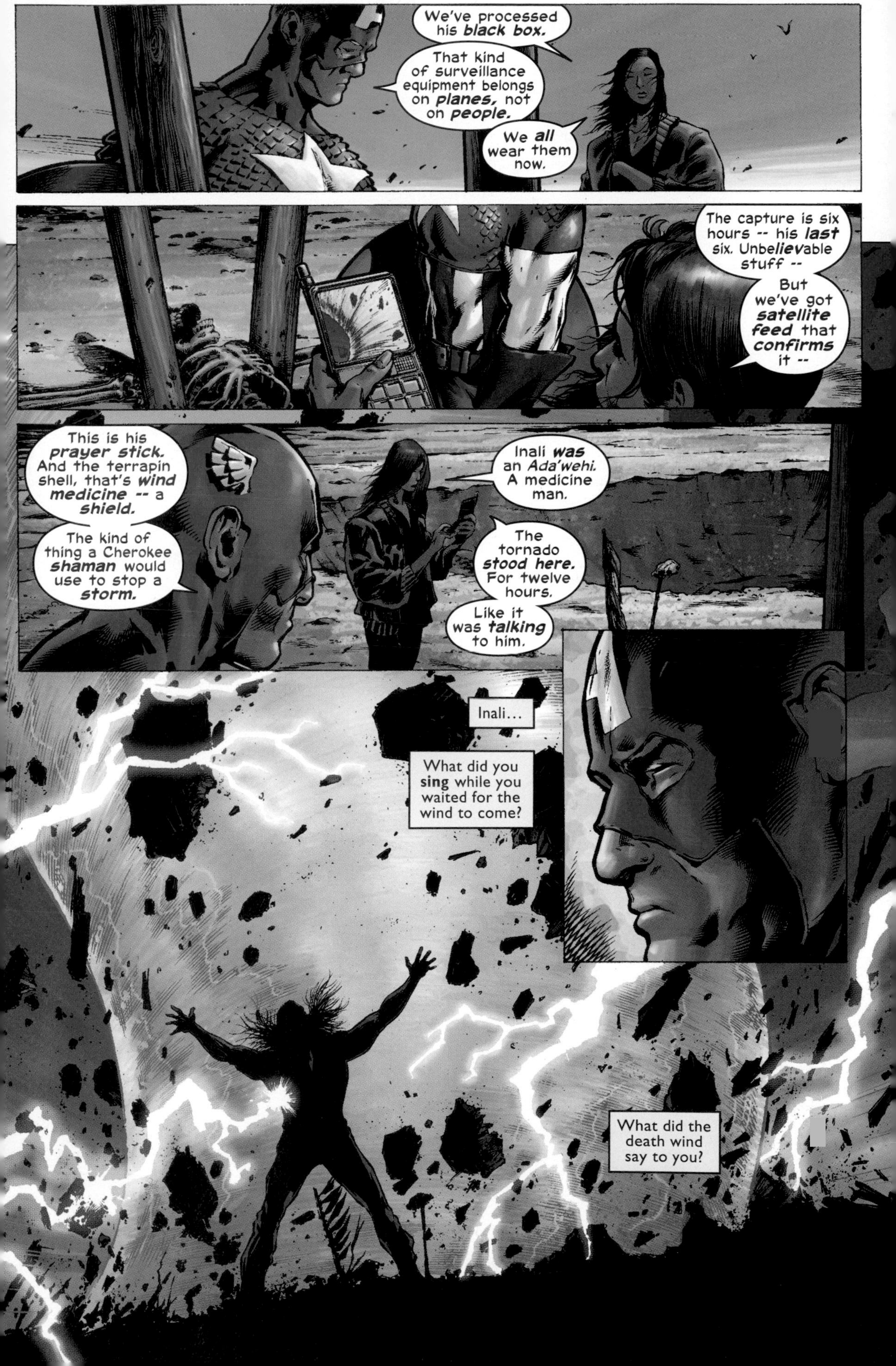

We've processed his black box.
That kind of surveillance equipment belongs on planes, not on people.
We all wear them now.
The capture is six hours -- his last six. Unbelievable stuff --
But we've got satellite feed that confirms it --
This is his prayer stick. And the terrapin shell, that's wind medicine -- a shield.
The kind of thing a Cherokee shaman would use to stop a storm.
Inali was an Ada'wehi. A medicine man.
The tornado stood here. For twelve hours.
Like it was talking to him.
Inali...
What did you sing while you waited for the wind to come?
What did the death wind say to you?

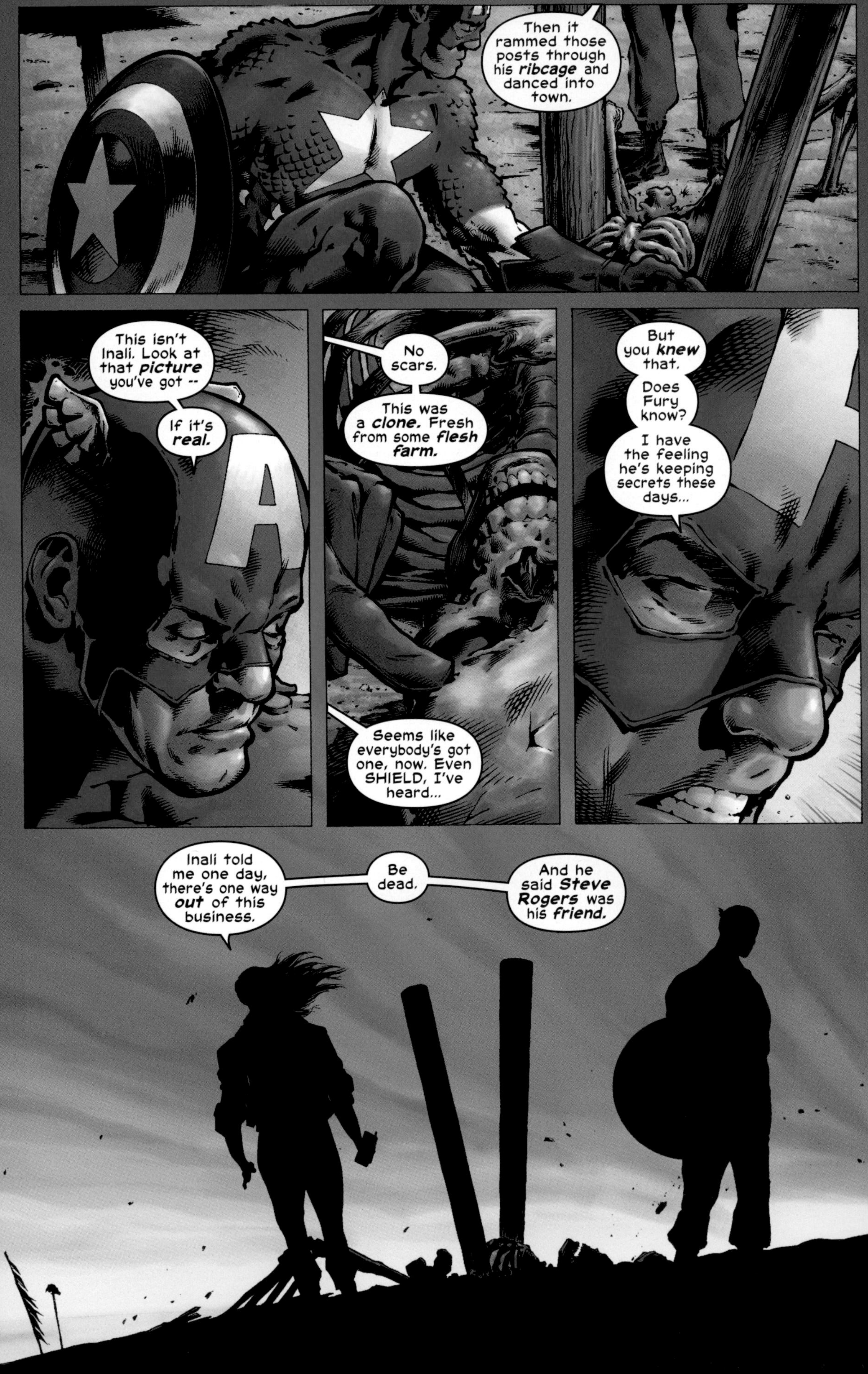

Then it rammed those posts through his ribcage and danced into town.
This isn't Inali. Look at that picture you've got --
If it's real.
No scars.
This was a clone. Fresh from some flesh farm.
Seems like everybody's got one, now. Even SHIELD, I've heard...
But you knew that.
Does Fury know?
I have the feeling he's keeping secrets these days...
Inali told me one day, there's one way out of this business.
Be dead.
And he said Steve Rogers was his friend.

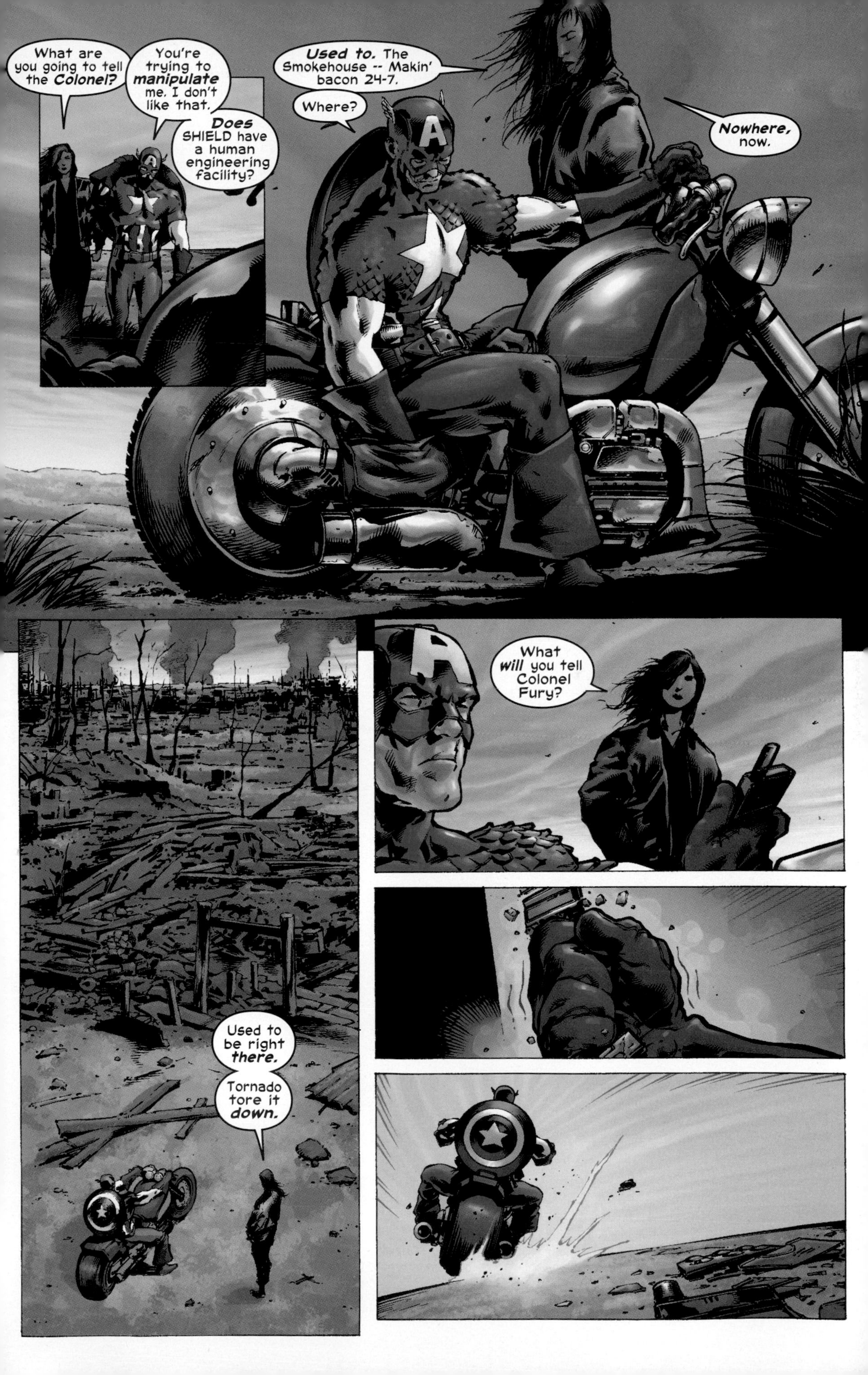
What are you going to tell the *Colonel?*
You're trying to *manipulate* me. I don't like that.
Does SHIELD have a human engineering facility?
Used to. The Smokehouse -- Makin' bacon 24-7.
Where?
Nowhere, now.
Used to be right *there.*
Tornado tore it *down.*
What *will* you tell Colonel Fury?

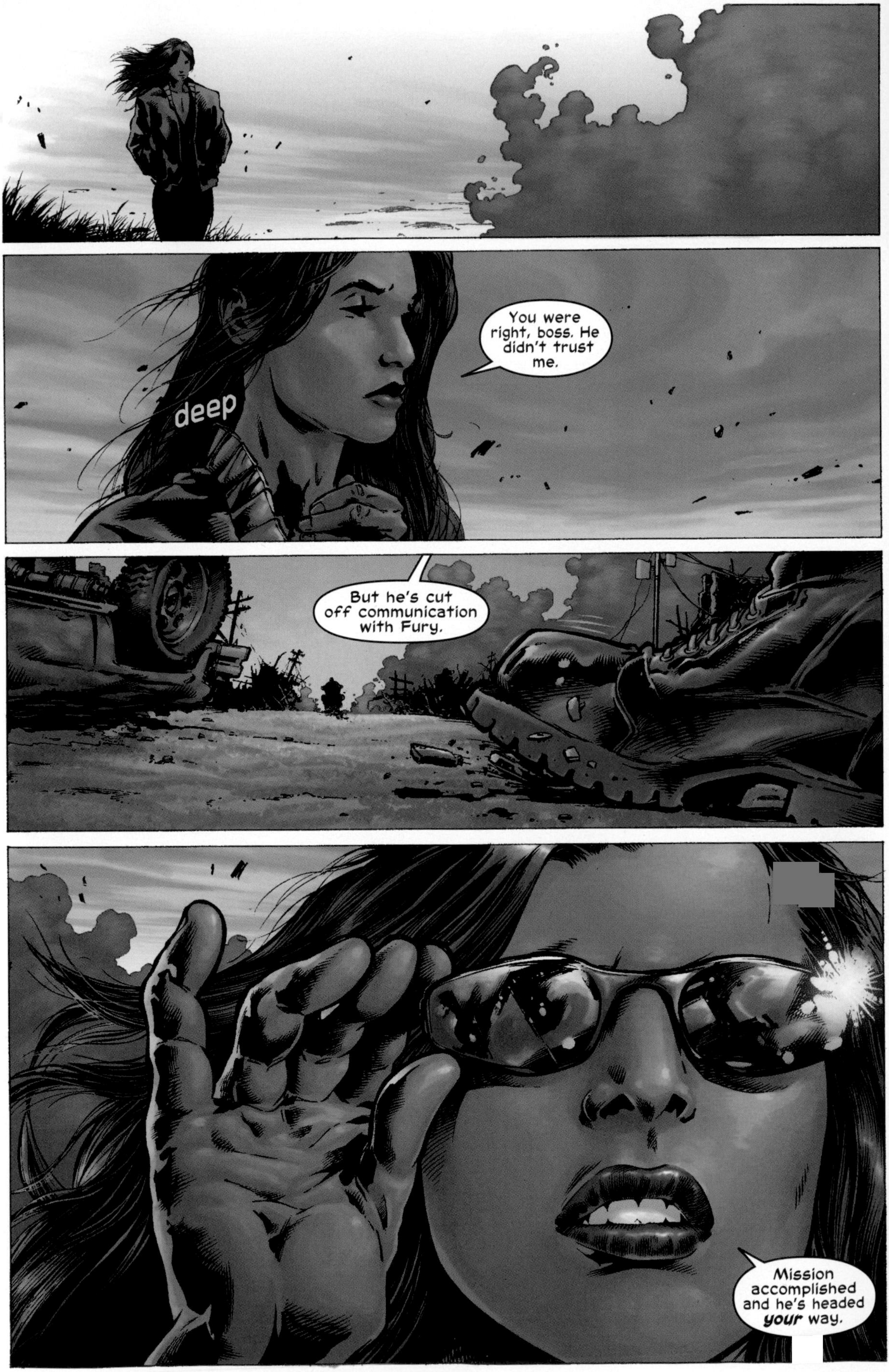
deep
You were right, boss. He didn't trust me.
But he's cut off communication with Fury.
Mission accomplished and he's headed *your* way.

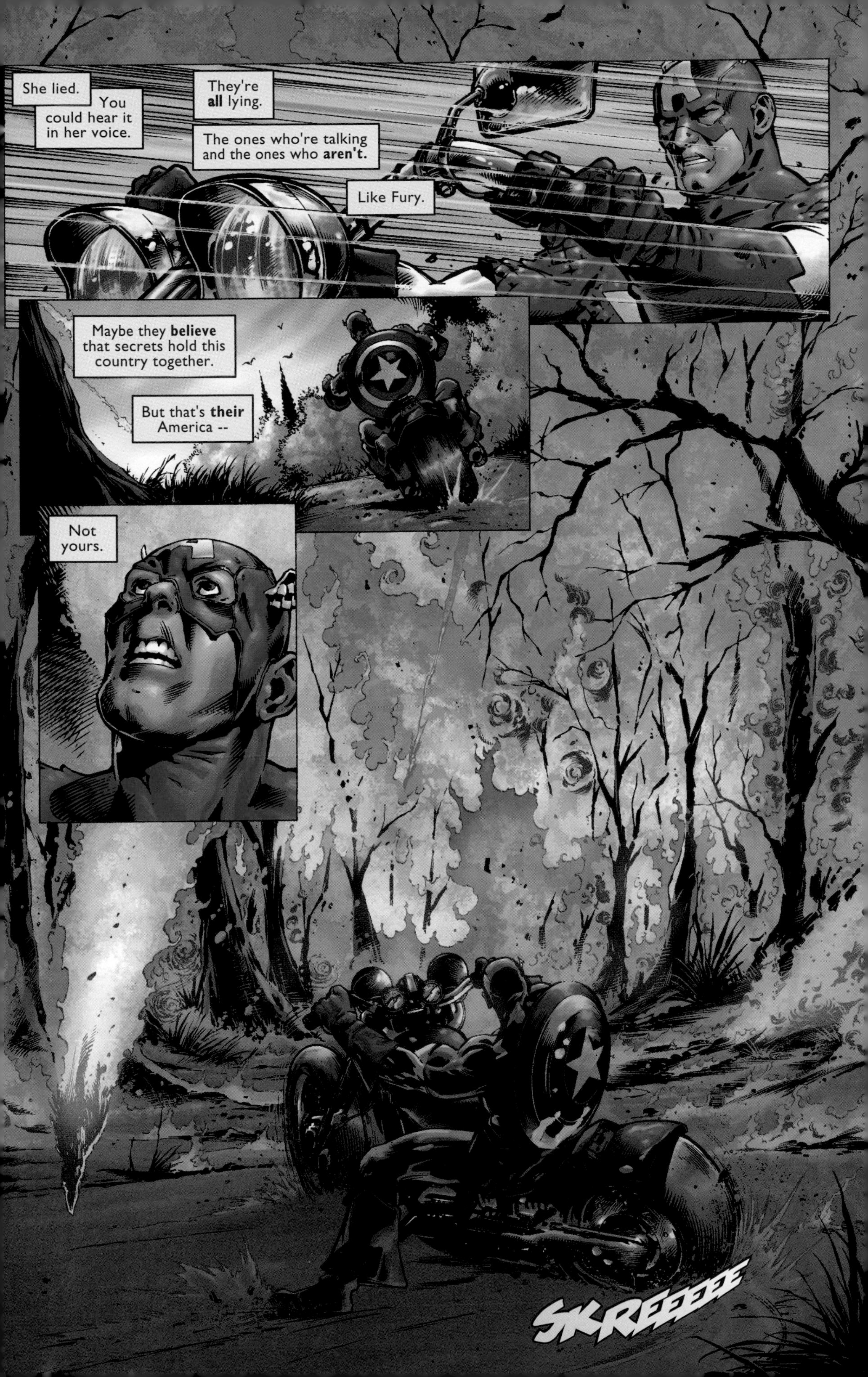
She lied.
You could hear it in her voice.
They're **all** lying.
The ones who're talking and the ones who **aren't.**
Like Fury.
Maybe they **believe** that secrets hold this country together.
But that's **their** America --
Not yours.
SKREEEEEE

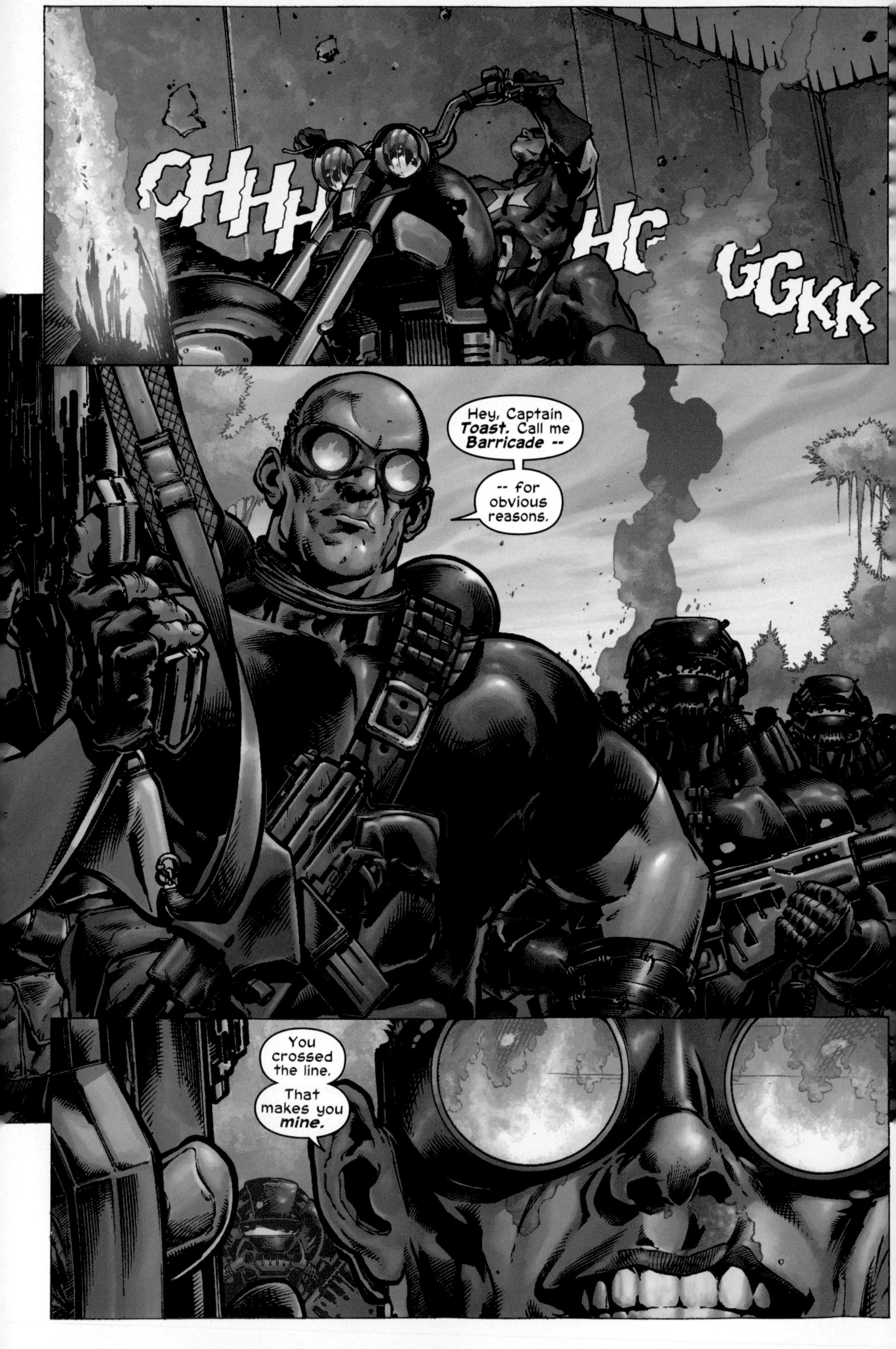
CHHHHHHHGGKK
Hey, Captain *Toast.* Call me *Barricade --*
-- for obvious reasons.
You crossed the line.
That makes you *mine.*

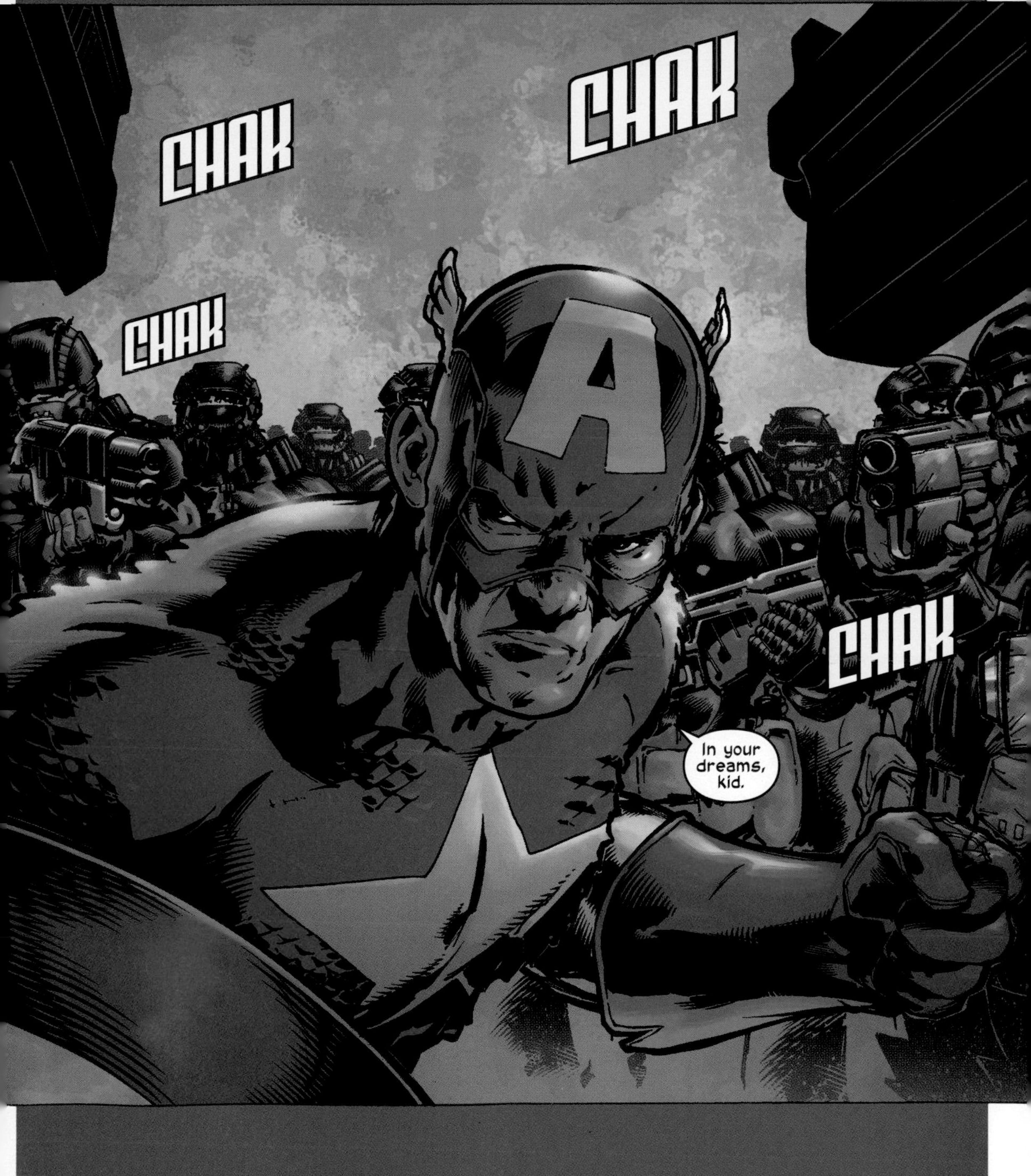
CHAK
CHAK
CHAK
CHAK
In your dreams, kid.

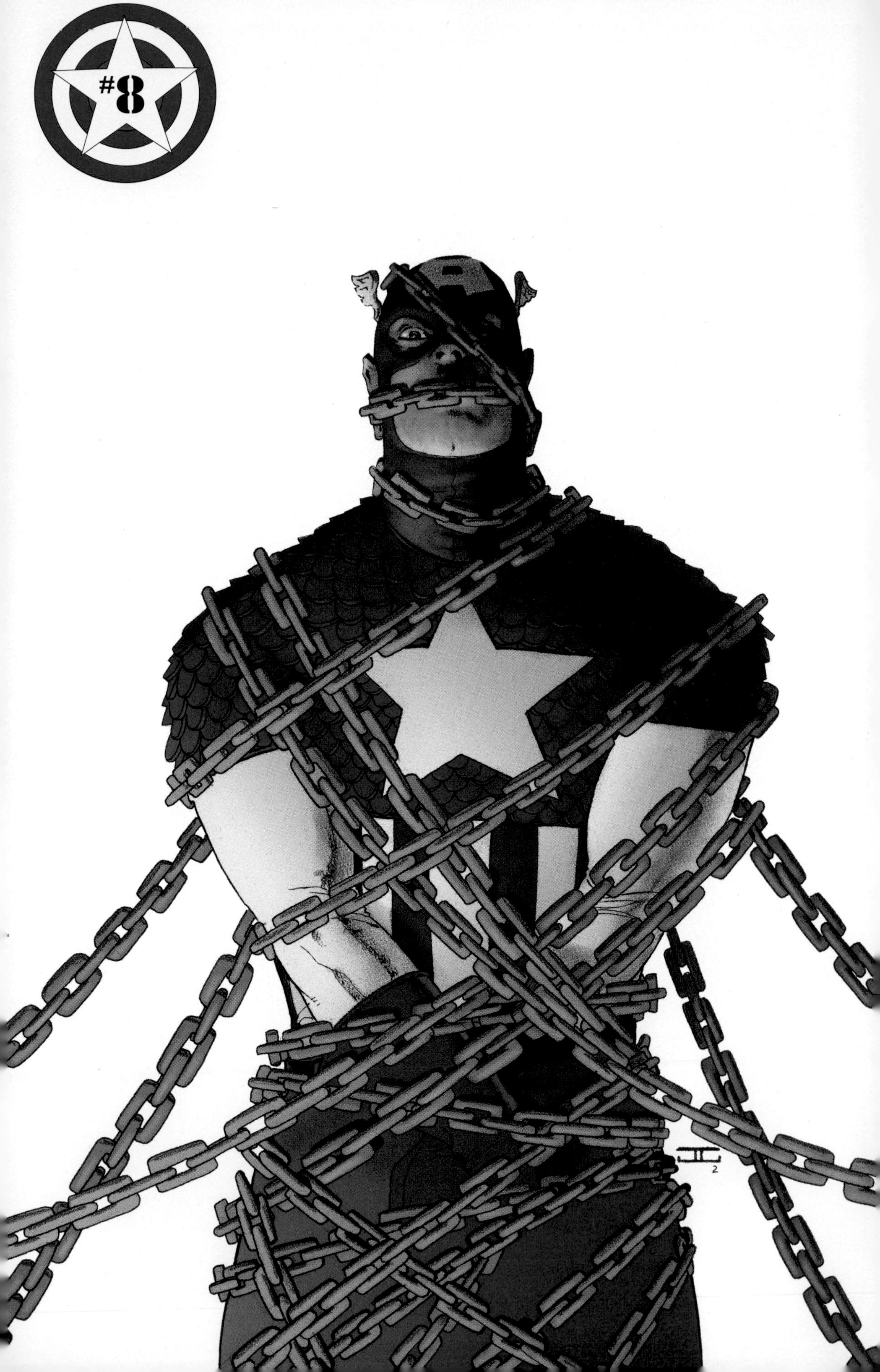
#8

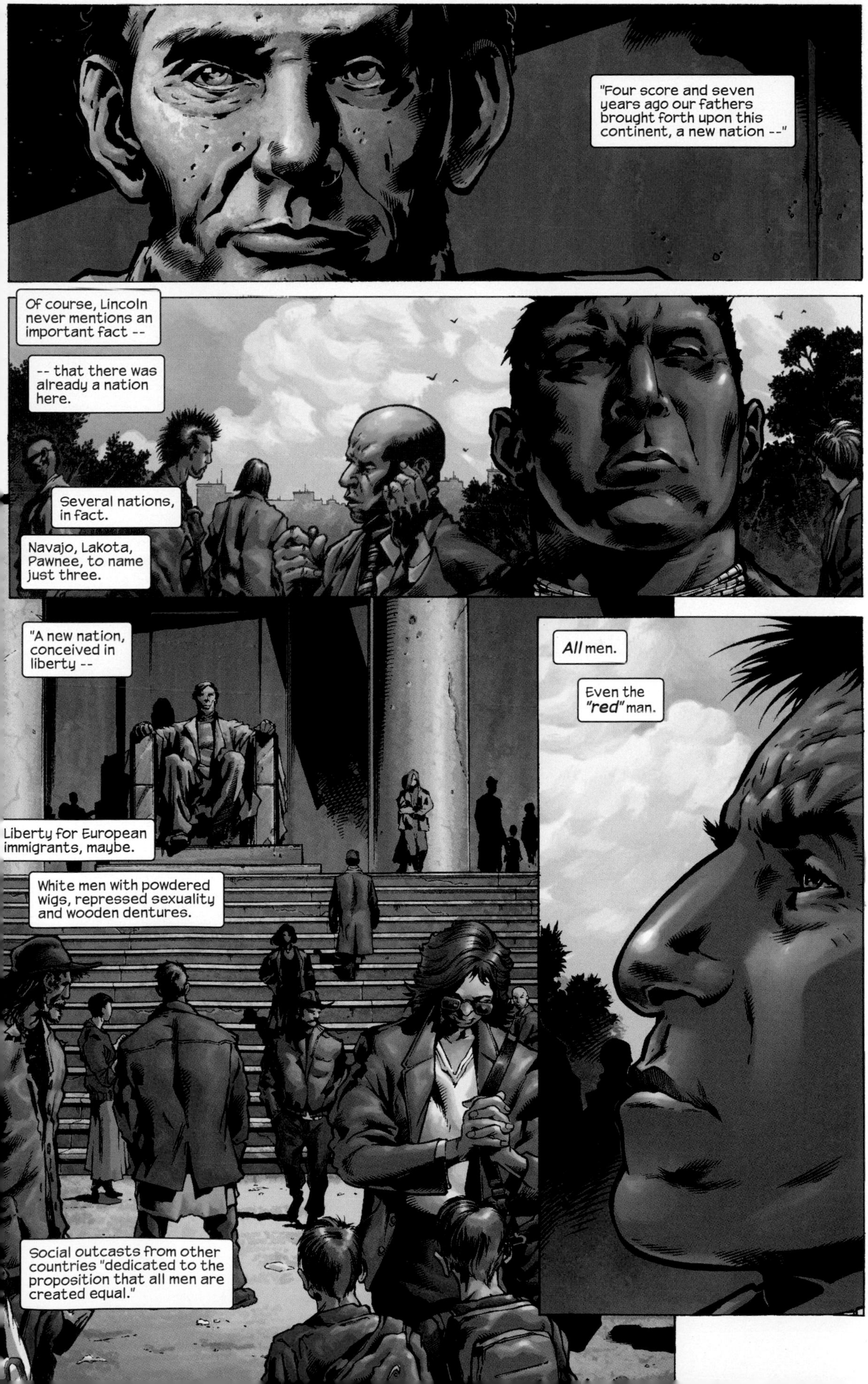
"Four score and seven years ago our fathers brought forth upon this continent, a new nation --"
Of course, Lincoln never mentions an important fact --
-- that there was already a nation here.
Several nations, in fact.
Navajo, Lakota, Pawnee, to name just three.
"A new nation, conceived in liberty --
Liberty for European immigrants, maybe.
White men with powdered wigs, repressed sexuality and wooden dentures.
Social outcasts from other countries "dedicated to the proposition that all men are created equal."
All men.
Even the "red" man.

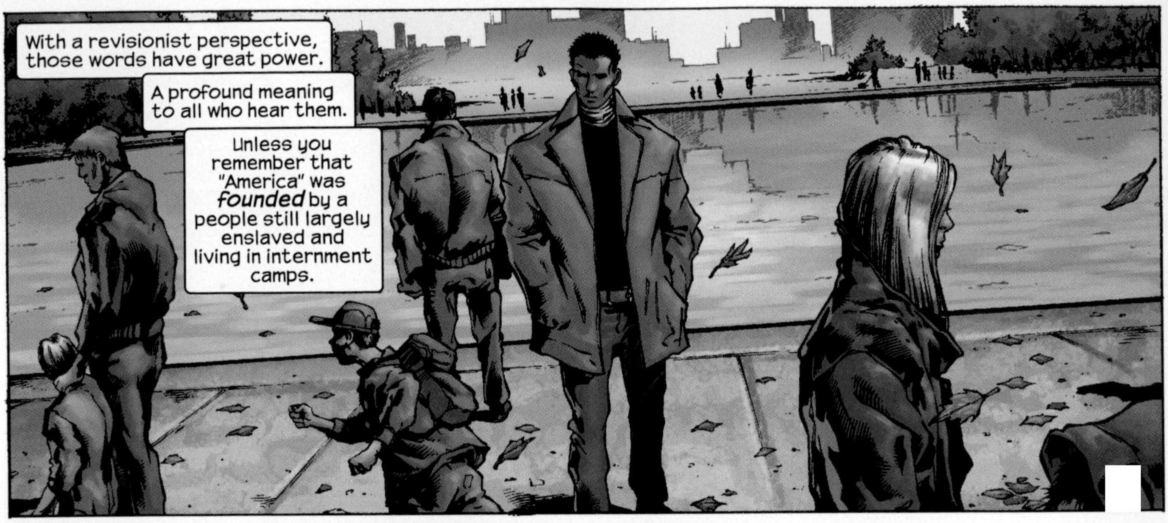
With a revisionist perspective, those words have great power.
A profound meaning to all who hear them.
Unless you remember that "America" was *founded* by a people still largely enslaved and living in internment camps.

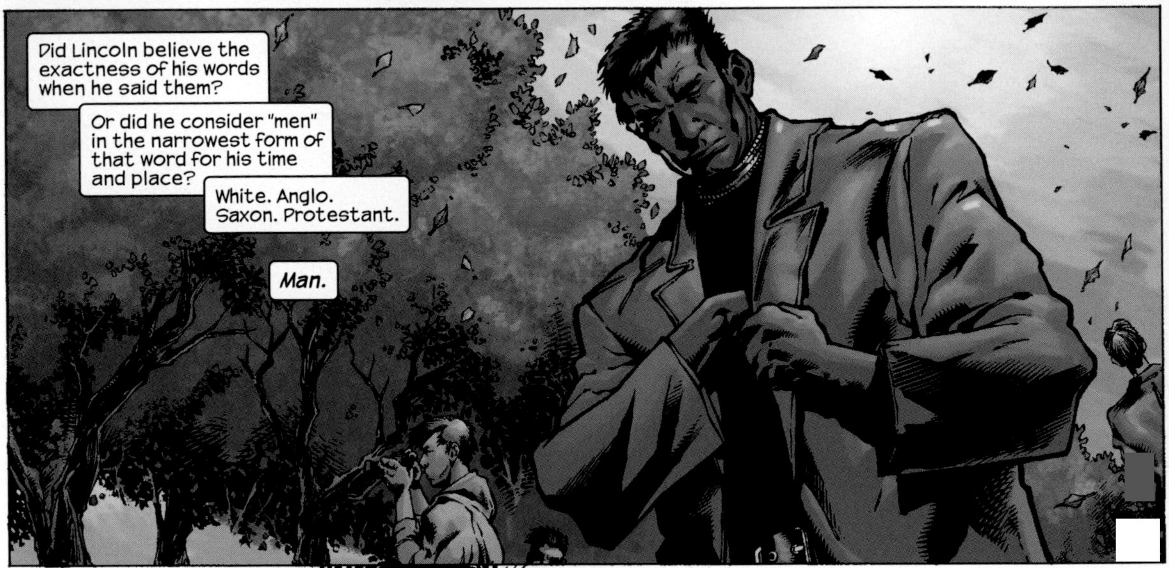
Did Lincoln believe the exactness of his words when he said them?
Or did he consider "men" in the narrowest form of that word for his time and place?
White. Anglo. Saxon. Protestant.
Man.

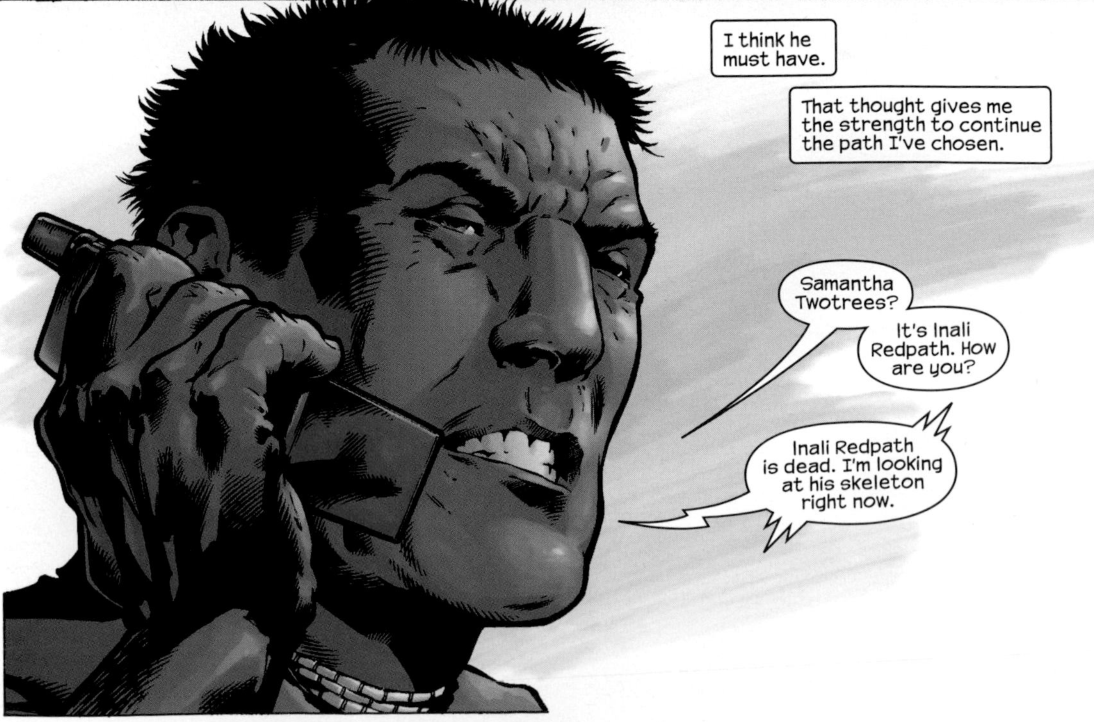
I think he must have.
That thought gives me the strength to continue the path I've chosen.
Samantha Twotrees?
It's Inali Redpath. How are you?
Inali Redpath is dead. I'm looking at his skeleton right now.

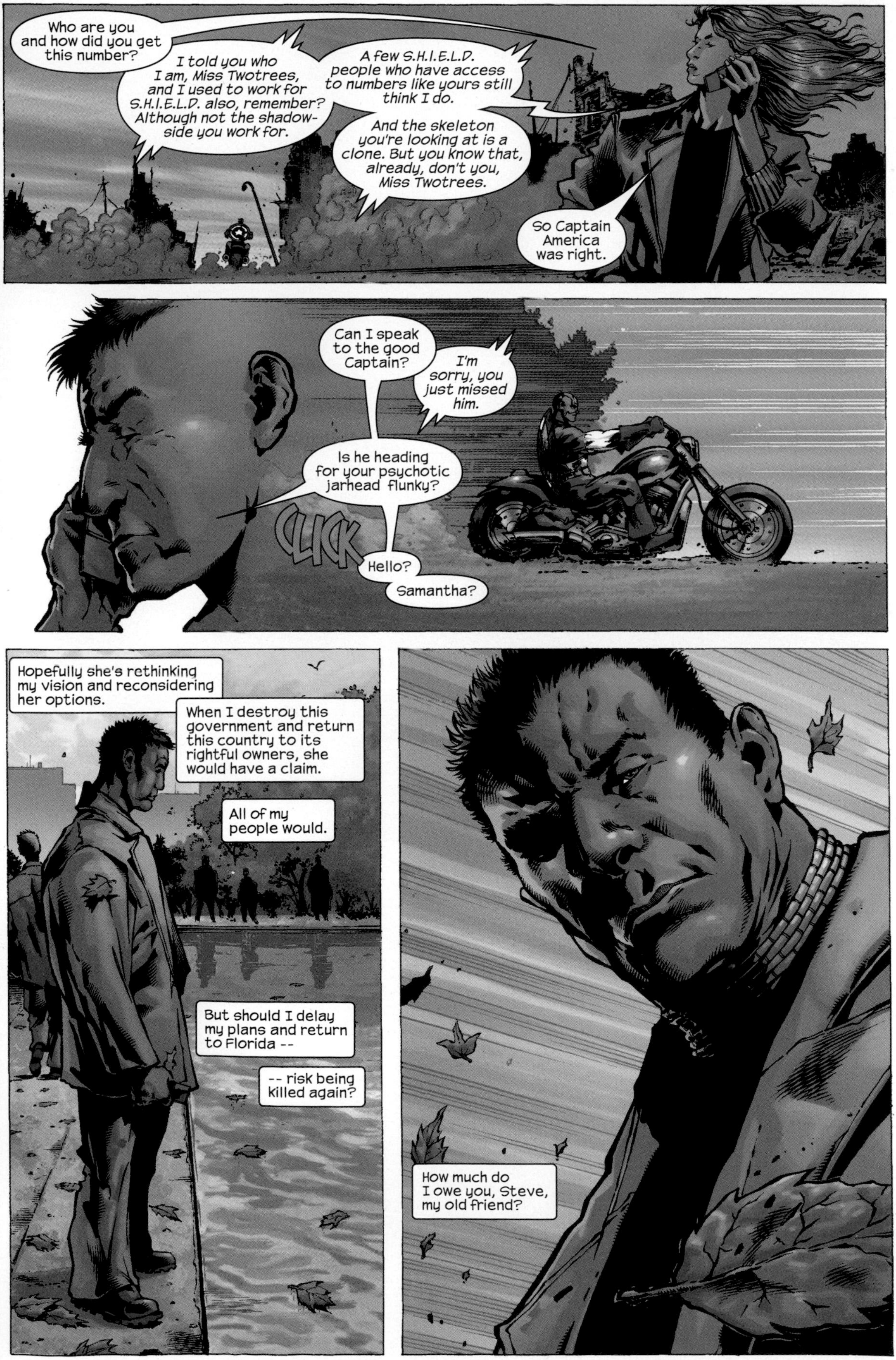
Who are you and how did you get this number?
I told you who I am, Miss Twotrees, and I used to work for S.H.I.E.L.D. also, remember? Although not the shadow-side you work for.
A few S.H.I.E.L.D. people who have access to numbers like yours still think I do.
And the skeleton you're looking at is a clone. But you know that, already, don't you, Miss Twotrees.
So Captain America was right.
Can I speak to the good Captain?
I'm sorry, you just missed him.
Is he heading for your psychotic jarhead flunky?
CLICK
Hello?
Samantha?
Hopefully she's rethinking my vision and reconsidering her options.
When I destroy this government and return this country to its rightful owners, she would have a claim.
All of my people would.
But should I delay my plans and return to Florida --
-- risk being killed again?
How much do I owe you, Steve, my old friend?

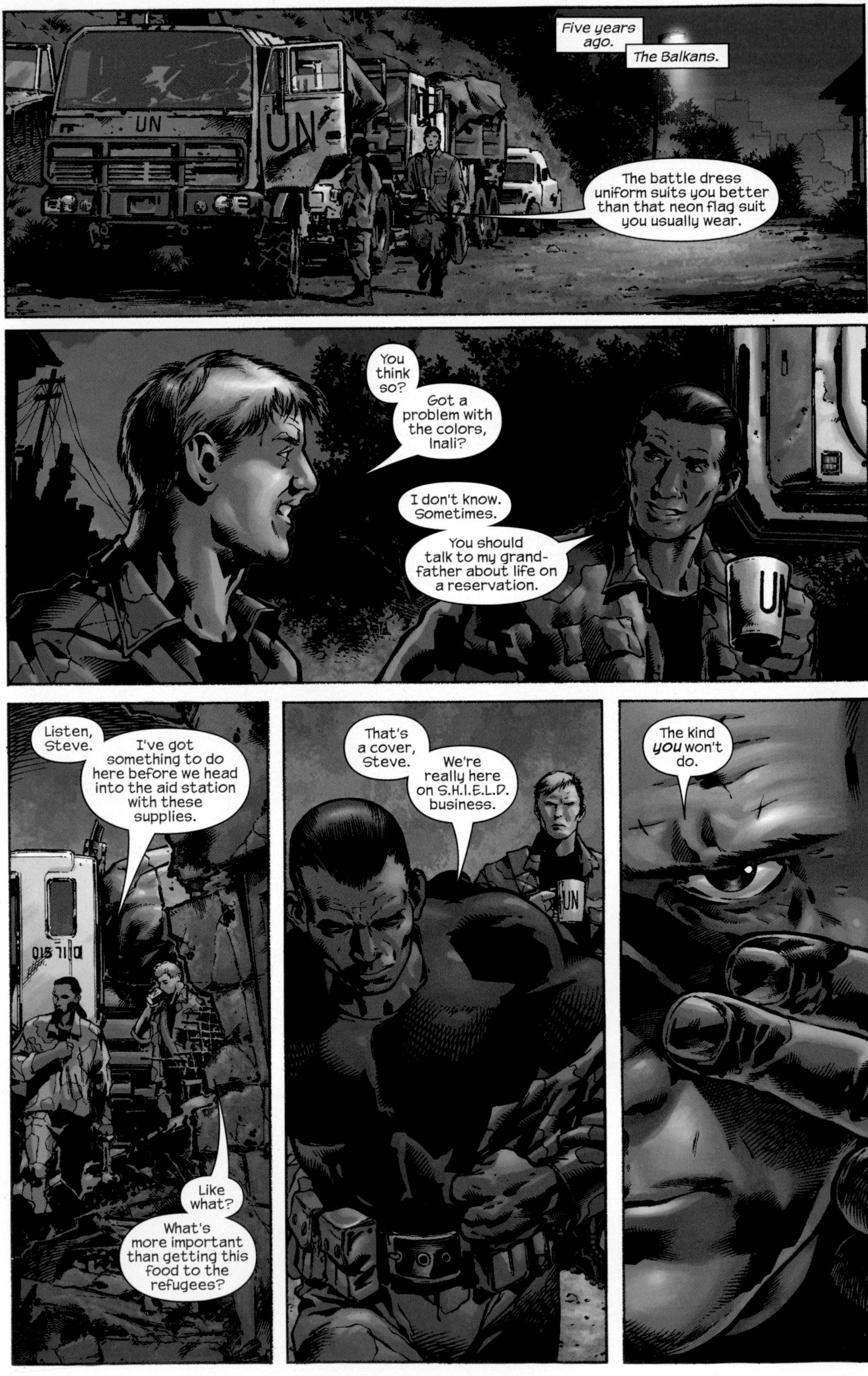
Five years ago.
The Balkans.
The battle dress uniform suits you better than that neon flag suit you usually wear.
You think so?
Got a problem with the colors, Inali?
I don't know. Sometimes.
You should talk to my grand-father about life on a reservation.
Listen, Steve.
I've got something to do here before we head into the aid station with these supplies.
Like what?
What's more important than getting this food to the refugees?
That's a cover, Steve.
We're really here on S.H.I.E.L.D. business.
The kind *you* won't do.

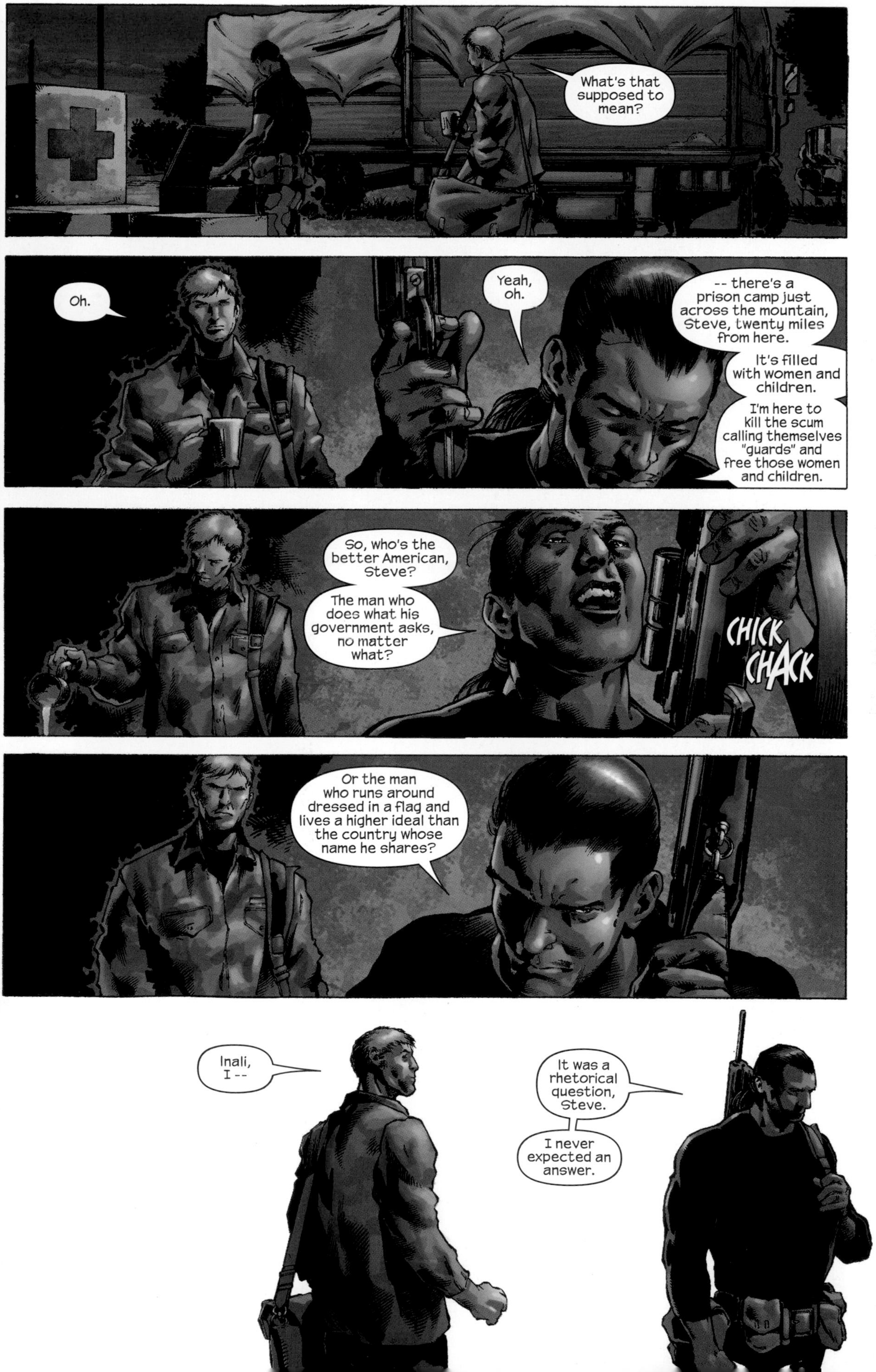
What's that supposed to mean?
Oh.
Yeah, oh.
-- there's a prison camp just across the mountain, Steve, twenty miles from here.
It's filled with women and children.
I'm here to kill the scum calling themselves "guards" and free those women and children.
So, who's the better American, Steve?
The man who does what his government asks, no matter what?
CHICK CHACK
Or the man who runs around dressed in a flag and lives a higher ideal than the country whose name he shares?
Inali, I --
It was a rhetorical question, Steve.
I never expected an answer.

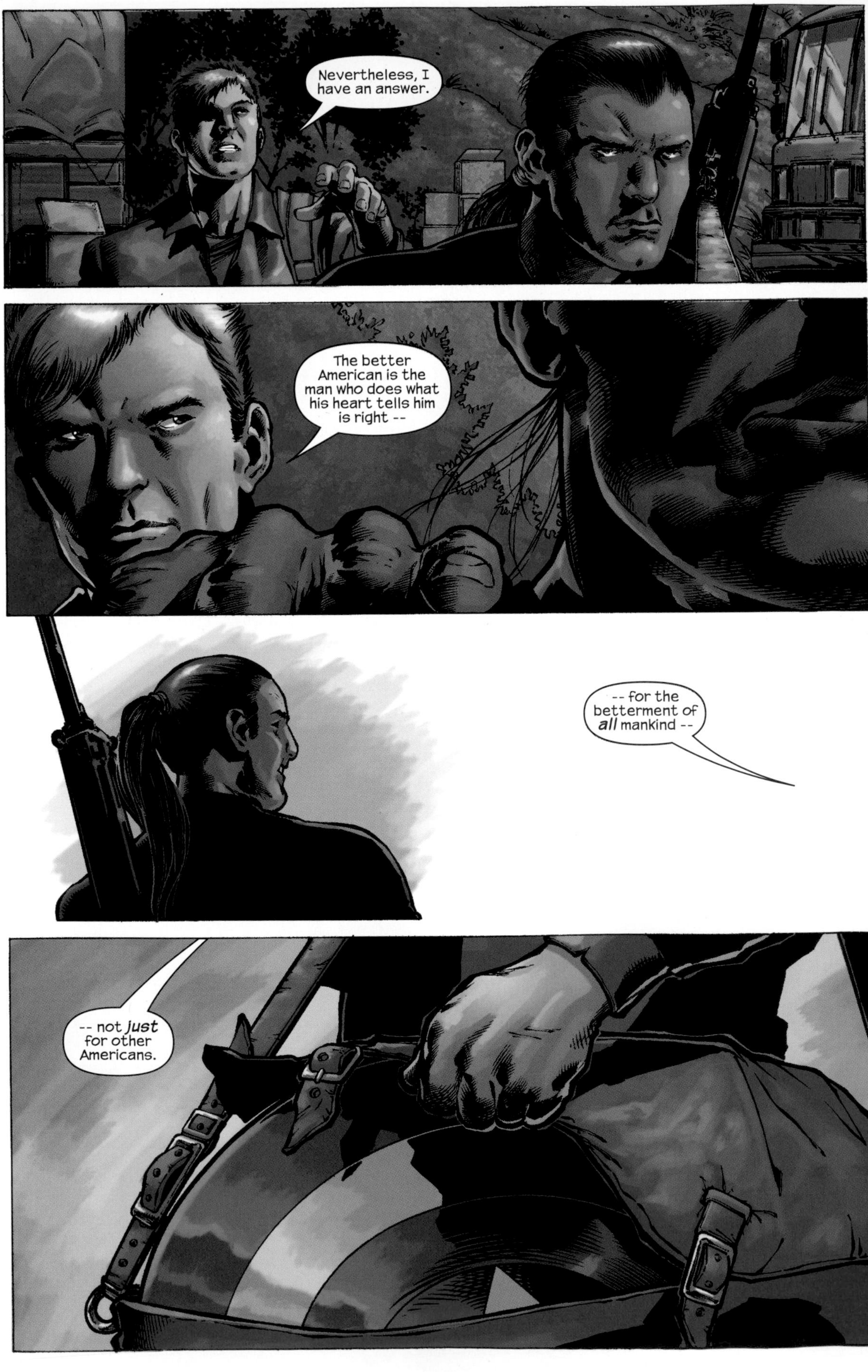
Nevertheless, I have an answer.
The better American is the man who does what his heart tells him is right --
-- for the betterment of *all* mankind --
-- not *just* for other Americans.

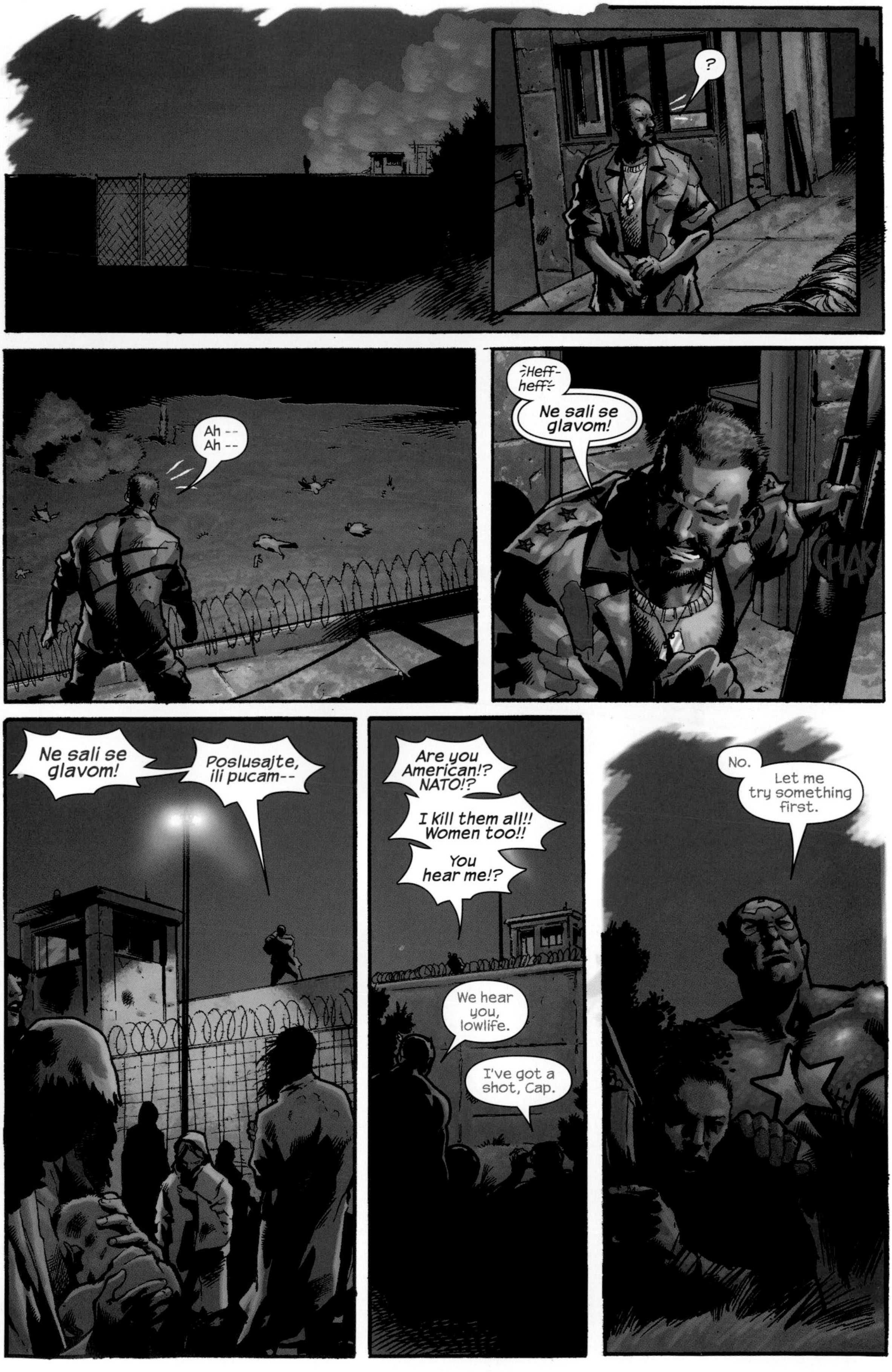
?
Ah -- Ah --
-Heff- heff-
Ne sali se glavom!
CHAK
Ne sali se glavom!
Poslusajte, ili pucam--
Are you American!? NATO!?
I kill them all!! Women too!!
You hear me!?
We hear you, lowlife.
I've got a shot, Cap.
No.
Let me try something first.

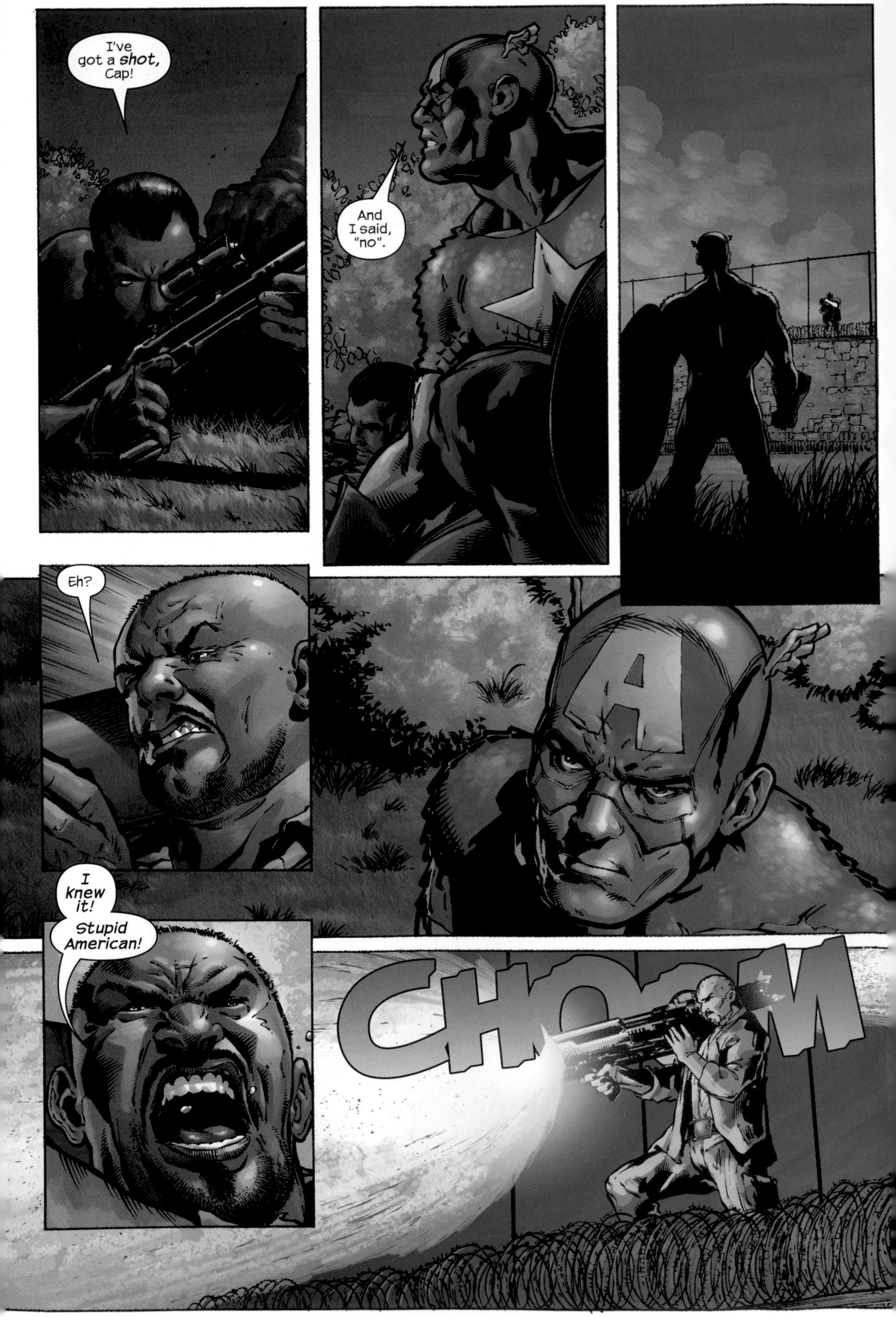
I've got a shot, Cap!
And I said, "no".
Eh?
I knew it!
Stupid American!
CHOOM

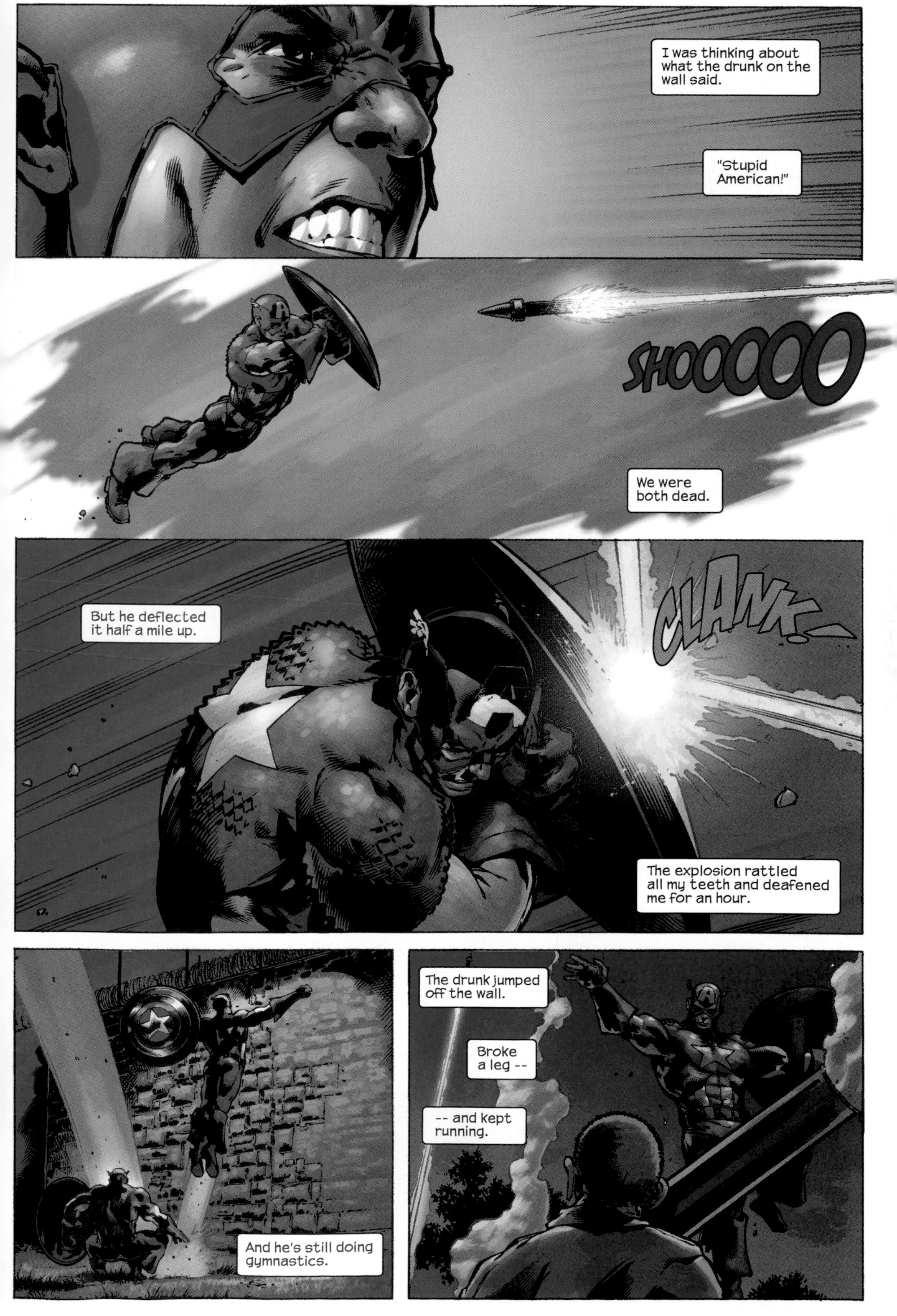
I was thinking about what the drunk on the wall said.
"Stupid American!"
SHOOOOO
We were both dead.
But he deflected it half a mile up.
CLANK!
The explosion rattled all my teeth and deafened me for an hour.
And he's still doing gymnastics.
The drunk jumped off the wall.
Broke a leg --
-- and kept running.

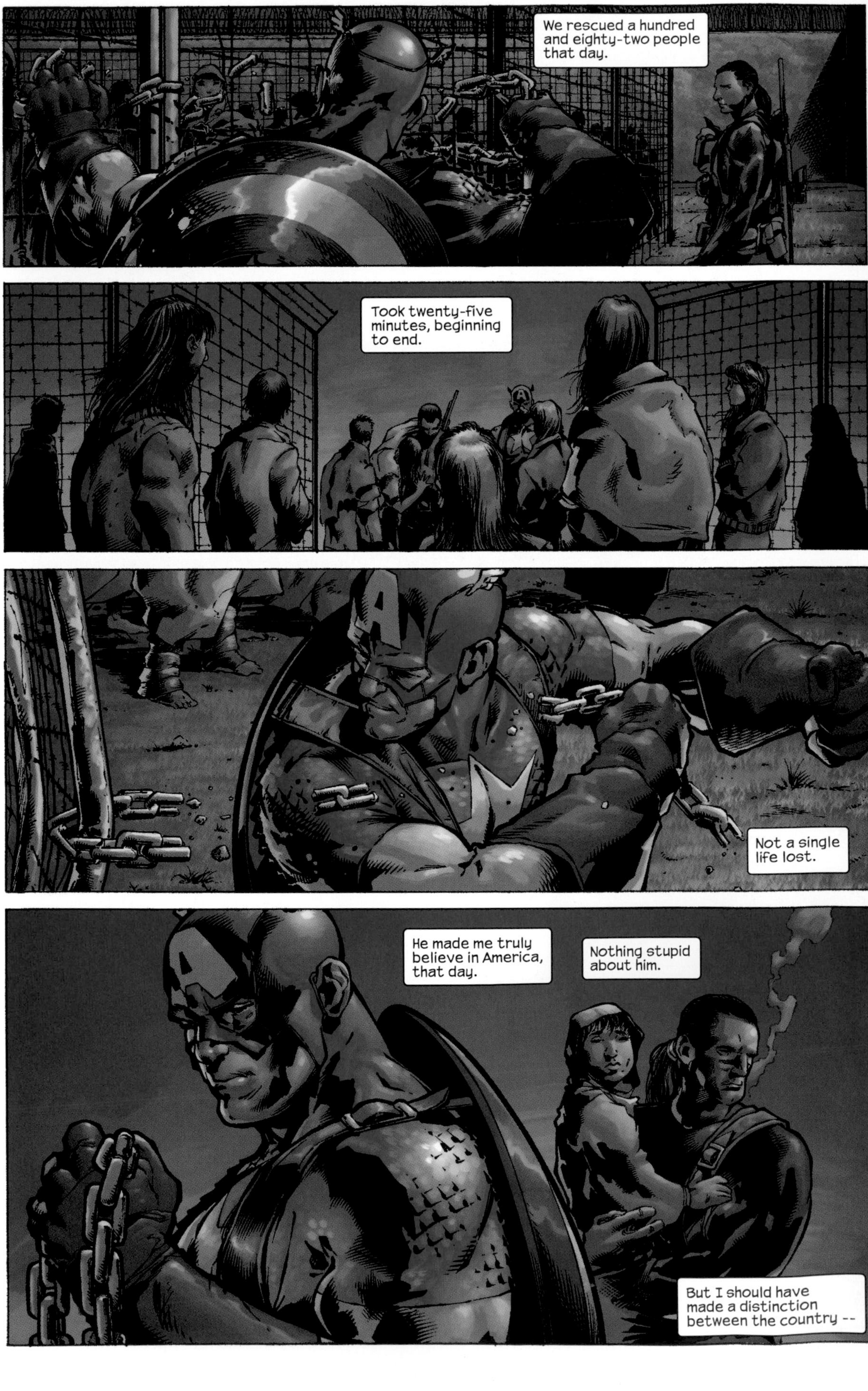

We rescued a hundred and eighty-two people that day.
Took twenty-five minutes, beginning to end.
Not a single life lost.
He made me truly believe in America, that day.
Nothing stupid about him.
But I should have made a distinction between the country --

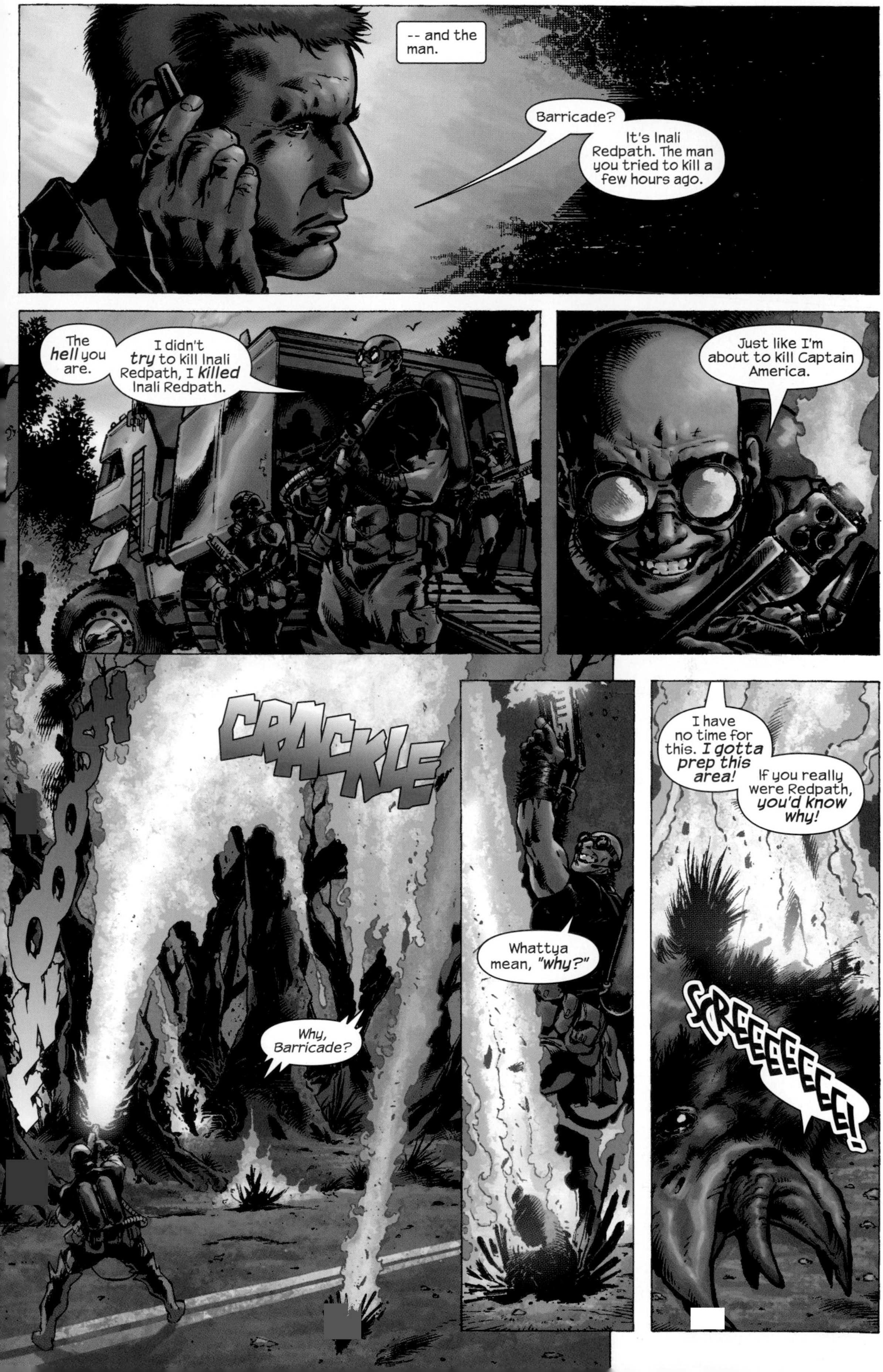
-- and the man.
Barricade?
It's Inali Redpath. The man you tried to kill a few hours ago.
The *hell* you are.
I didn't *try* to kill Inali Redpath, I *killed* Inali Redpath.
Just like I'm about to kill Captain America.
CRACKLE
Why, Barricade?
Whattya mean, *"why?"*
I have no time for this. *I gotta prep this area!*
If you really were Redpath, *you'd know why!*

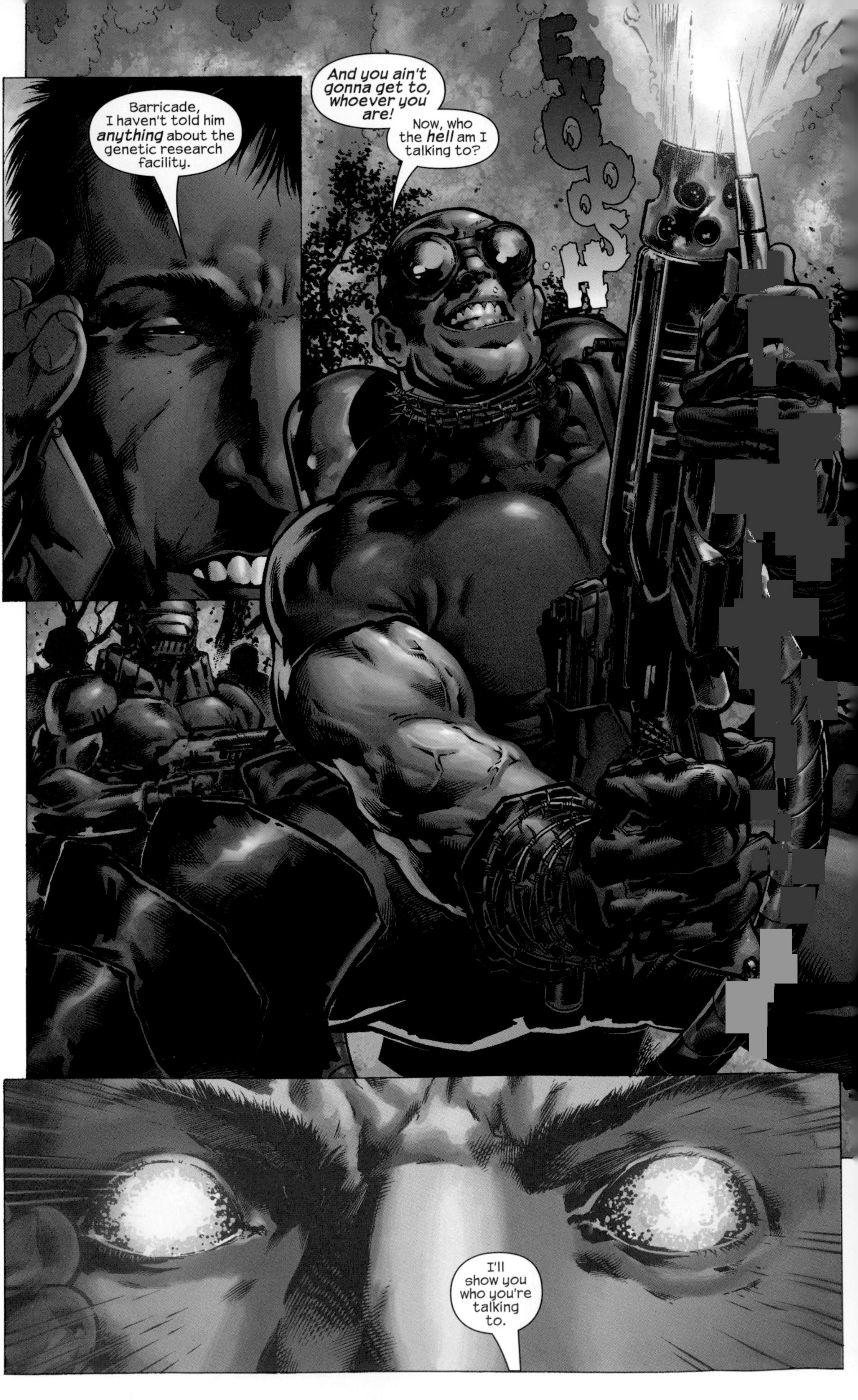
Barricade, I haven't told him anything about the genetic research facility.
And you ain't gonna get to, whoever you are!
Now, who the hell am I talking to?
I'll show you who you're talking to.

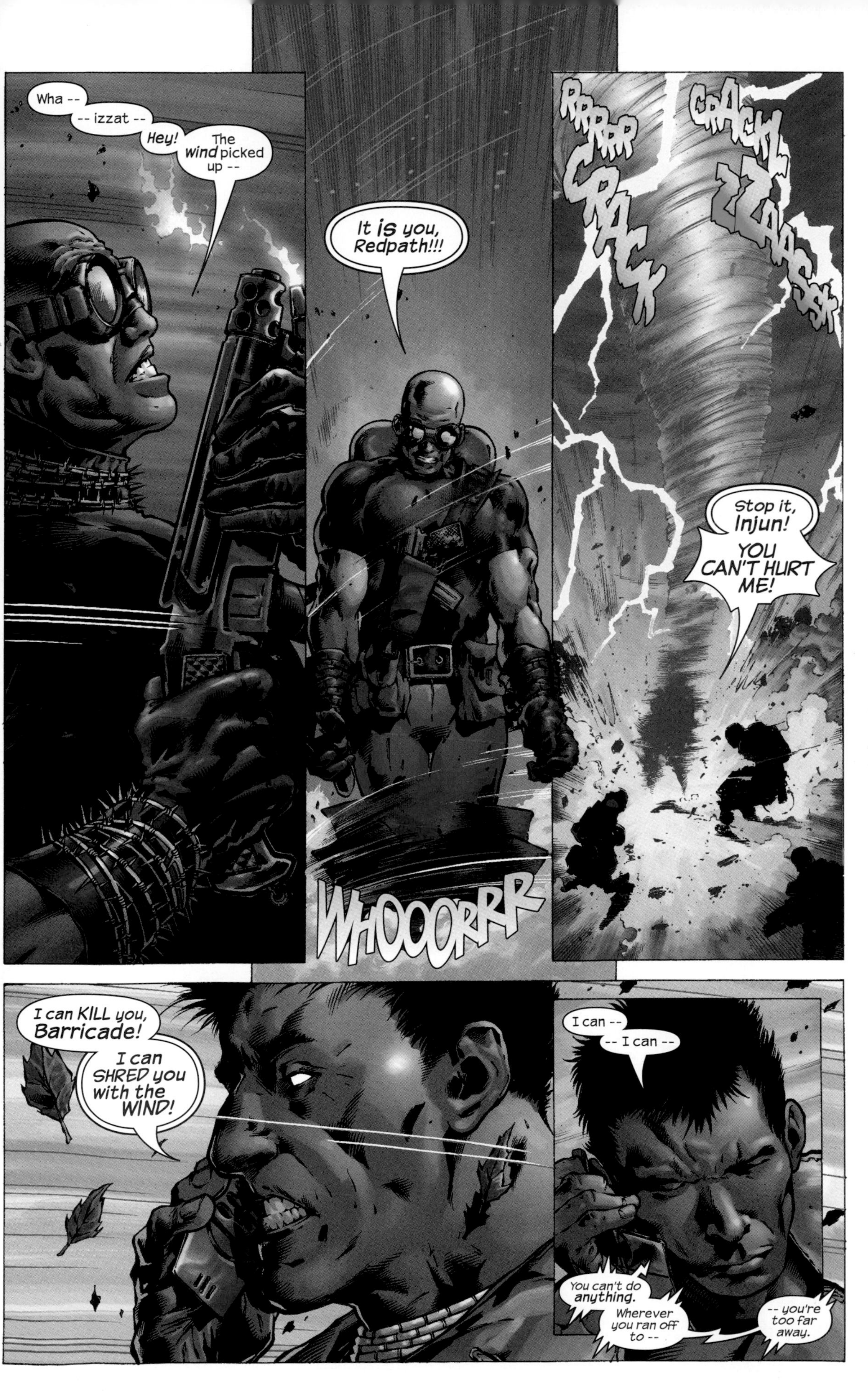
Wha --
-- izzat --
Hey!
The wind picked up --
It is you, Redpath!!!
WHOOORRR
RRRRR CRACK
CRACKL ZZAPSSK
Stop it, Injun! YOU CAN'T HURT ME!
I can KILL you, Barricade!
I can SHRED you with the WIND!
I can --
-- I can --
You can't do anything.
Wherever you ran off to --
-- you're too far away.

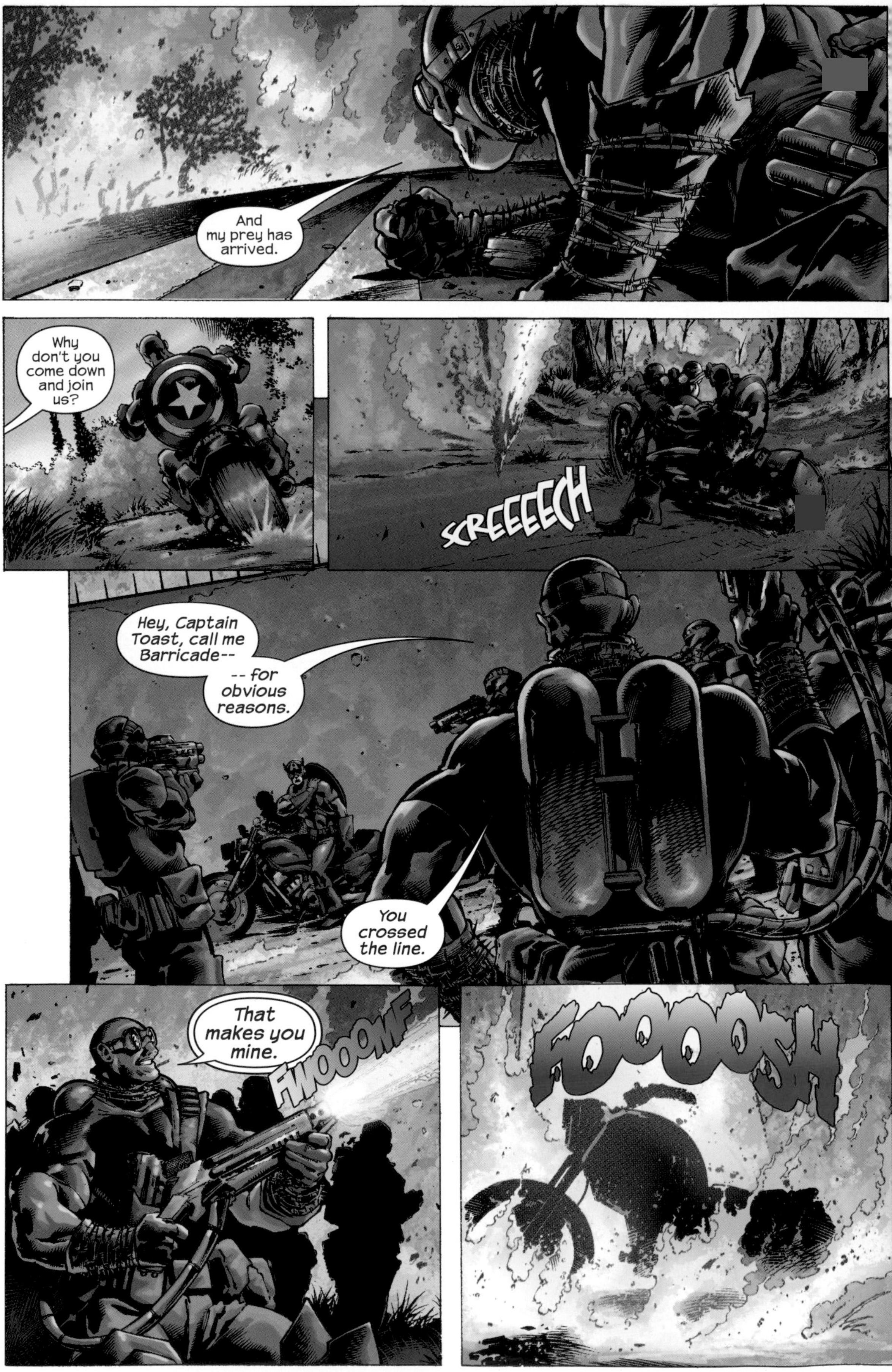
And my prey has arrived.
Why don't you come down and join us?
SCREEEECH
Hey, Captain Toast, call me Barricade--
-- for obvious reasons.
You crossed the line.
That makes you mine.
FWOOOMF
FOOOOSH

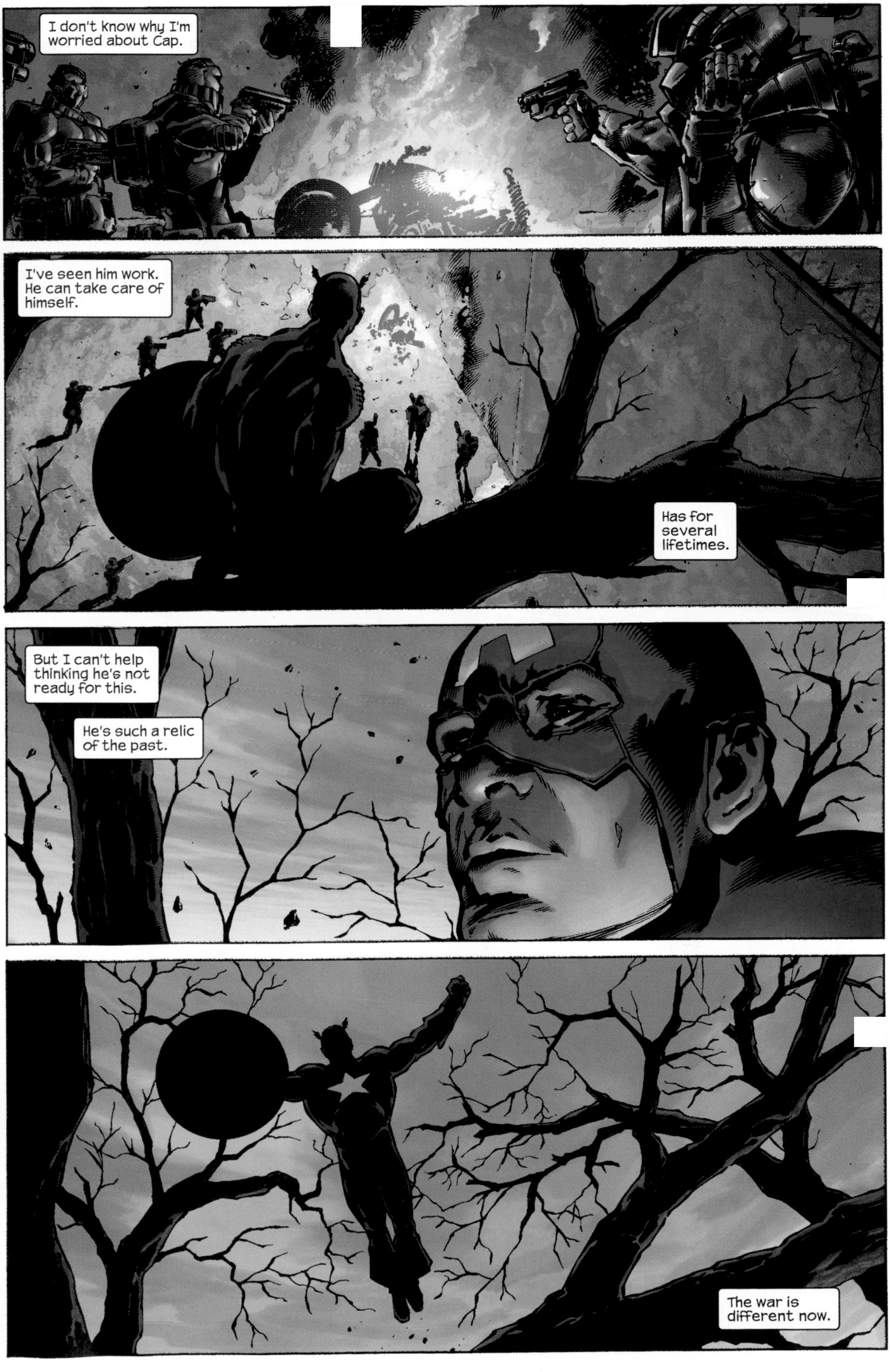
I don't know why I'm worried about Cap.
I've seen him work. He can take care of himself.
Has for several lifetimes.
But I can't help thinking he's not ready for this.
He's such a relic of the past.
The war is different now.

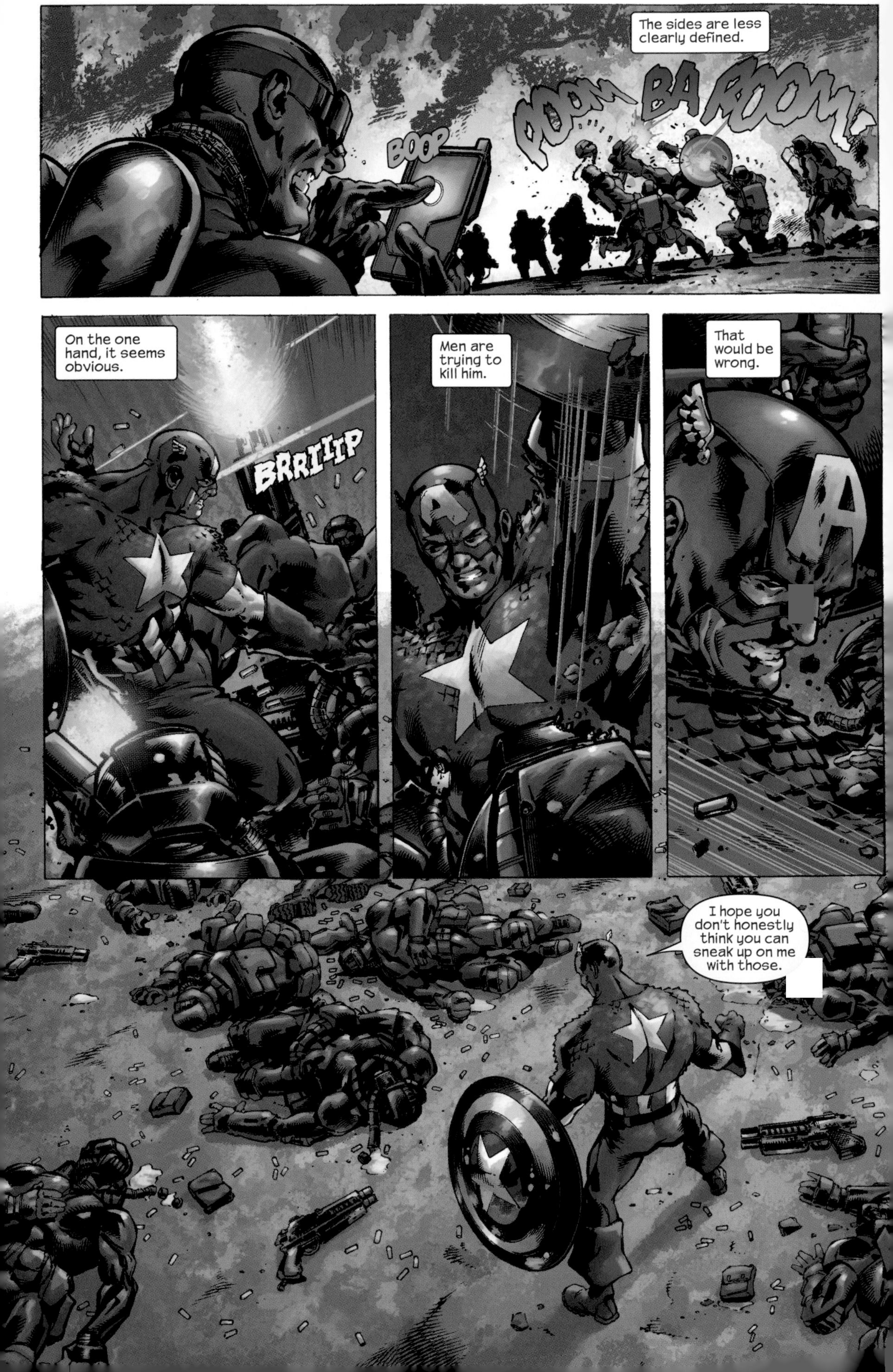

The sides are less clearly defined.
BOOP
POOM BA ROOM!
On the one hand, it seems obvious.
BRRIIIP
Men are trying to kill him.
That would be wrong.
I hope you don't honestly think you can sneak up on me with those.

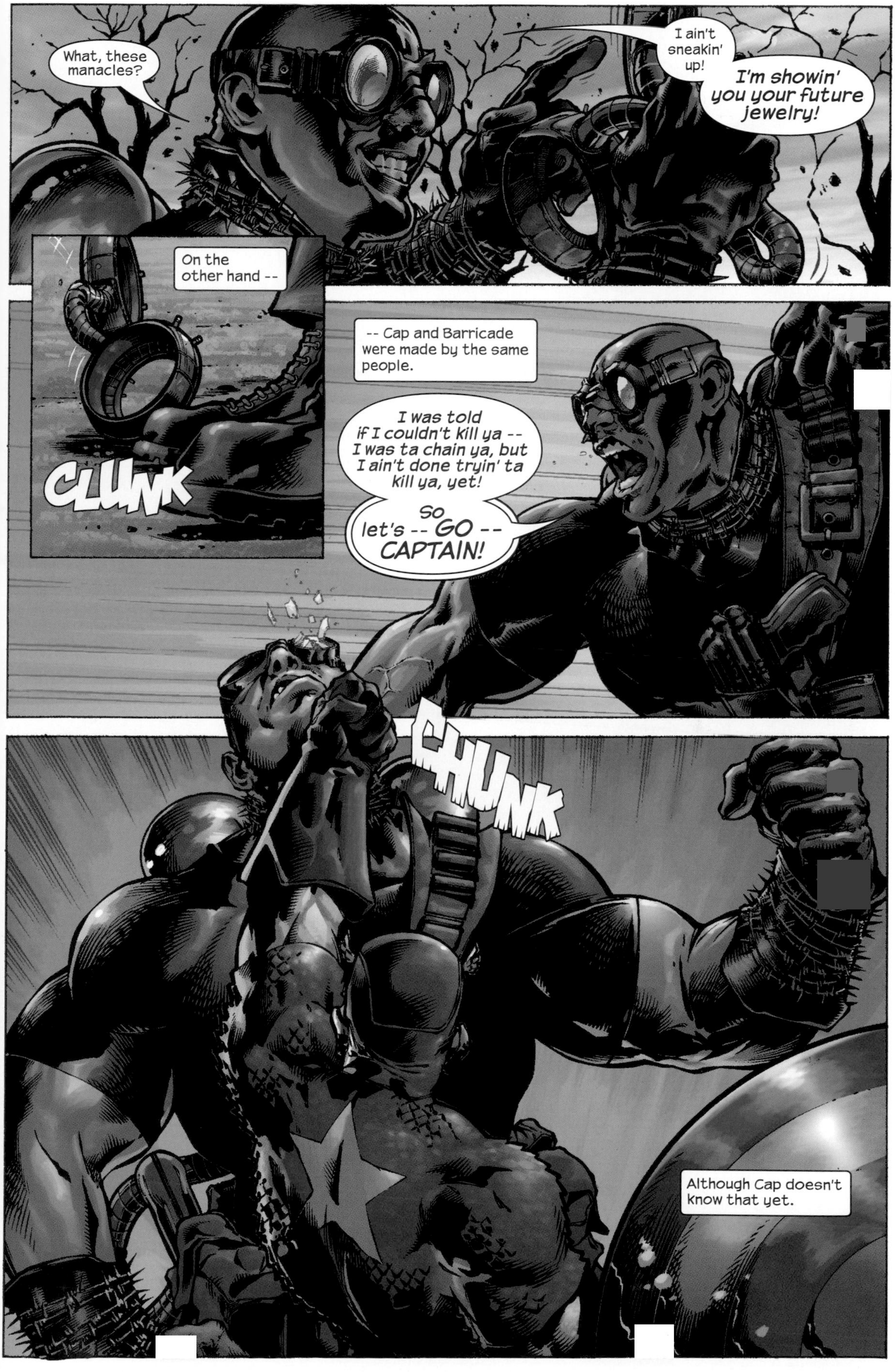
What, these manacles?
I ain't sneakin' up!
I'm showin' you your future jewelry!
On the other hand --
CLUNK
-- Cap and Barricade were made by the same people.
I was told if I couldn't kill ya -- I was ta chain ya, but I ain't done tryin' ta kill ya, yet!
So let's -- GO -- CAPTAIN!
CHUNK
Although Cap doesn't know that yet.

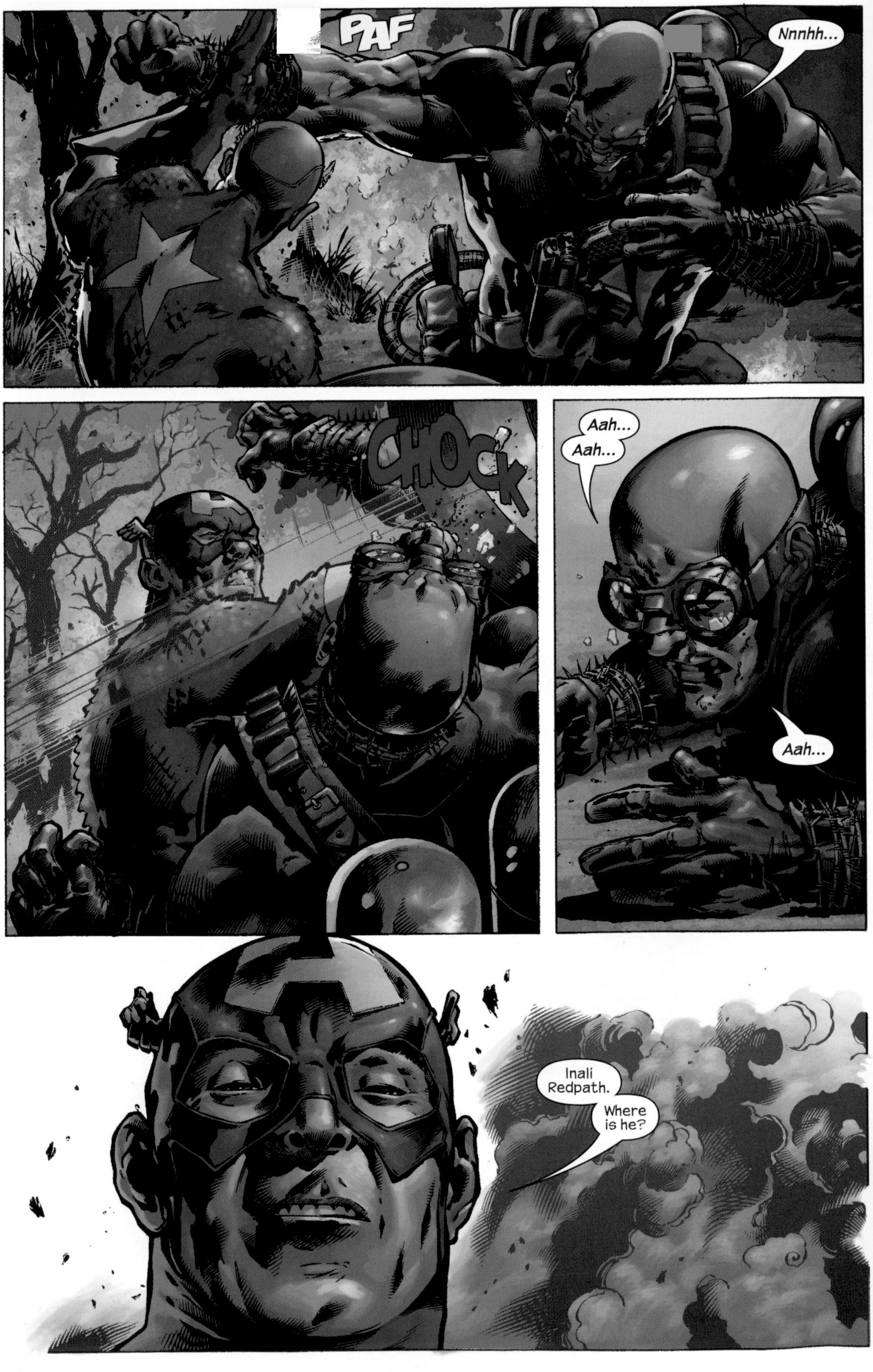
PAF
Nnnhh...
CHOCK
Aah... Aah...
Aah...
Inali Redpath. Where is he?

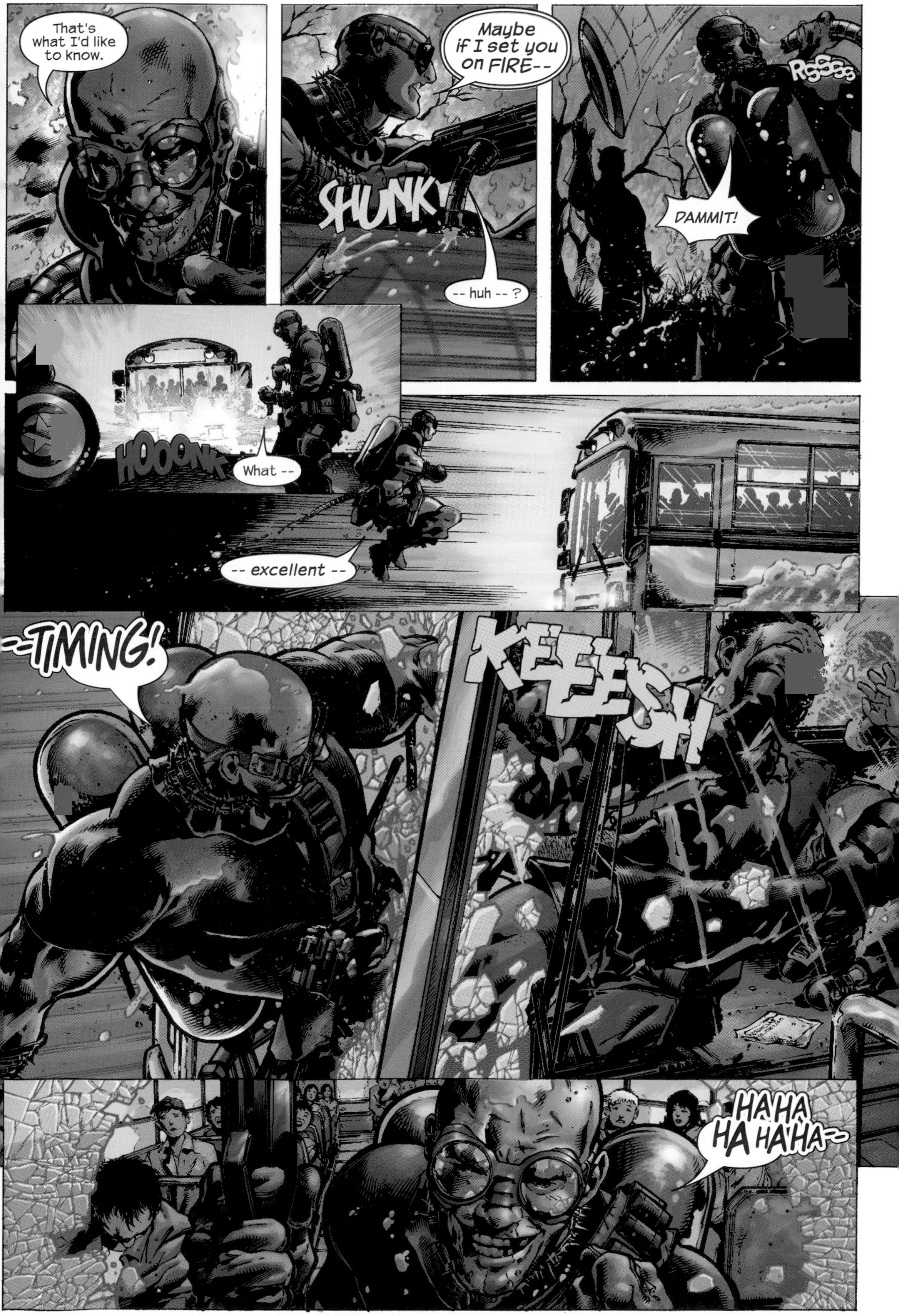
That's what I'd like to know.
Maybe if I set you on FIRE--
SHUNK
-- huh -- ?
RSSSS
DAMMIT!
HOOONK
What --
-- excellent --
--TIMING!
KEEESH!
HAHA HA HAHA--

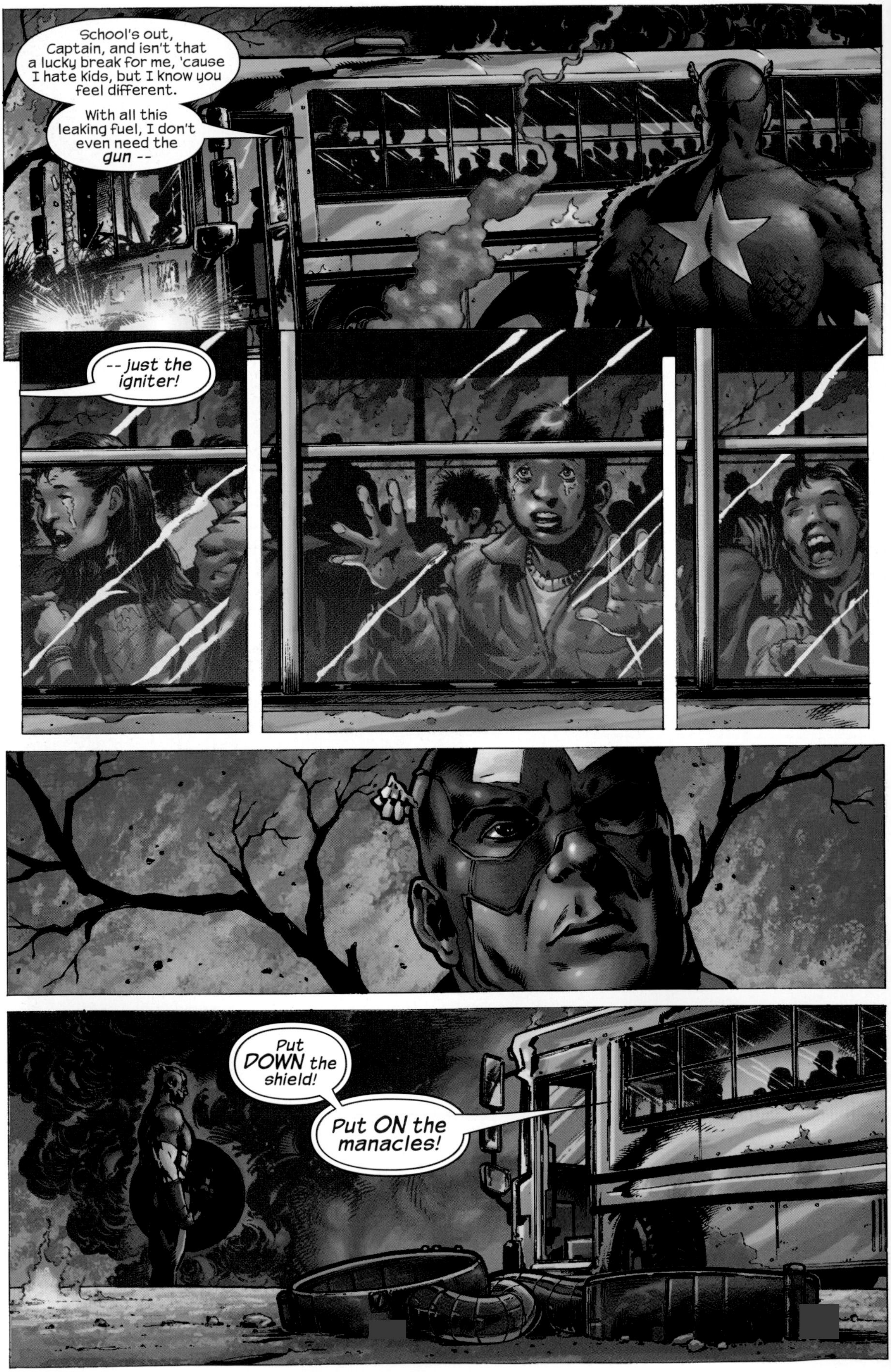
School's out, Captain, and isn't that a lucky break for me, 'cause I hate kids, but I know you feel different.
With all this leaking fuel, I don't even need the *gun* --
-- just the igniter!
Put DOWN the shield!
Put ON the manacles!

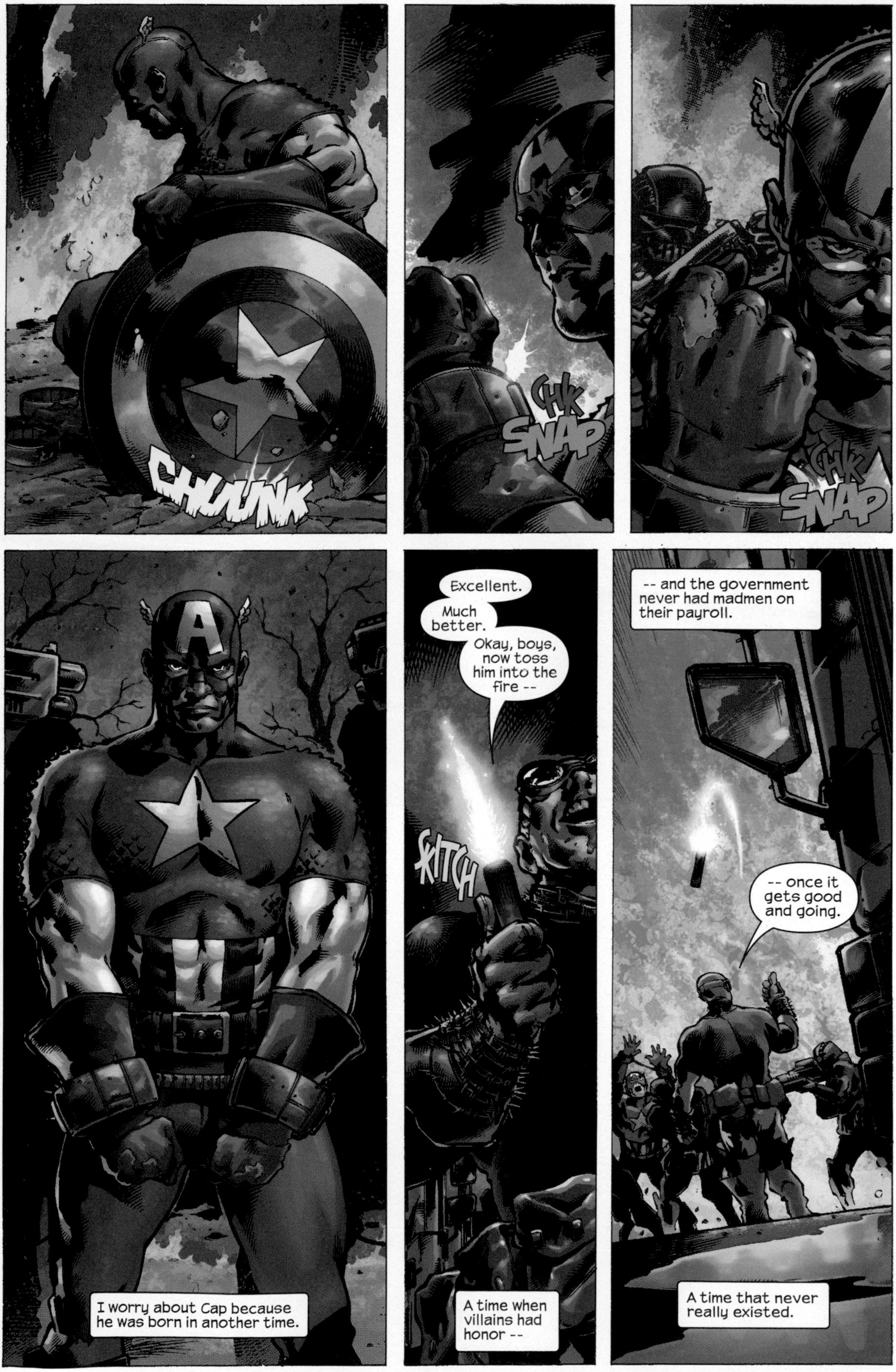
CHUUNK
CHK
SNAP
CHK
SNAP
I worry about Cap because he was born in another time.
Excellent.
Much better.
Okay, boys, now toss him into the fire --
SKITCH
A time when villains had honor --
-- and the government never had madmen on their payroll.
-- once it gets good and going.
A time that never really existed.

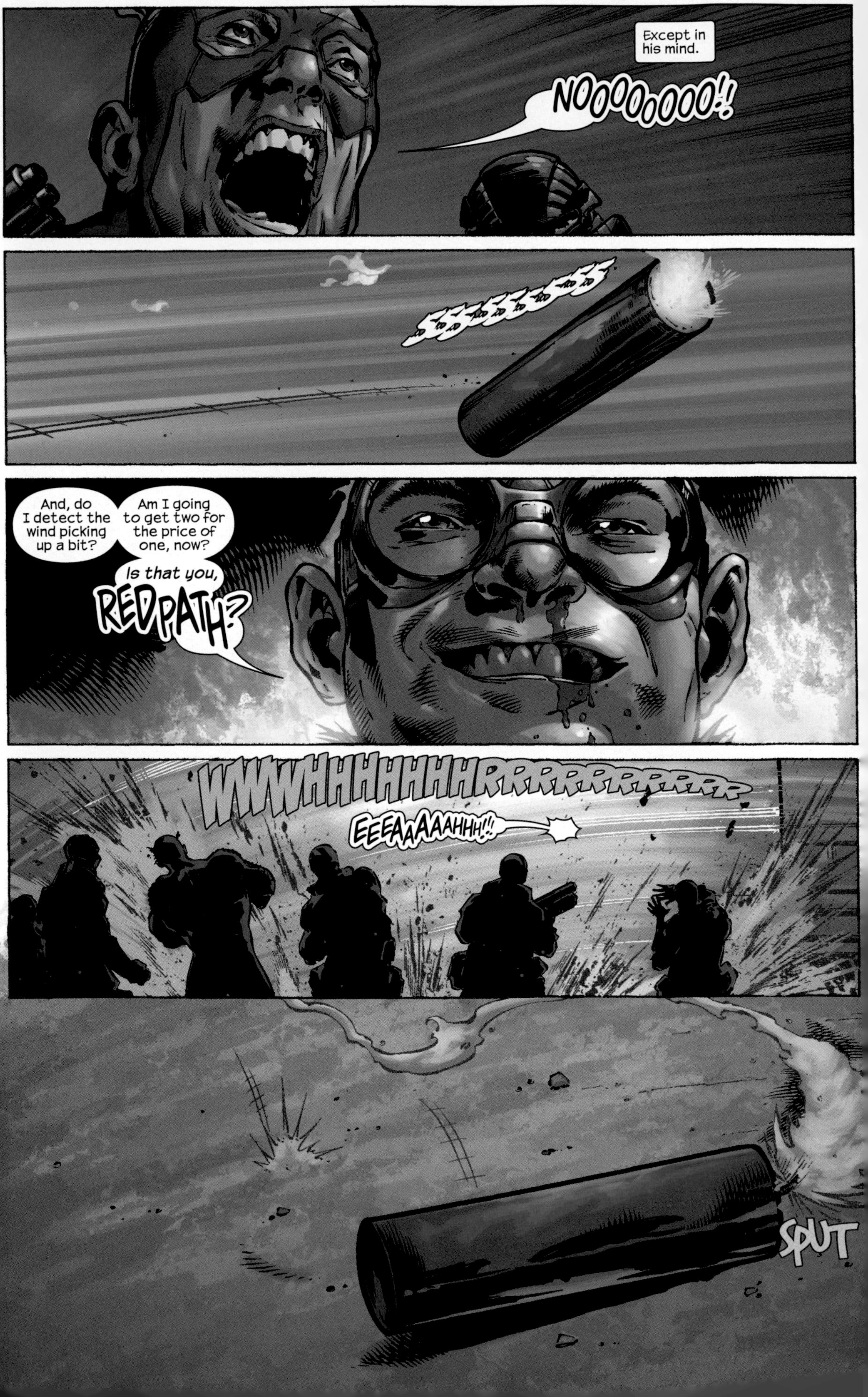
Except in his mind.
NOOOOOOOO!!
SSSSSSSSSSS
And, do I detect the wind picking up a bit?
Am I going to get two for the price of one, now?
Is that you, REDPATH?
WWWHHHHHHHRRRRRRRRRRRR
EEEAAAAAHHH!!
SPUT

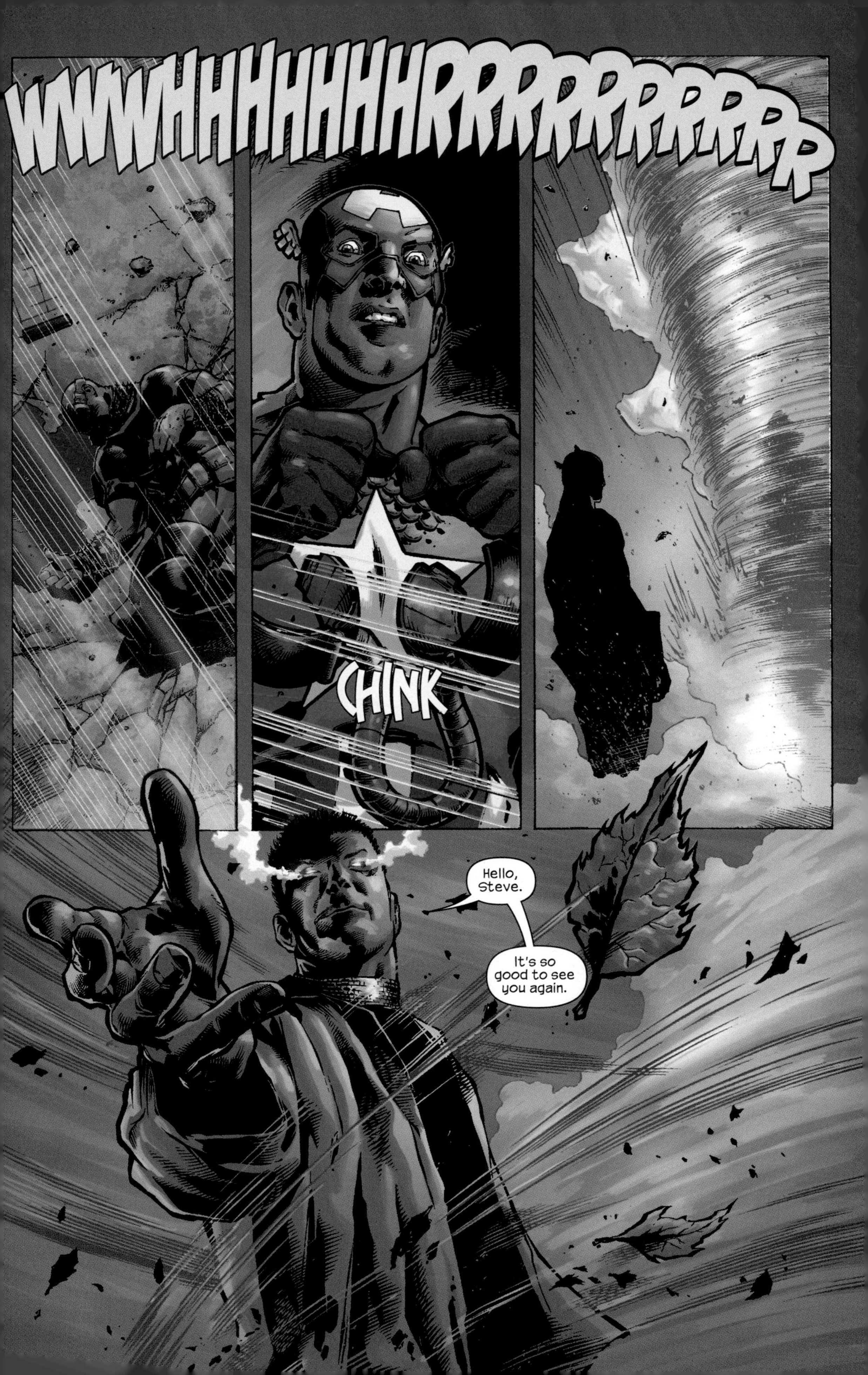
WWWHHHHHHRRRRRRRRRRRR
CHINK
Hello, Steve.
It's so good to see you again.

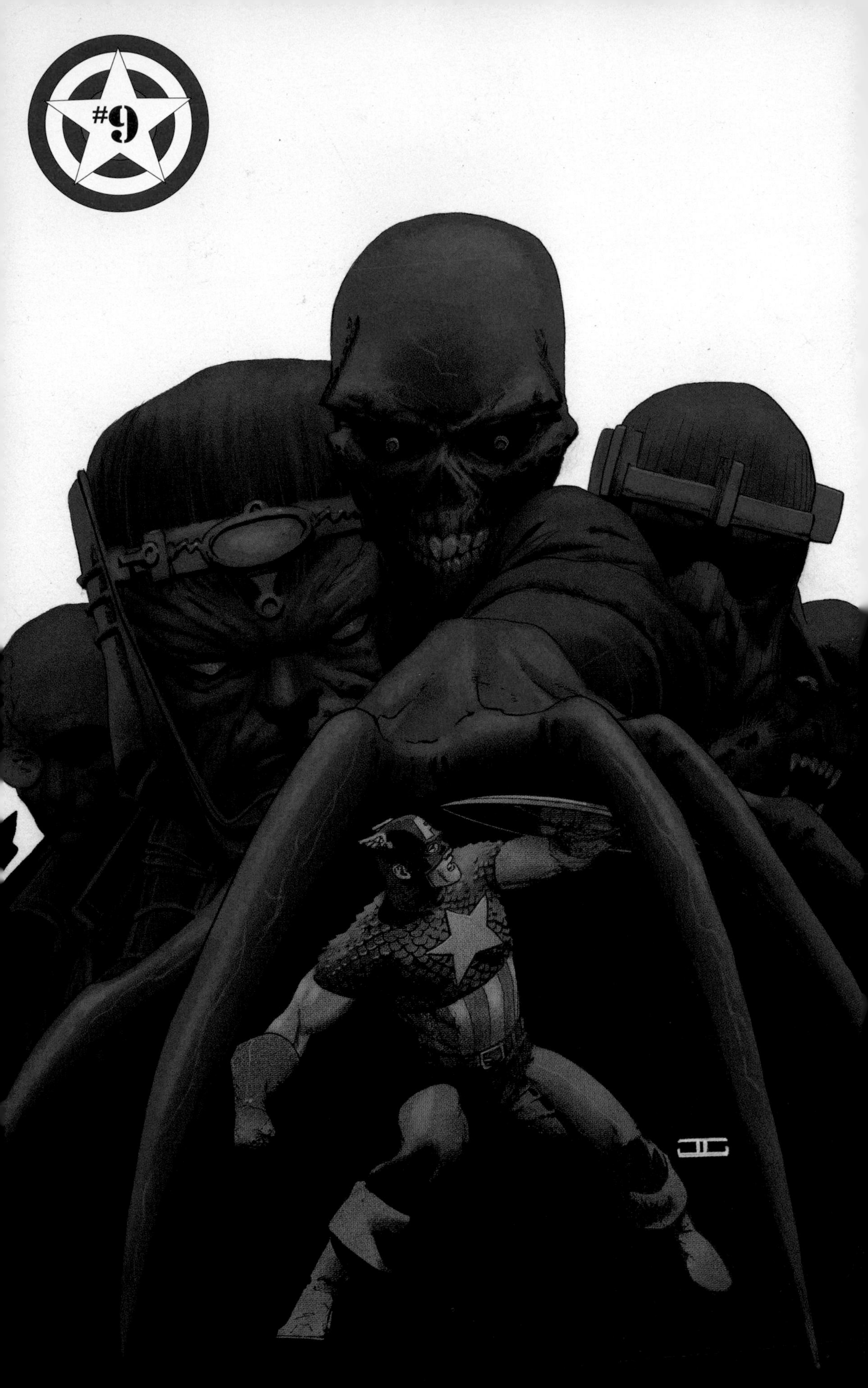
#9

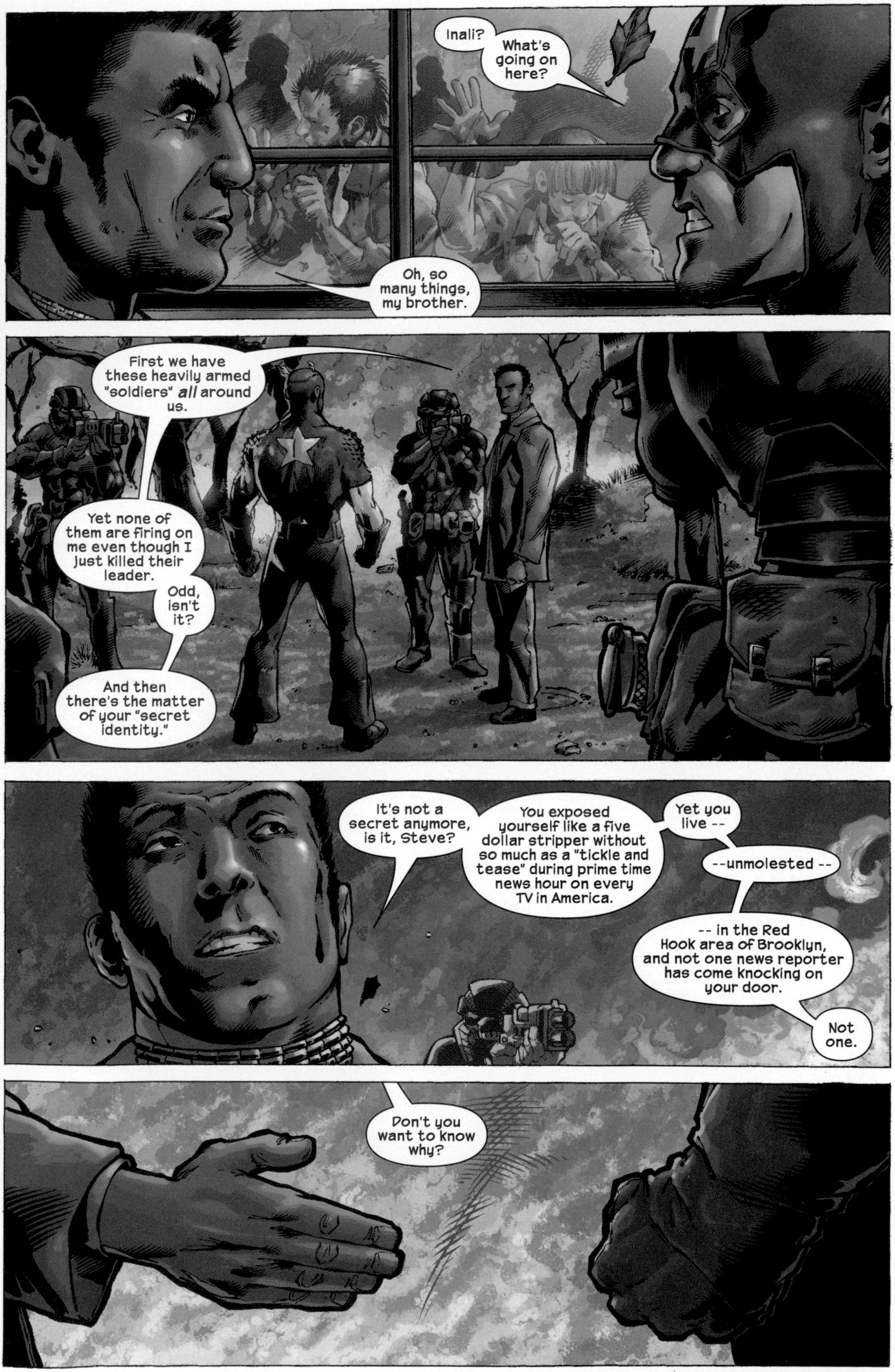
Inali?
What's going on here?
Oh, so many things, my brother.
First we have these heavily armed "soldiers" *all* around us.
Yet none of them are firing on me even though I just killed their leader.
Odd, isn't it?
And then there's the matter of your "secret identity."
It's not a secret anymore, is it, Steve?
You exposed yourself like a five dollar stripper without so much as a "tickle and tease" during prime time news hour on every TV in America.
Yet you live --
--unmolested --
-- in the Red Hook area of Brooklyn, and not one news reporter has come knocking on your door.
Not one.
Don't you want to know why?

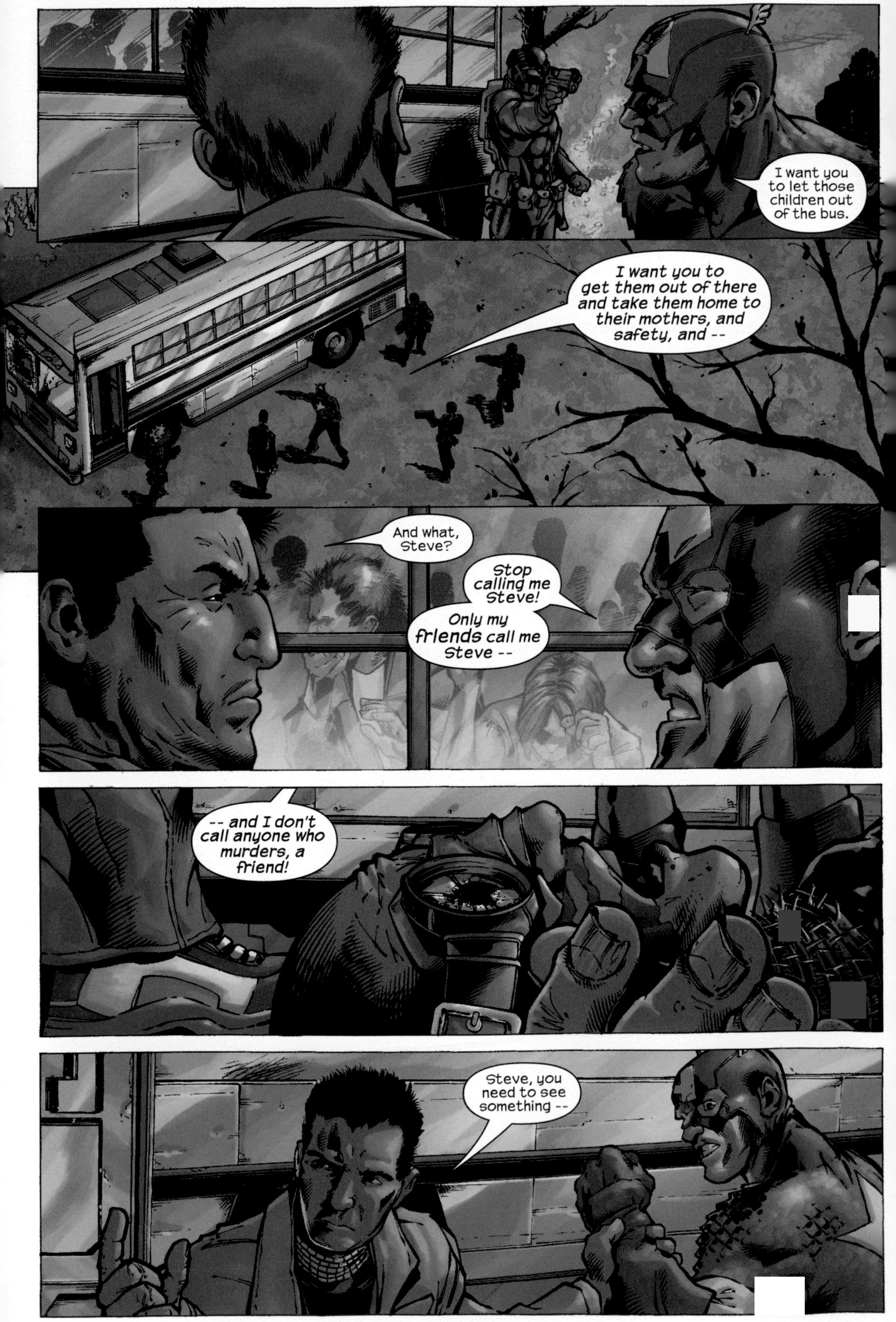
I want you to let those children out of the bus.
I want you to get them out of there and take them home to their mothers, and safety, and --
And what, Steve?
Stop calling me Steve!
Only my friends call me Steve --
-- and I don't call anyone who murders, a friend!
Steve, you need to see something --

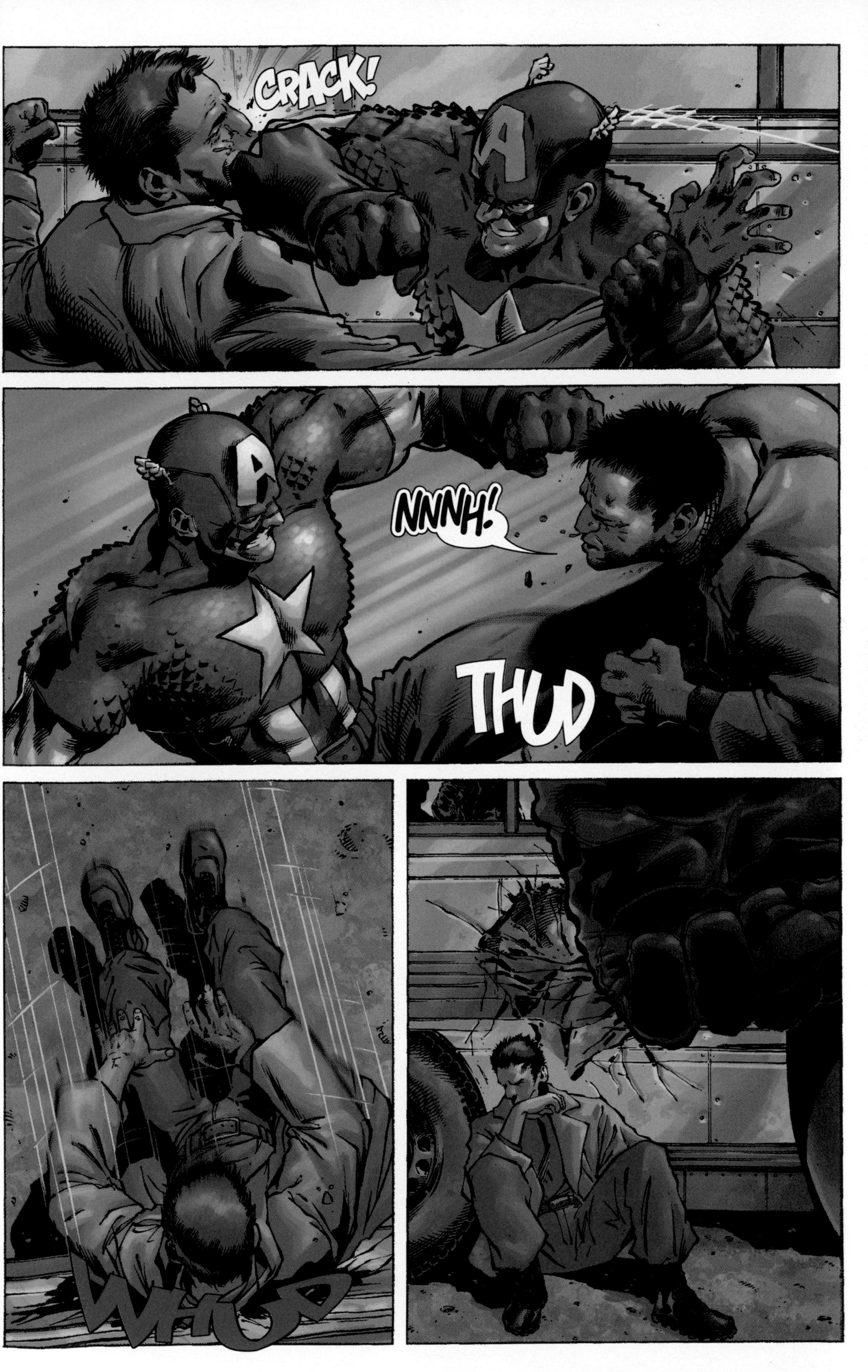
CRACK!
NNNH!
THUD
WHUD

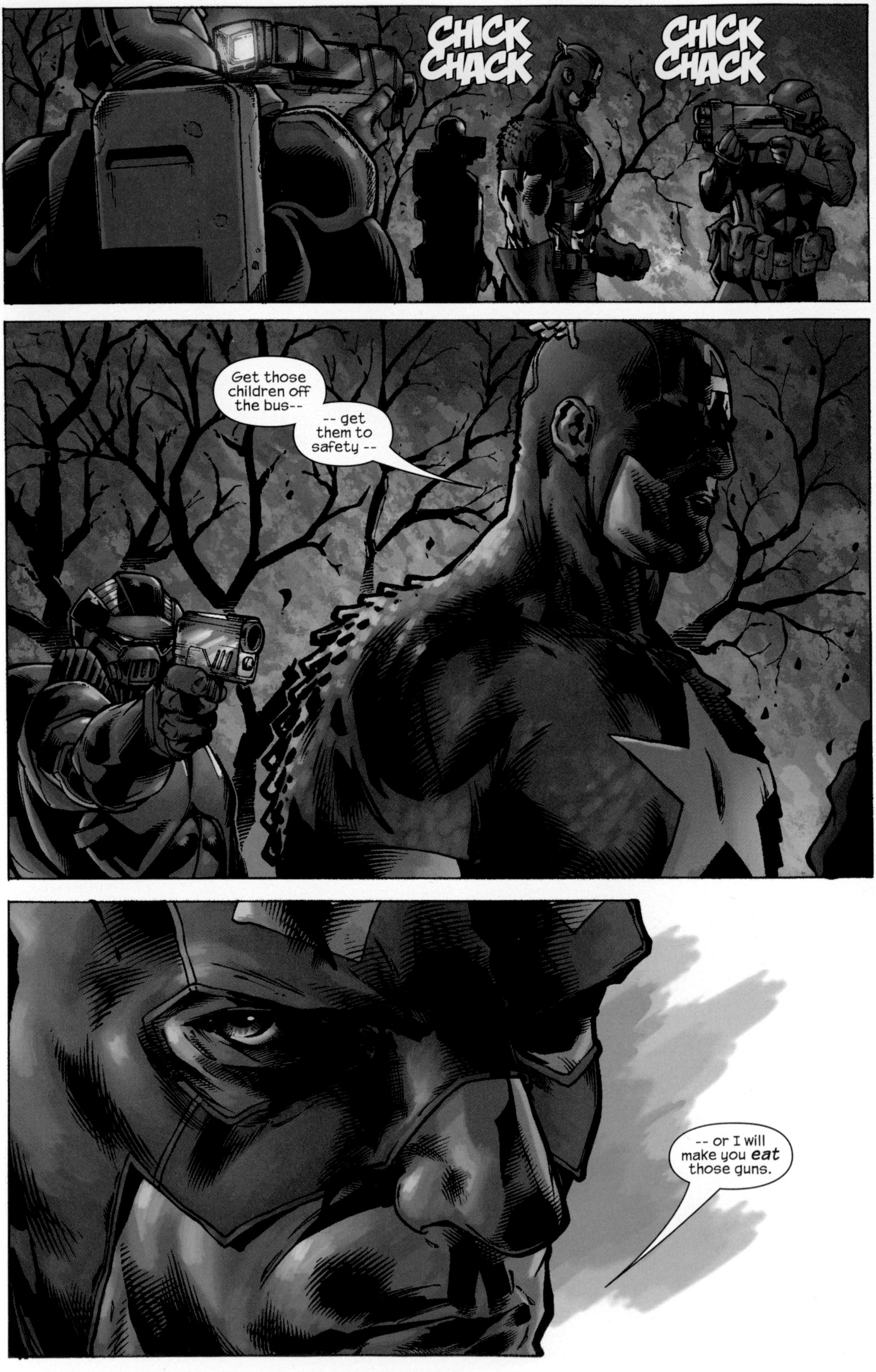
CHICK CHACK
CHICK CHACK
Get those children off the bus--
-- get them to safety --
-- or I will make you eat those guns.

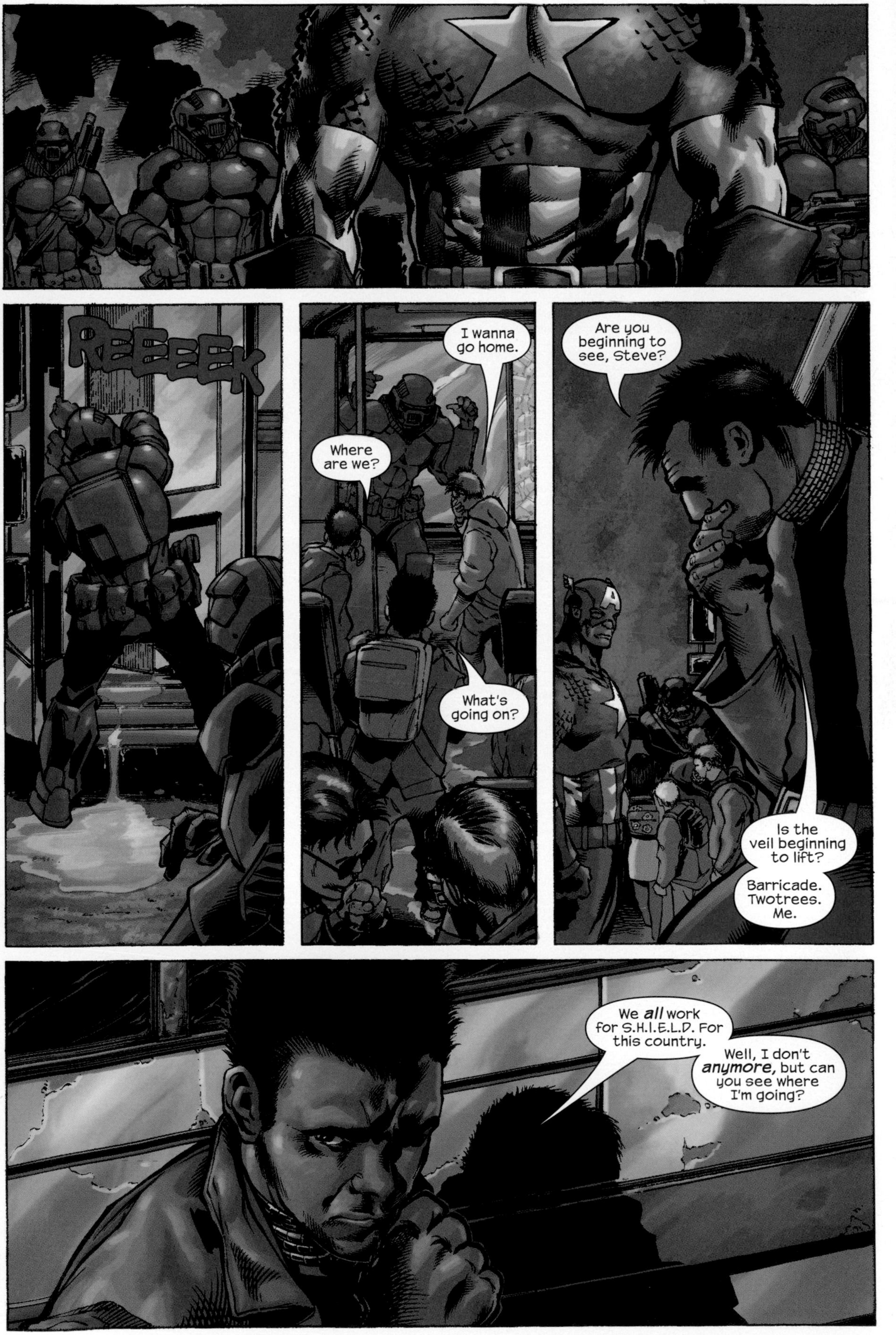
REEEEK
I wanna go home.
Where are we?
What's going on?
Are you beginning to see, Steve?
Is the veil beginning to lift?
Barricade. Twotrees. Me.
We *all* work for S.H.I.E.L.D. For this country.
Well, I don't *anymore,* but can you see where I'm going?

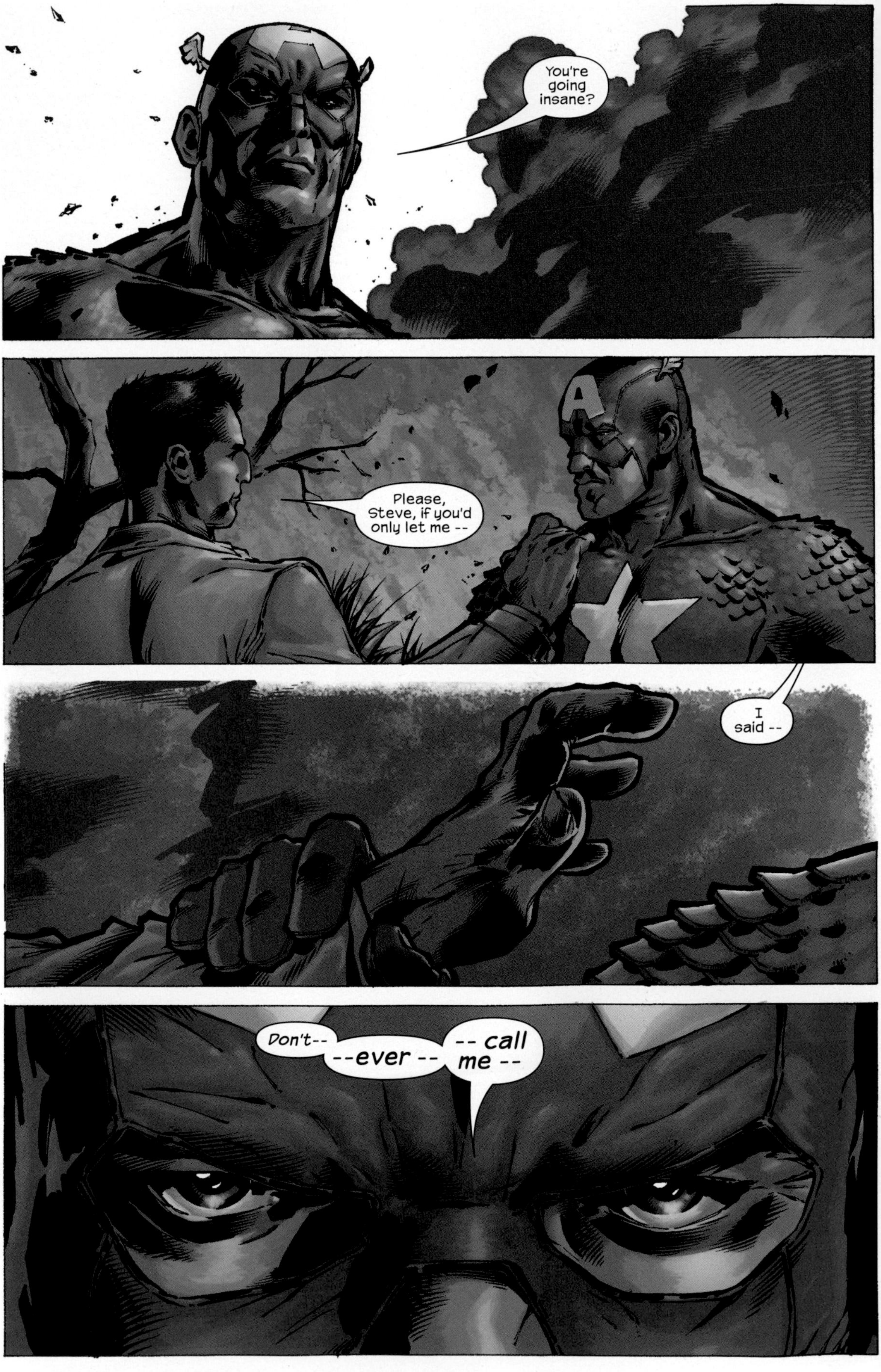
You're going insane?
Please, Steve, if you'd only let me --
I said --
Don't--
--ever --
-- call me --

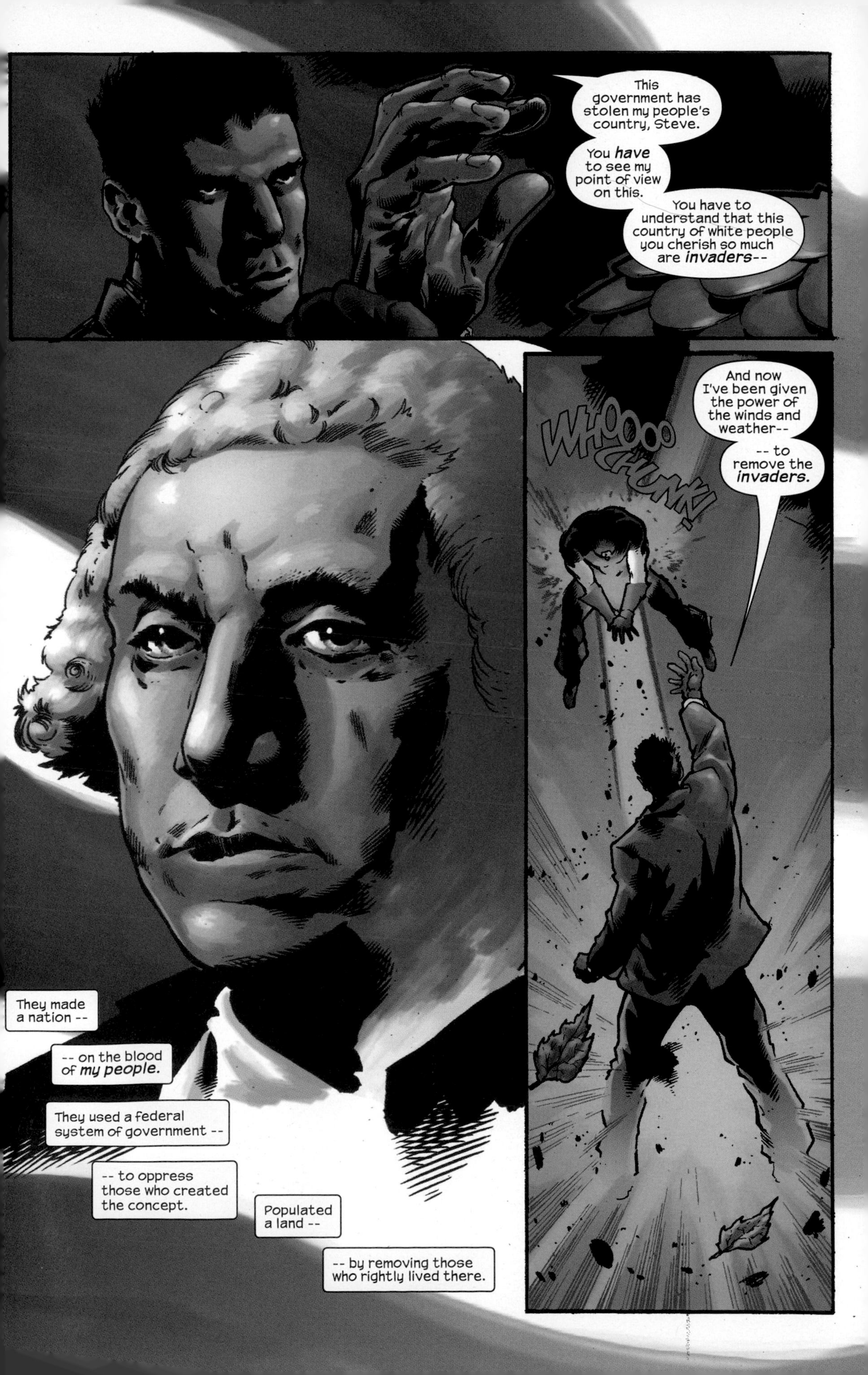
This government has stolen my people's country, Steve.
You have to see my point of view on this.
You have to understand that this country of white people you cherish so much are invaders--
And now I've been given the power of the winds and weather--
-- to remove the invaders.
WHOOOO
CHUNK!
They made a nation --
-- on the blood of my people.
They used a federal system of government --
-- to oppress those who created the concept.
Populated a land --
-- by removing those who rightly lived there.

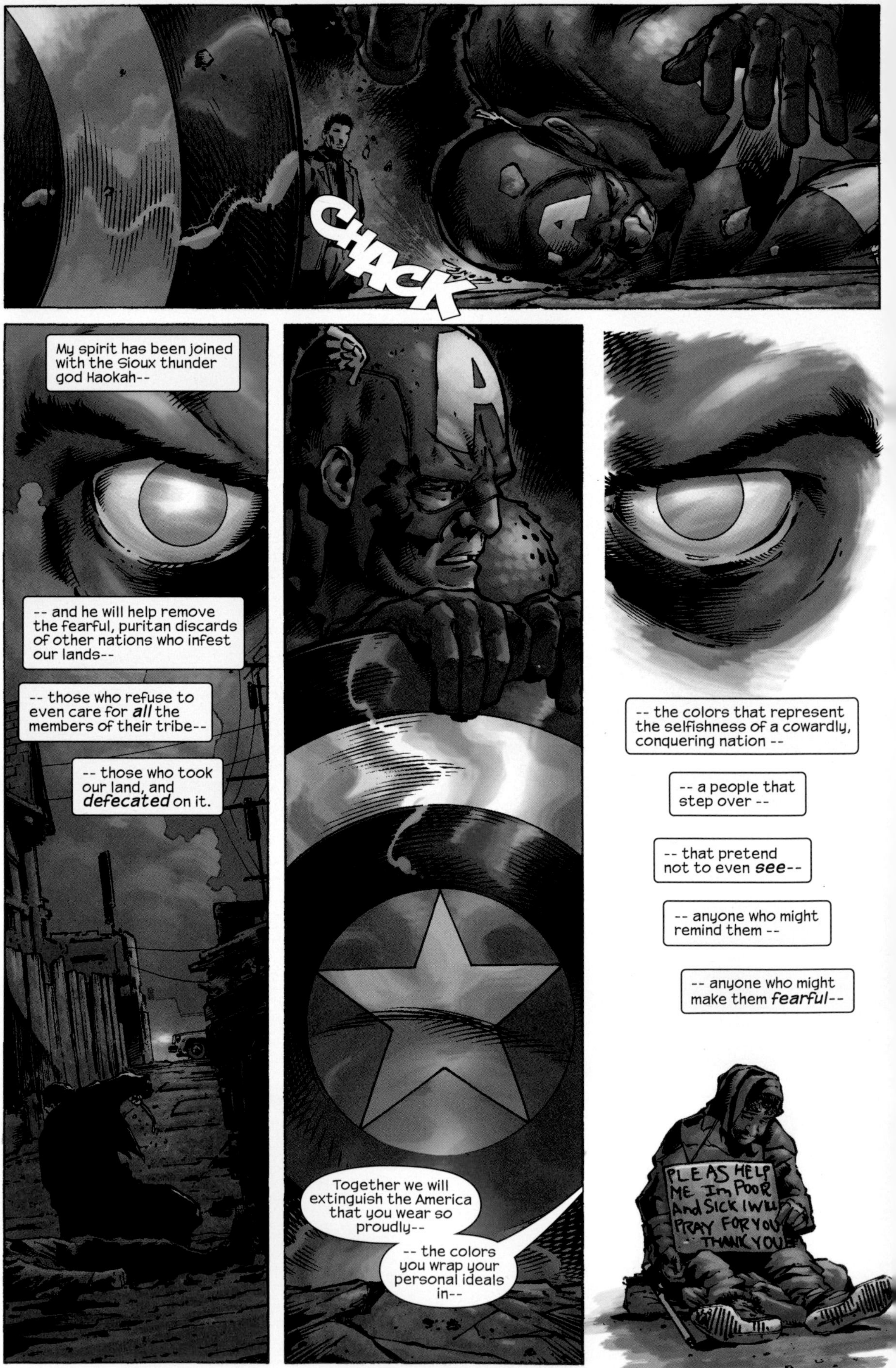
CHACK
My spirit has been joined with the Sioux thunder god Haokah--
-- and he will help remove the fearful, puritan discards of other nations who infest our lands--
-- those who refuse to even care for *all* the members of their tribe--
-- those who took our land, and *defecated* on it.
Together we will extinguish the America that you wear so proudly--
-- the colors you wrap your personal ideals in--
-- the colors that represent the selfishness of a cowardly, conquering nation --
-- a people that step over --
-- that pretend not to even *see*--
-- anyone who might remind them --
-- anyone who might make them *fearful*--
PLEAS HELP ME I'm POOR And SICK I WILL PRAY FOR YOU THANK YOU

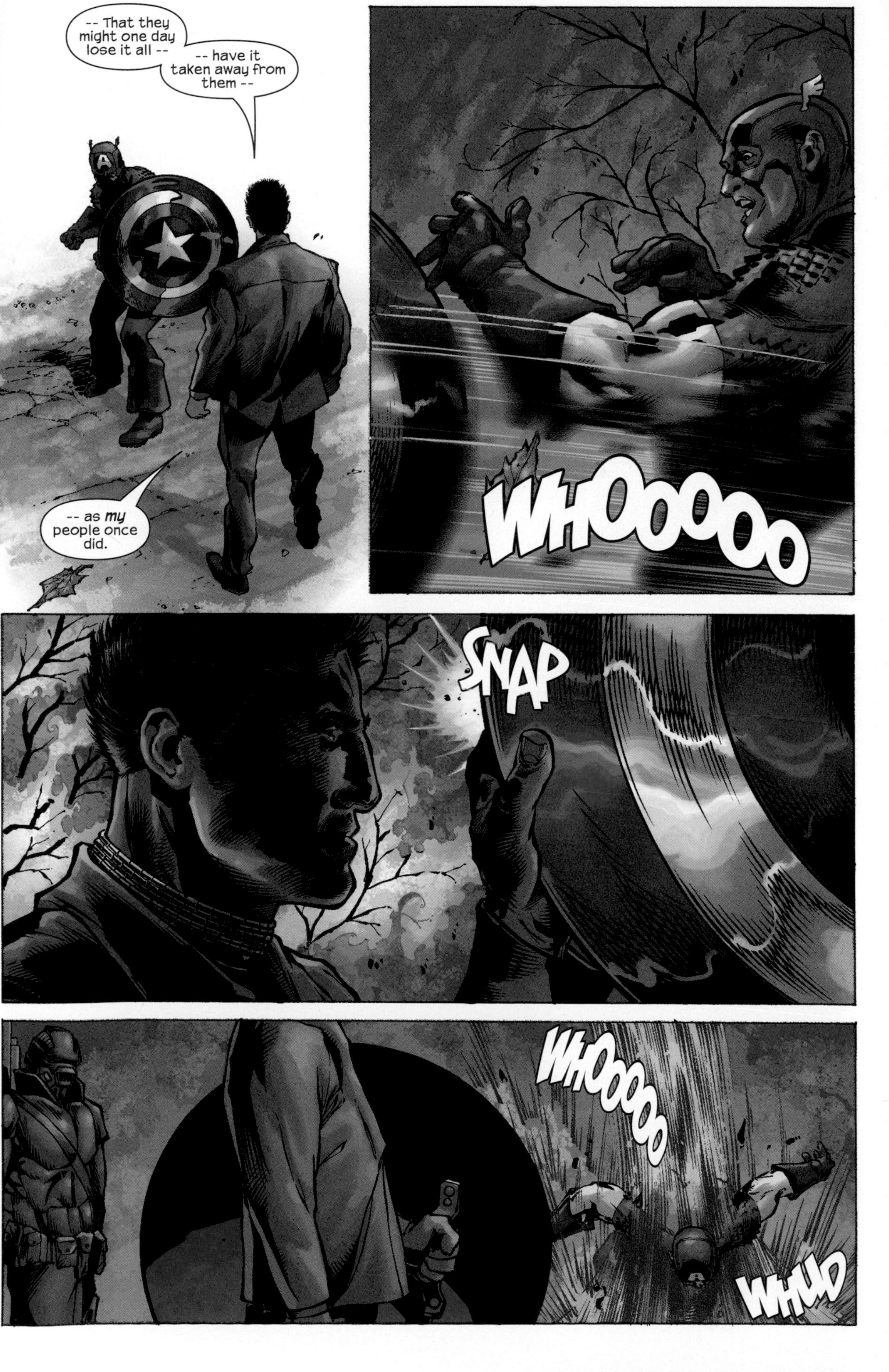
-- That they might one day lose it all --
-- have it taken away from them --
-- as *my* people once did.
WHOOOOO
SNAP
WHOOOOO
WHUD

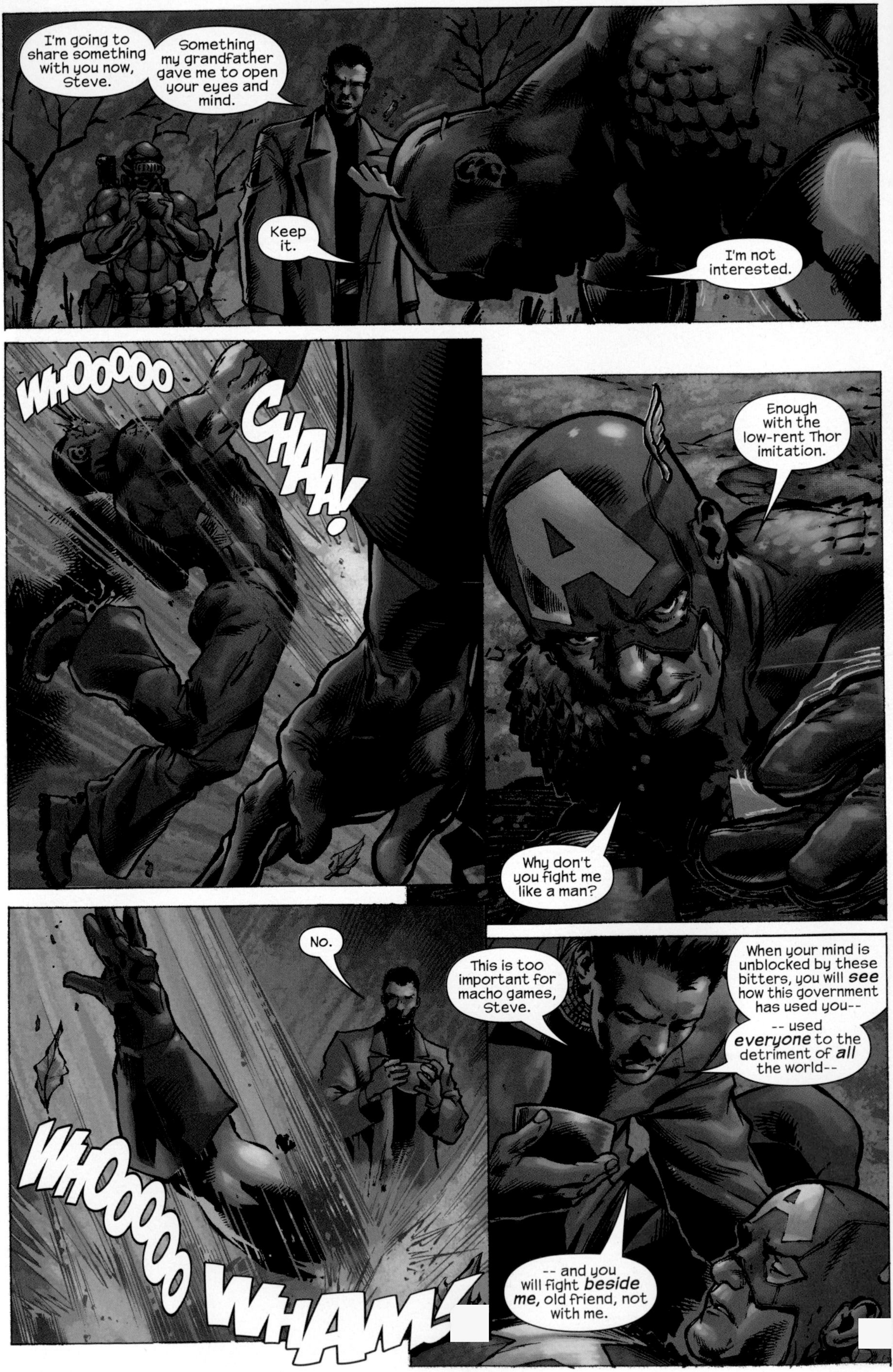
I'm going to share something with you now, Steve.
Something my grandfather gave me to open your eyes and mind.
Keep it.
I'm not interested.
WHOOOOO
CHAA!
Enough with the low-rent Thor imitation.
Why don't you fight me like a man?
No.
This is too important for macho games, Steve.
When your mind is unblocked by these bitters, you will *see* how this government has used you--
-- used *everyone* to the detriment of *all* the world--
-- and you will fight *beside me,* old friend, not with me.
WHOOOOOO
WHAM!

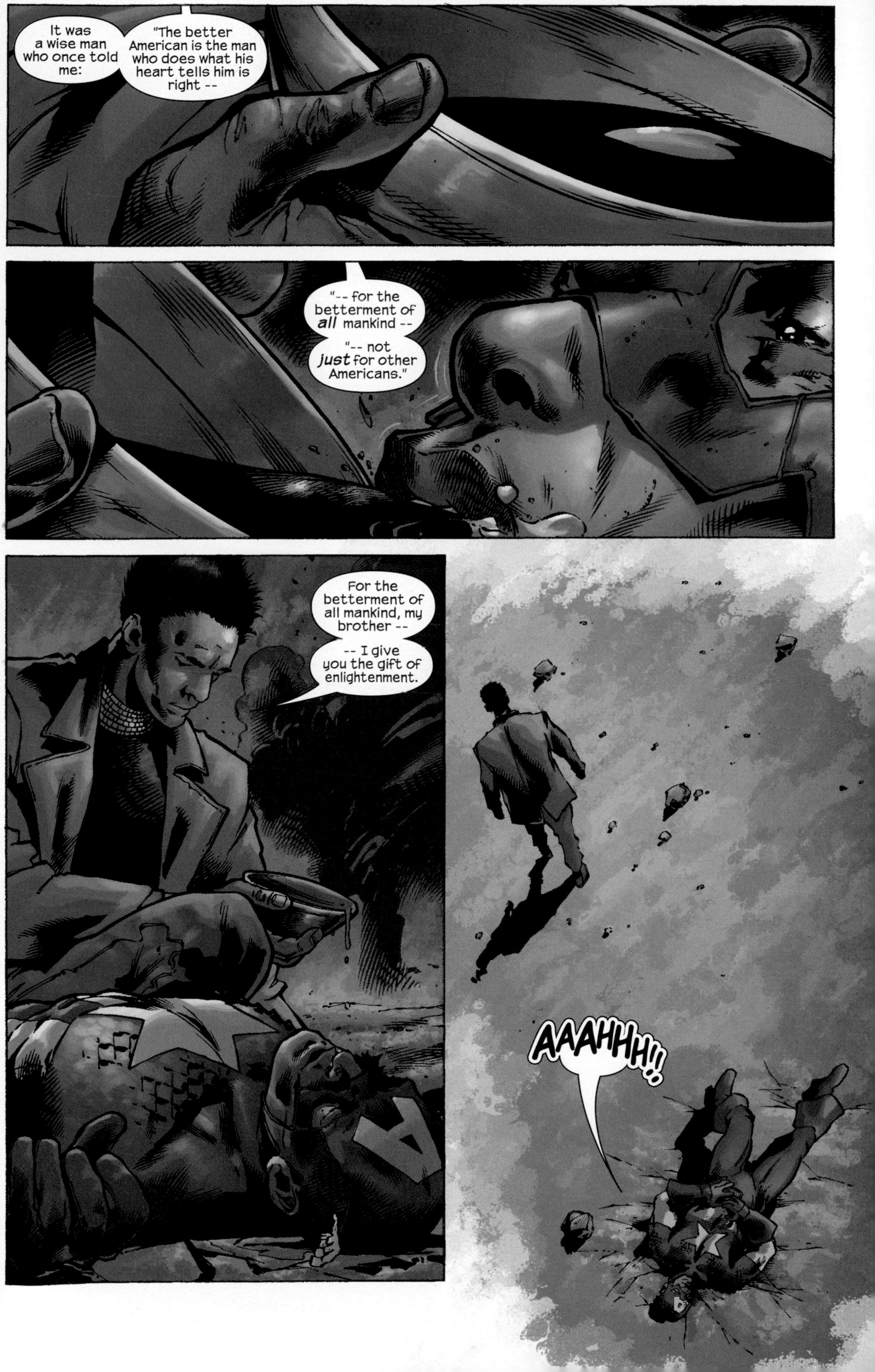
It was a wise man who once told me:
"The better American is the man who does what his heart tells him is right --
"-- for the betterment of *all* mankind --
"-- not *just* for other Americans."
For the betterment of all mankind, my brother --
-- I give you the gift of enlightenment.
AAAHHH!!

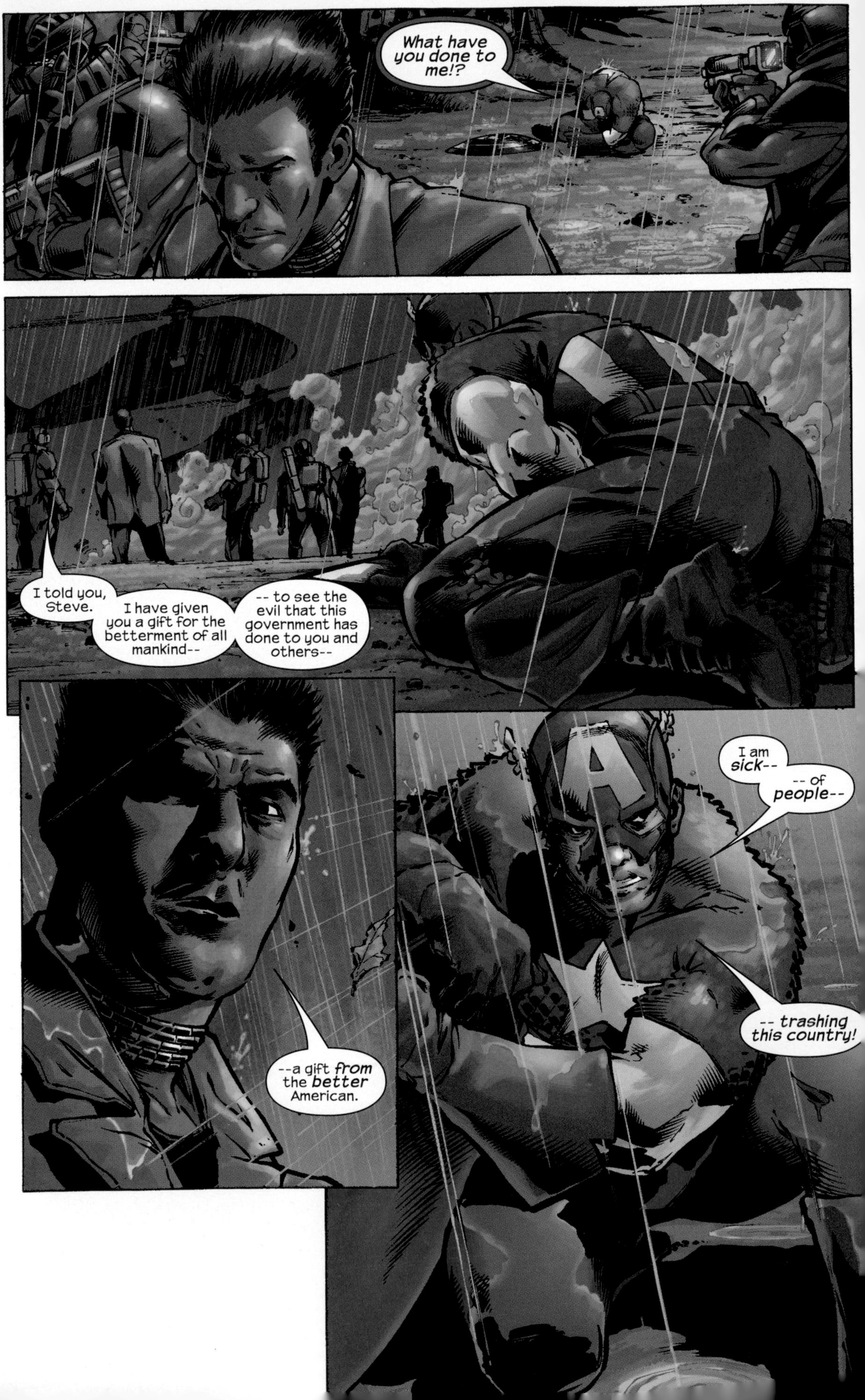
What have you done to me!?
I told you, Steve.
I have given you a gift for the betterment of all mankind--
-- to see the evil that this government has done to you and others--
--a gift *from* the *better* American.
I am *sick*--
-- of *people*--
-- *trashing this country!*

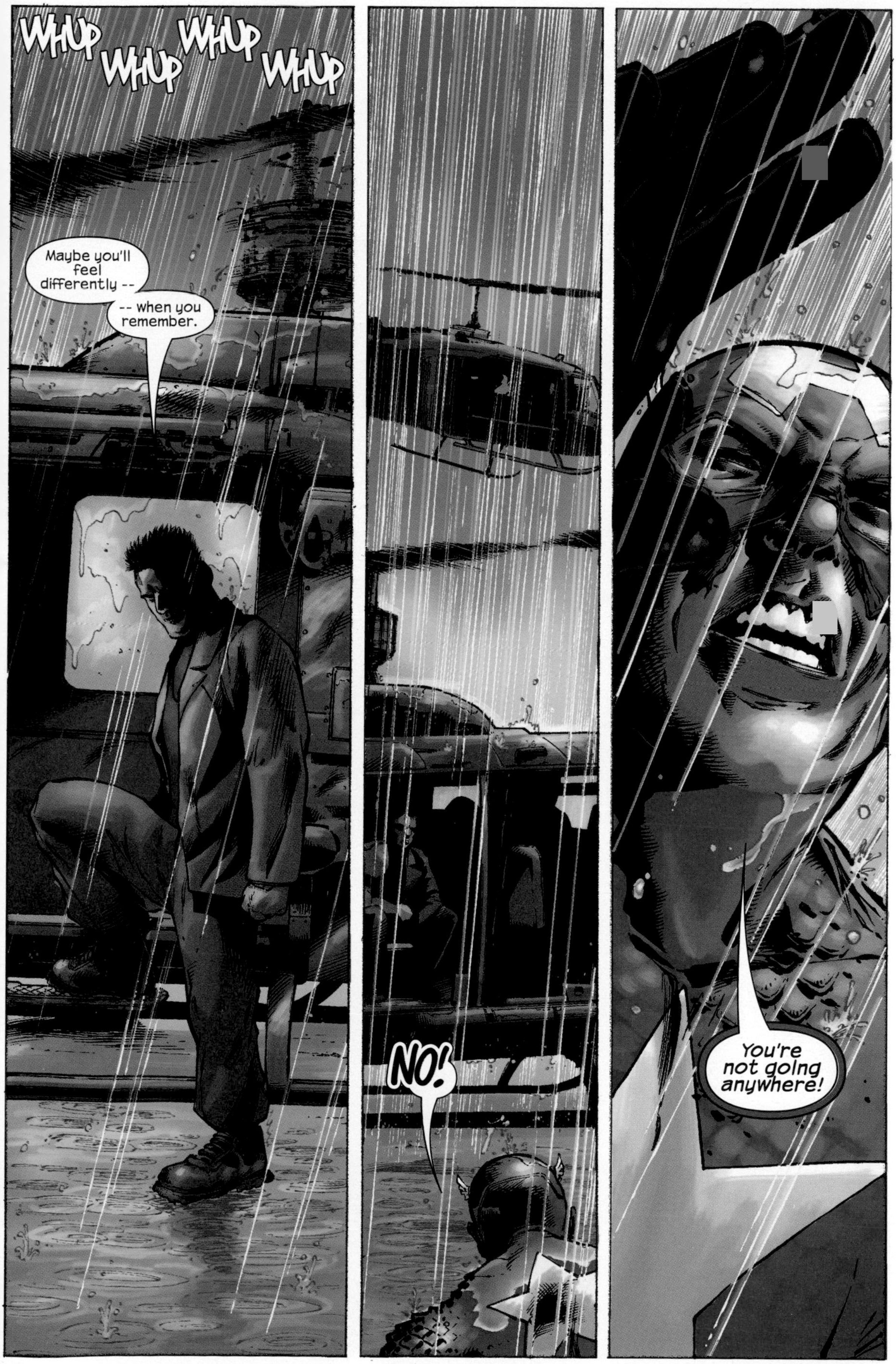
WHUP WHUP WHUP WHUP
Maybe you'll feel differently --
-- when you remember.
NO!
You're not going anywhere!

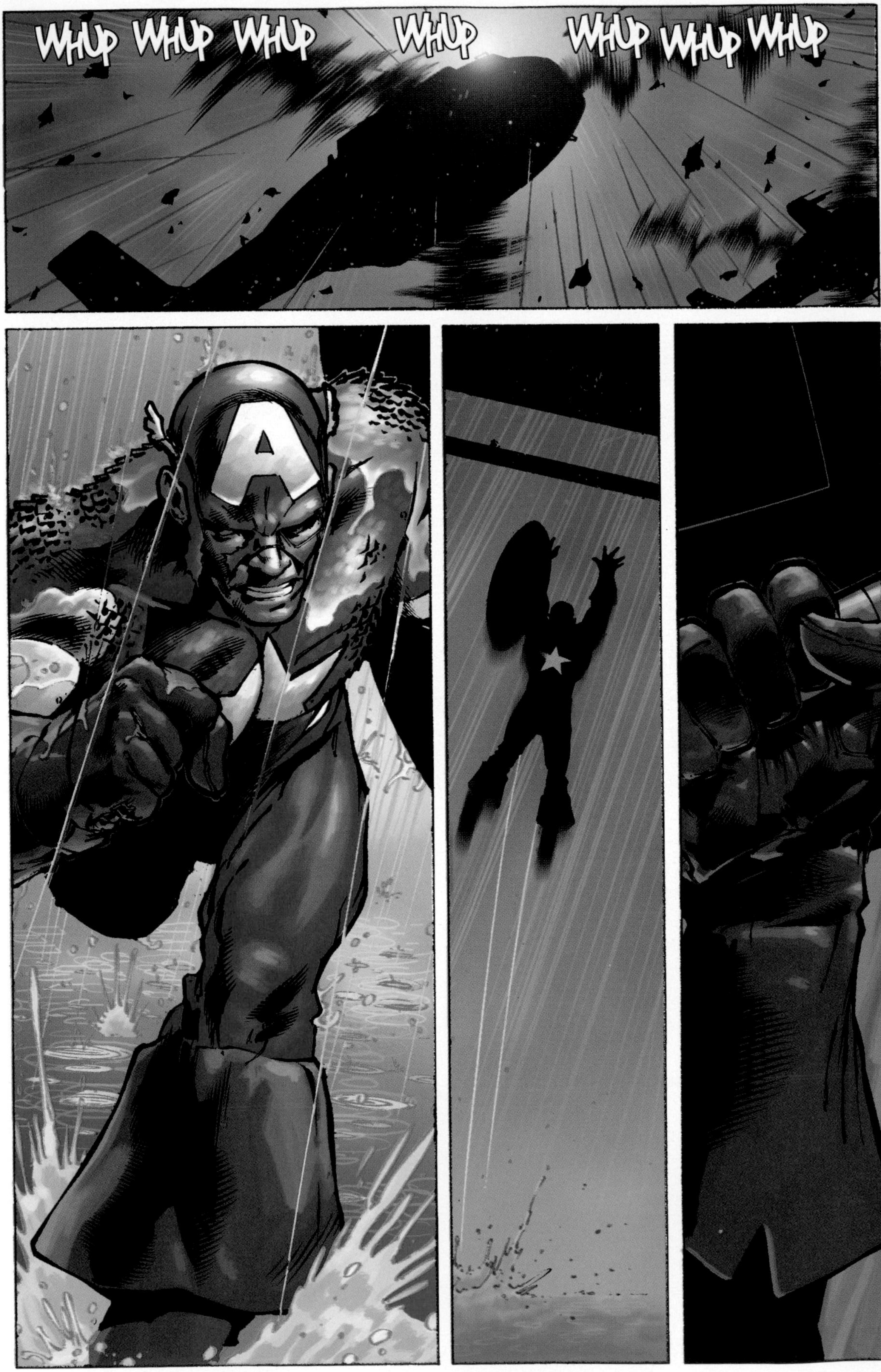
WHUP WHUP WHUP
WHUP
WHUP WHUP WHUP

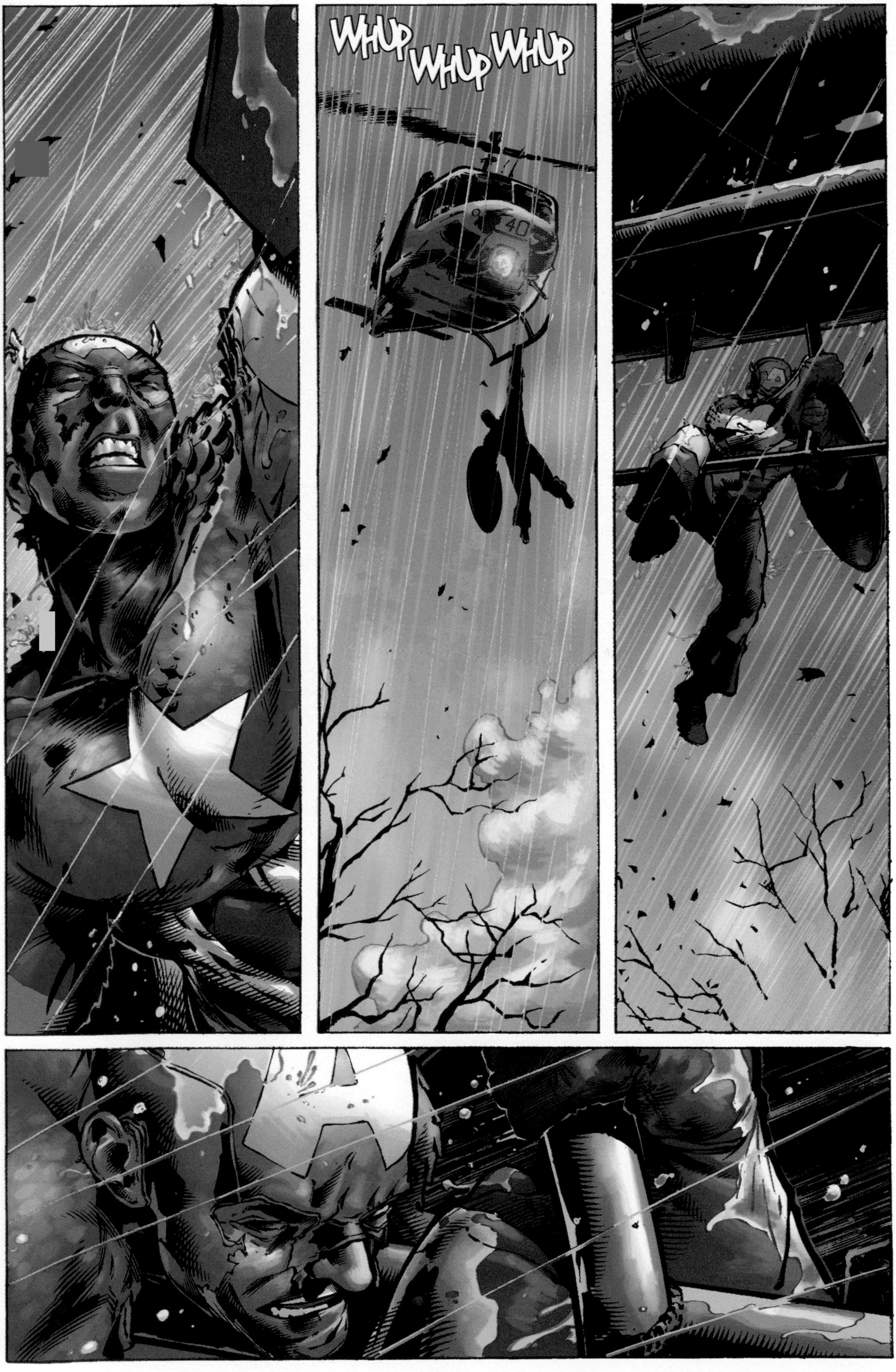
WHUP WHUP WHUP

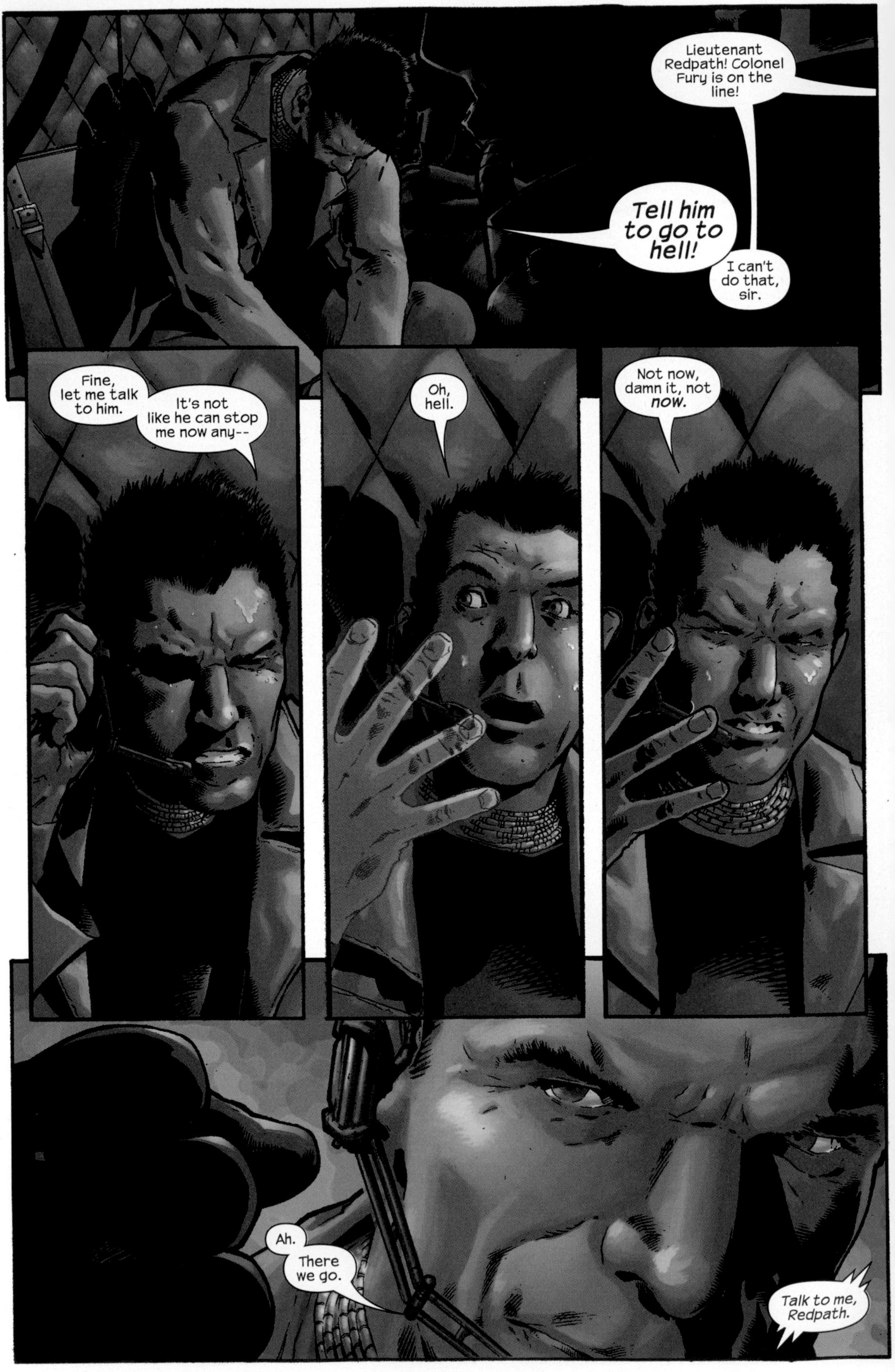
Lieutenant Redpath! Colonel Fury is on the line!
Tell him to go to hell!
I can't do that, sir.
Fine, let me talk to him.
It's not like he can stop me now any--
Oh, hell.
Not now, damn it, not now.
Ah.
There we go.
Talk to me, Redpath.

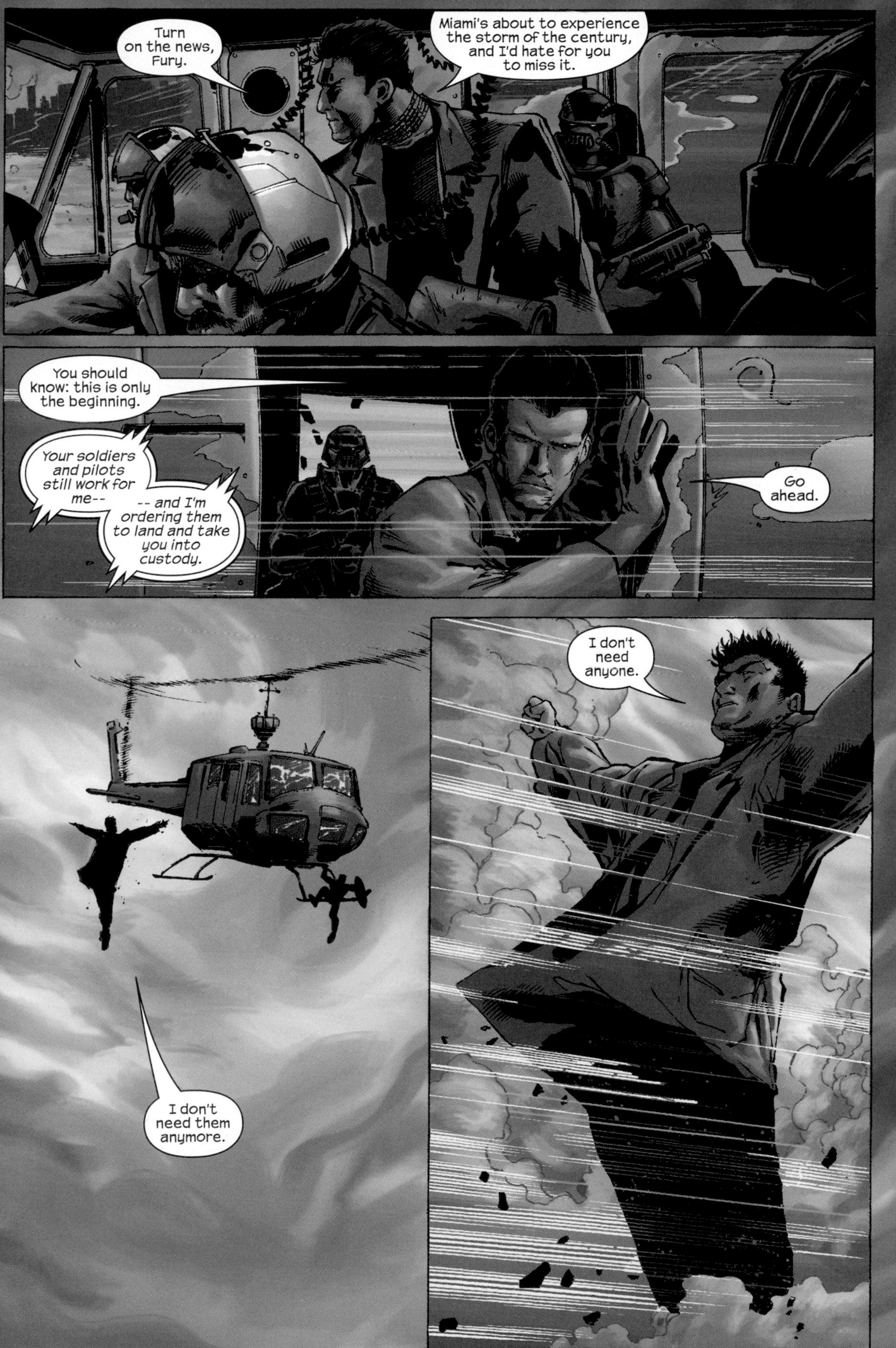
Turn on the news, Fury.
Miami's about to experience the storm of the century, and I'd hate for you to miss it.
You should know: this is only the beginning.
Your soldiers and pilots still work for me--
-- and I'm ordering them to land and take you into custody.
Go ahead.
I don't need them anymore.
I don't need anyone.

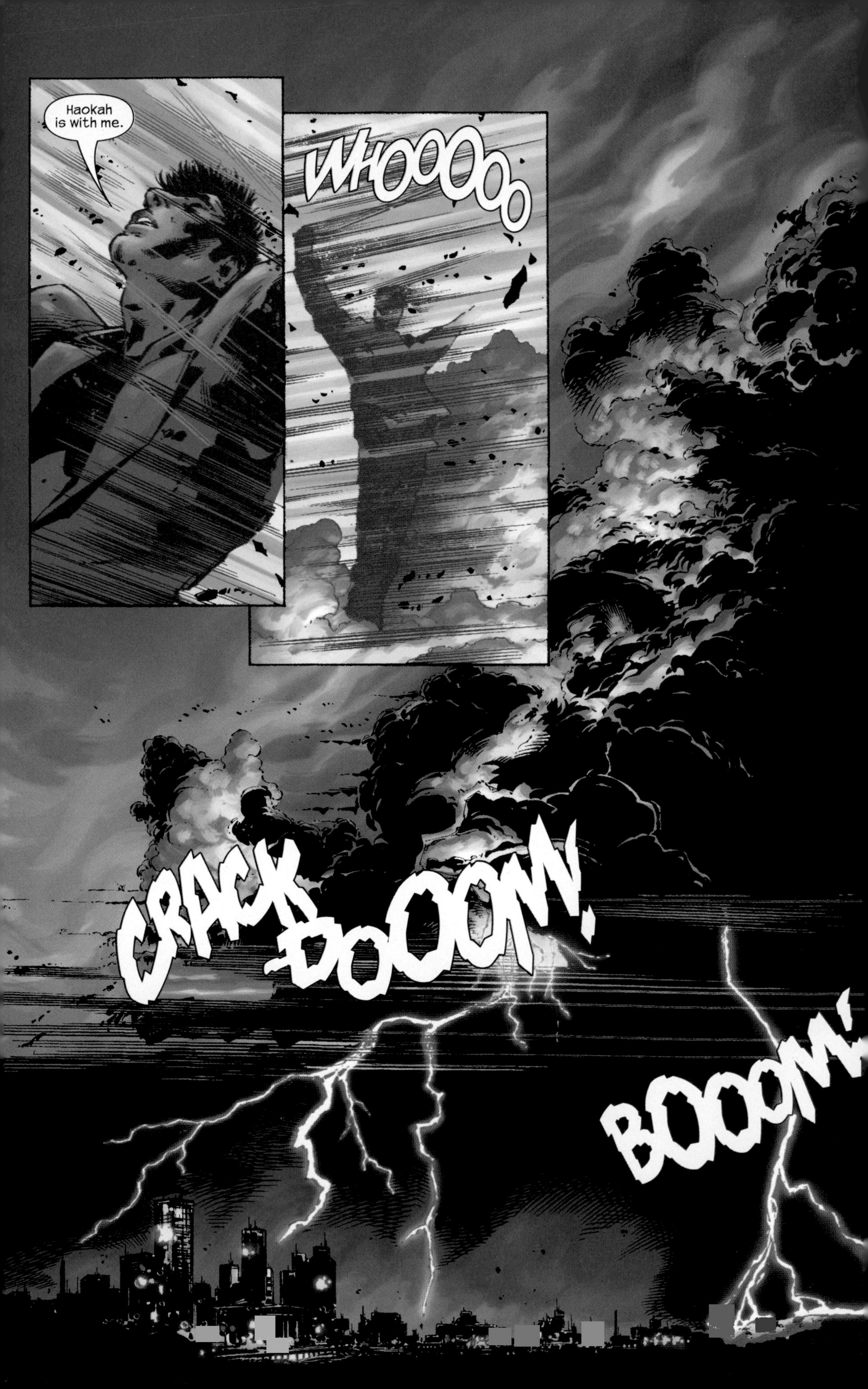
Haokah is with me.
WHOOOOO
CRACK-BOOOOM!
BOOOM!

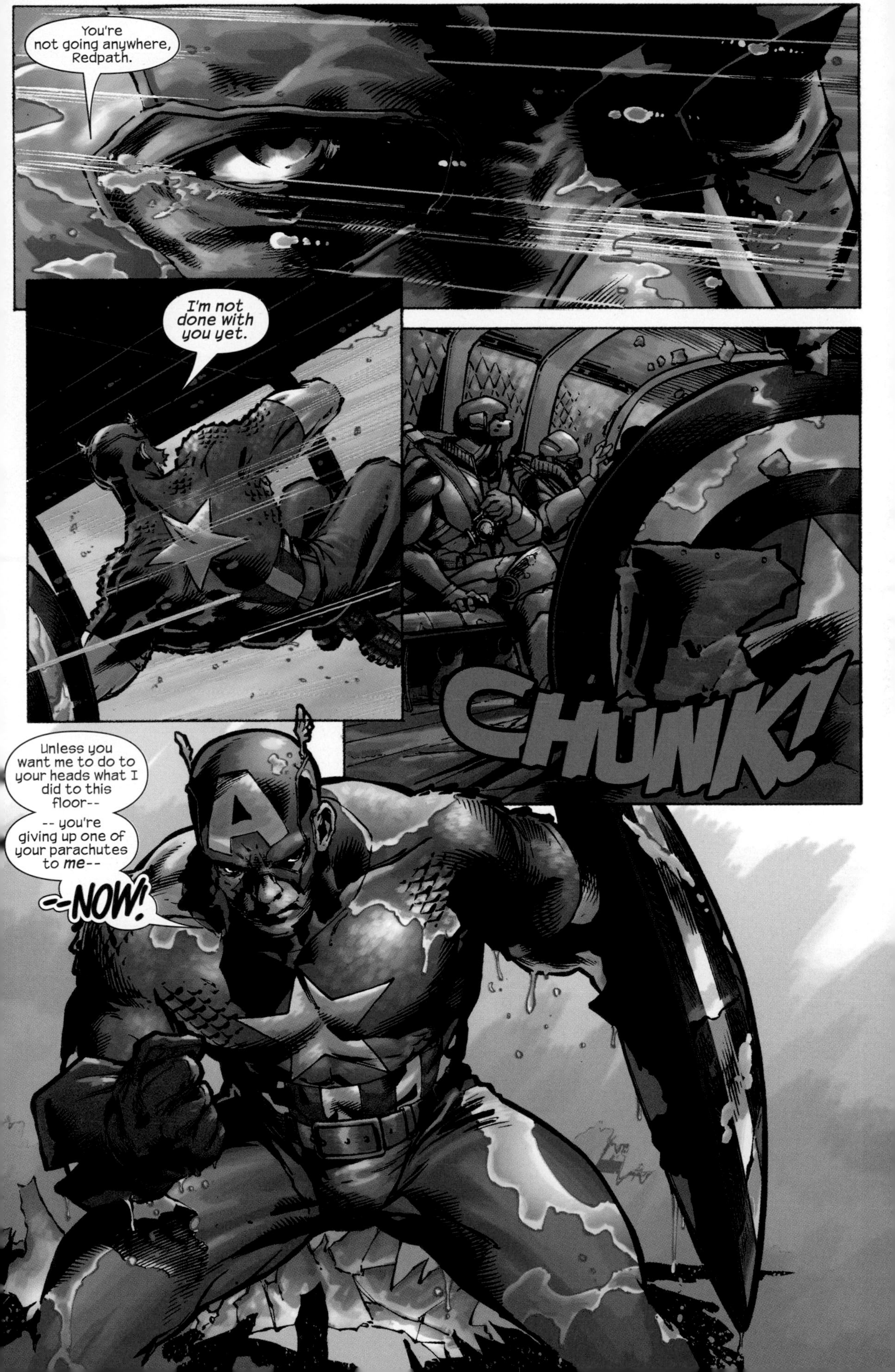
You're not going anywhere, Redpath.
I'm not done with you yet.
CHUNK!
Unless you want me to do to your heads what I did to this floor--
-- you're giving up one of your parachutes to *me*--
--NOW!

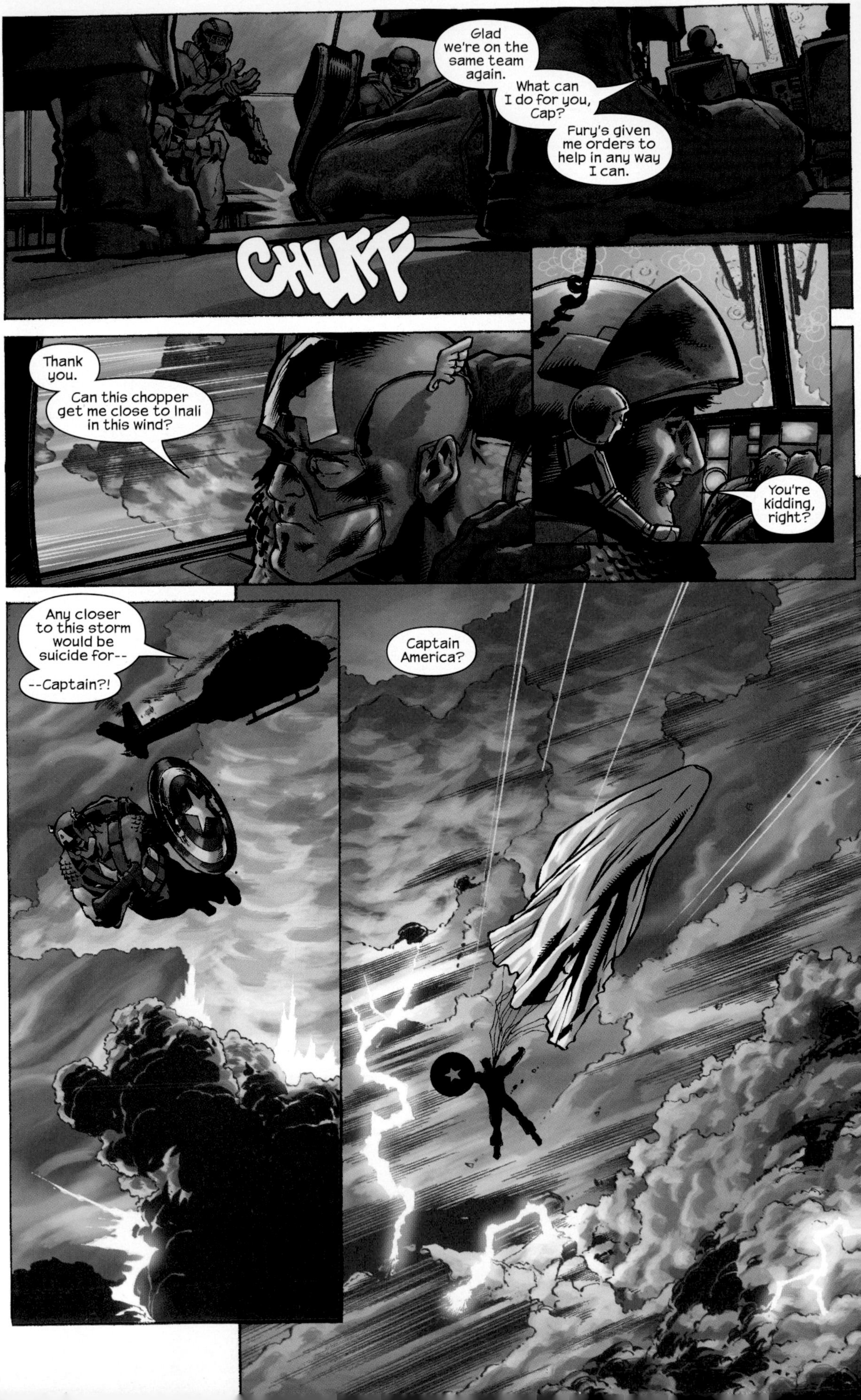
Glad we're on the same team again.
What can I do for you, Cap?
Fury's given me orders to help in any way I can.
CHUFF
Thank you.
Can this chopper get me close to Inali in this wind?
You're kidding, right?
Any closer to this storm would be suicide for--
--Captain?!
Captain America?

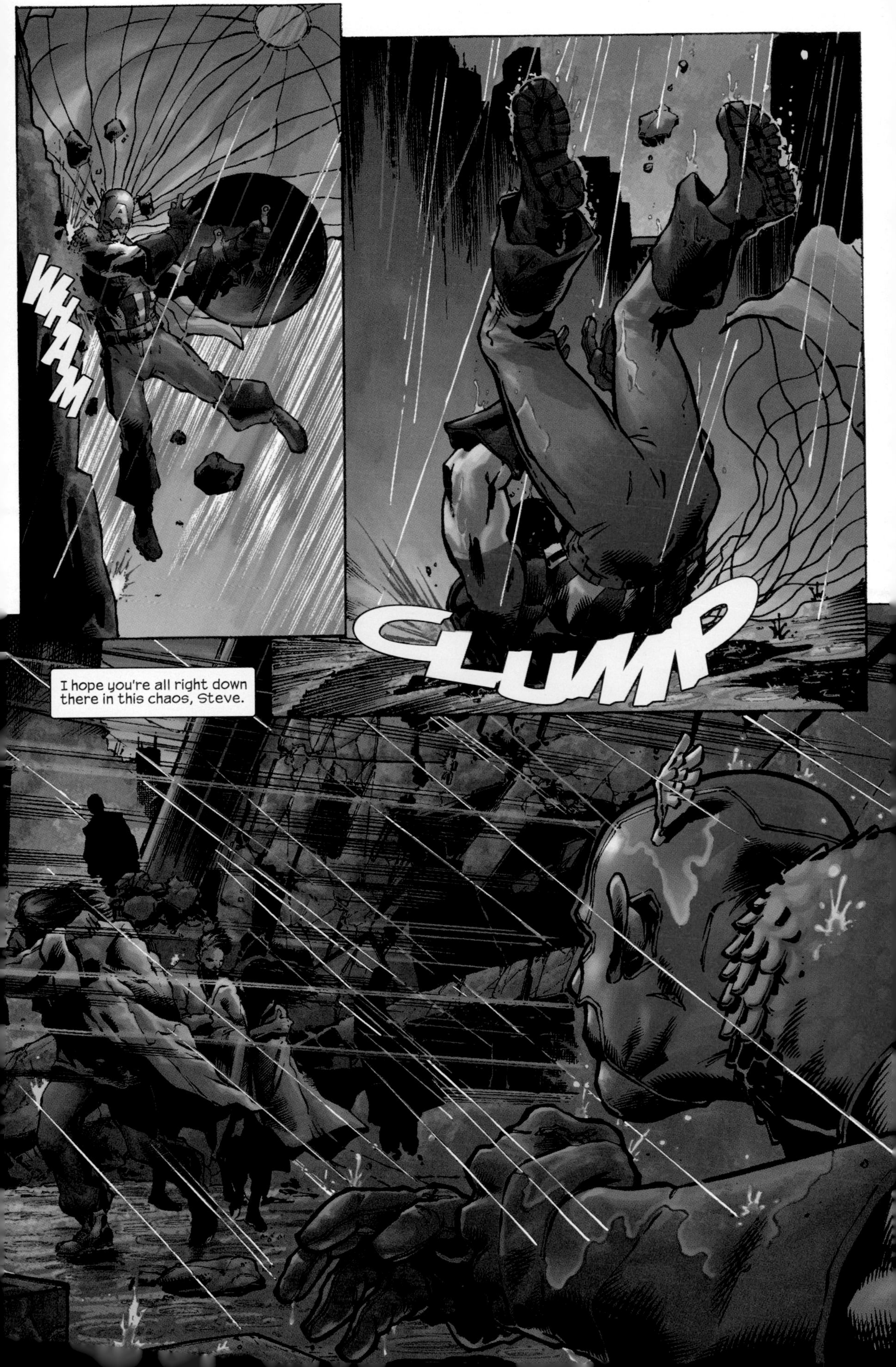
WHAM
CLUMP
I hope you're all right down there in this chaos, Steve.

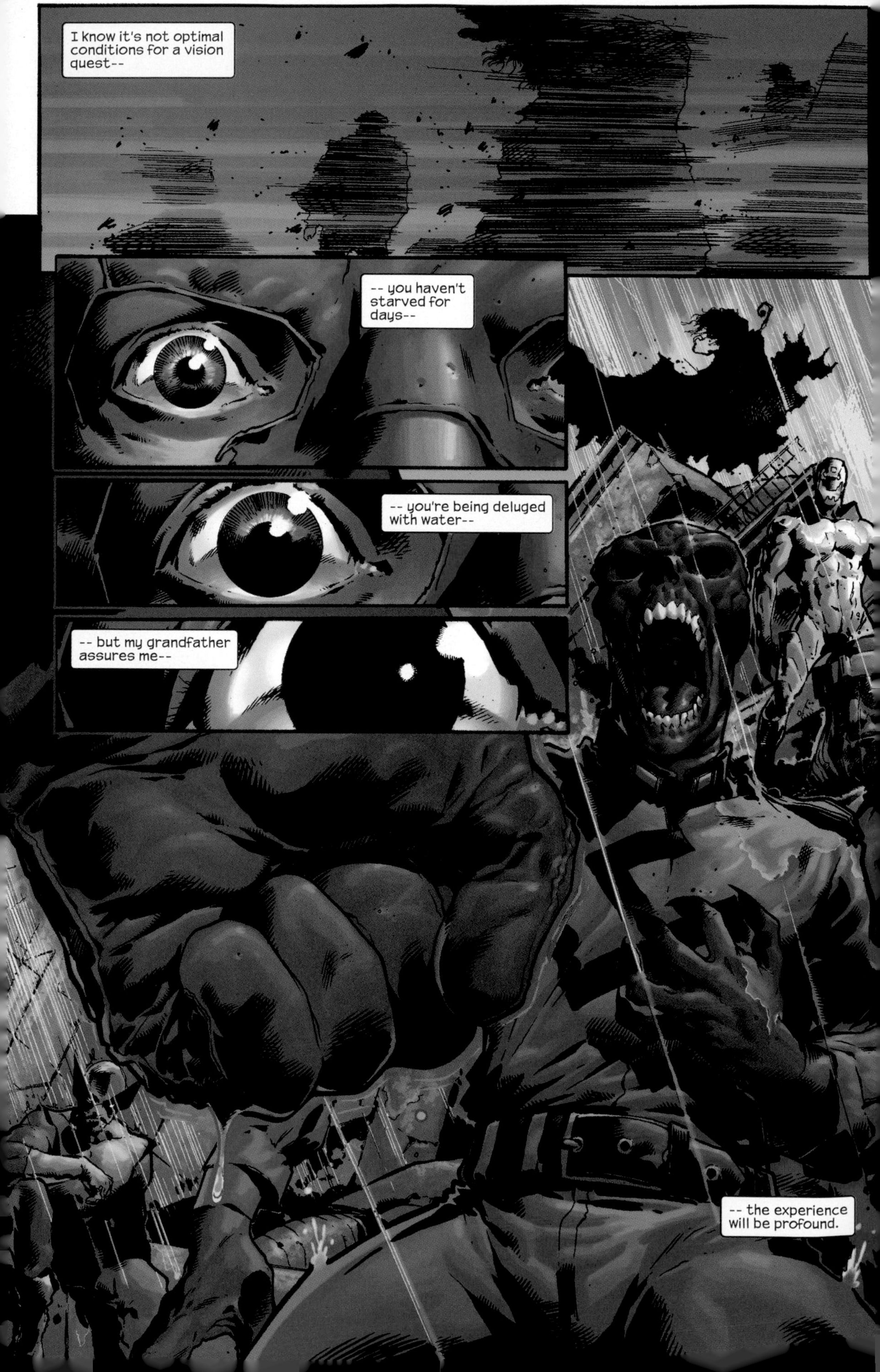
I know it's not optimal conditions for a vision quest--
-- you haven't starved for days--
-- you're being deluged with water--
-- but my grandfather assures me--
-- the experience will be profound.

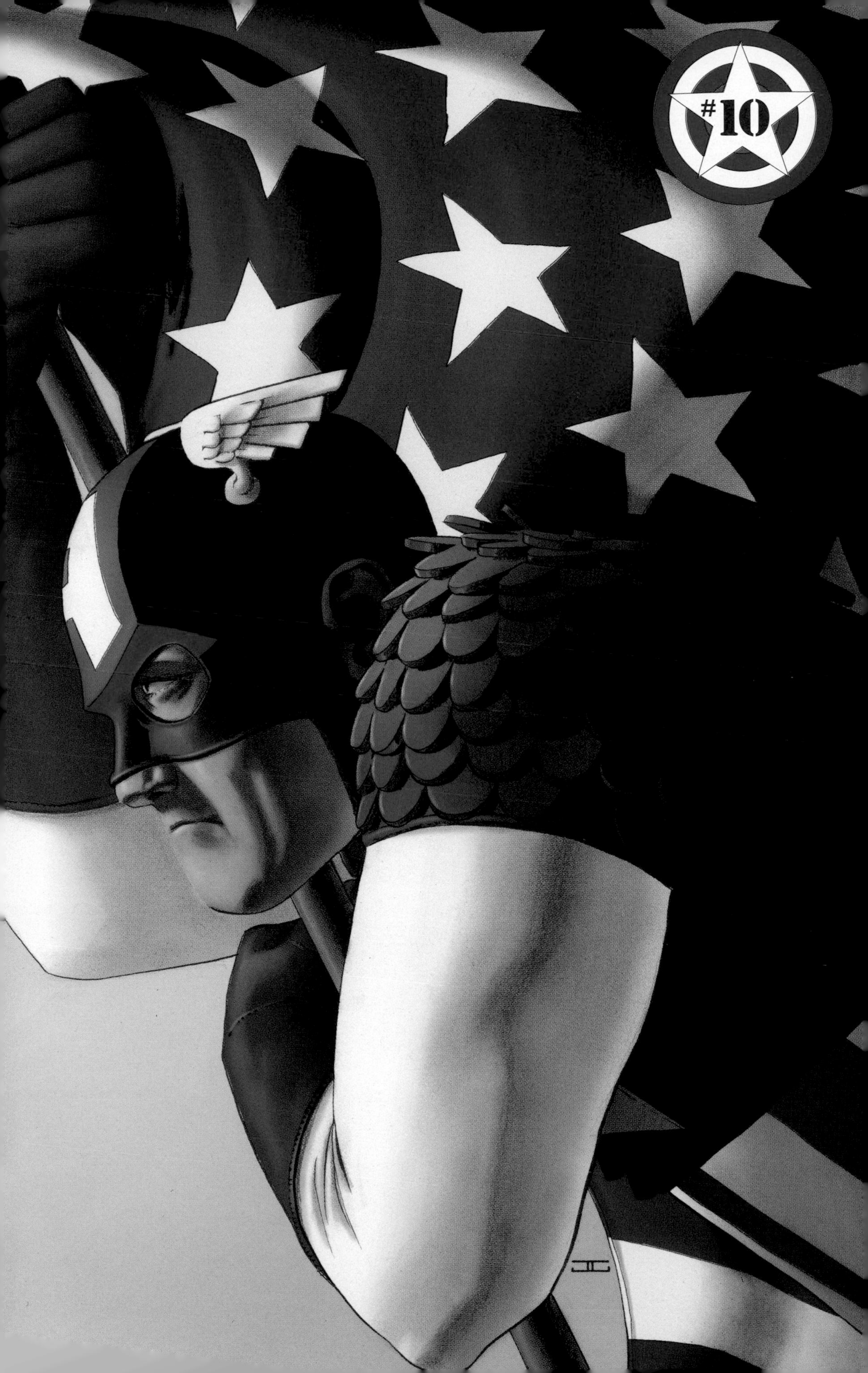
#10

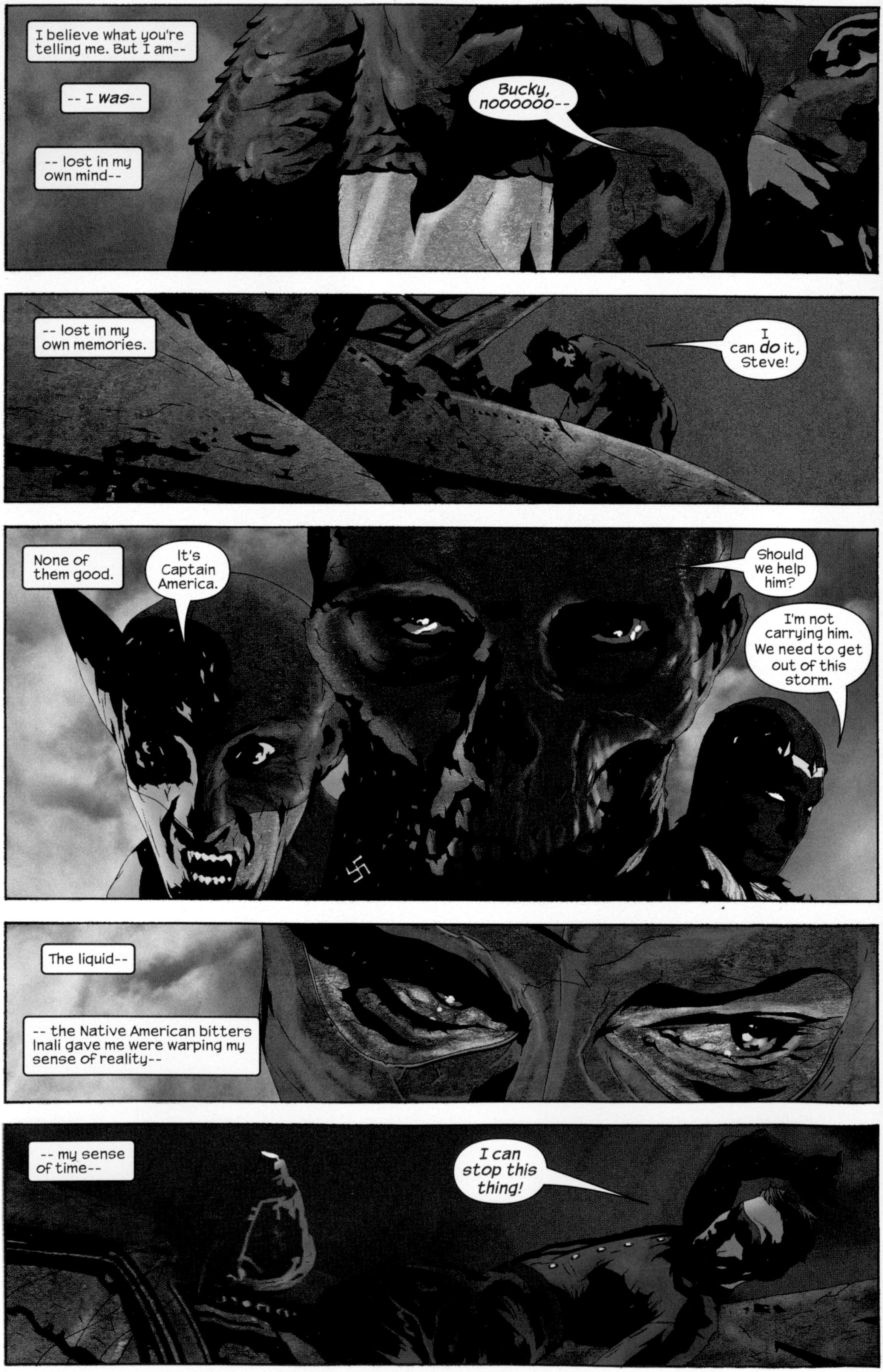

I believe what you're telling me. But I am--
-- I *was*--
-- lost in my own mind--
Bucky, nooooooo--
-- lost in my own memories.
I can *do* it, Steve!
None of them good.
It's Captain America.
Should we help him?
I'm not carrying him. We need to get out of this storm.
The liquid--
-- the Native American bitters Inali gave me were warping my sense of reality--
-- my sense of time--
I can stop this thing!

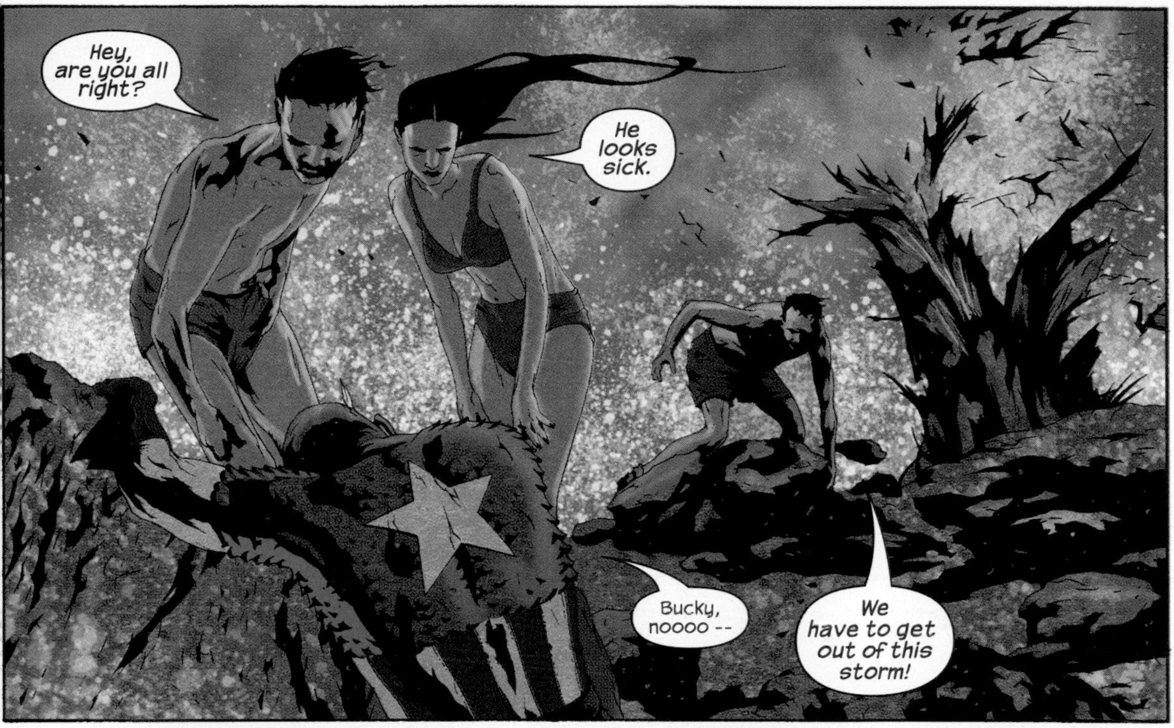
Hey, are you all right?
He looks sick.
Bucky, noooo --
We have to get out of this storm!
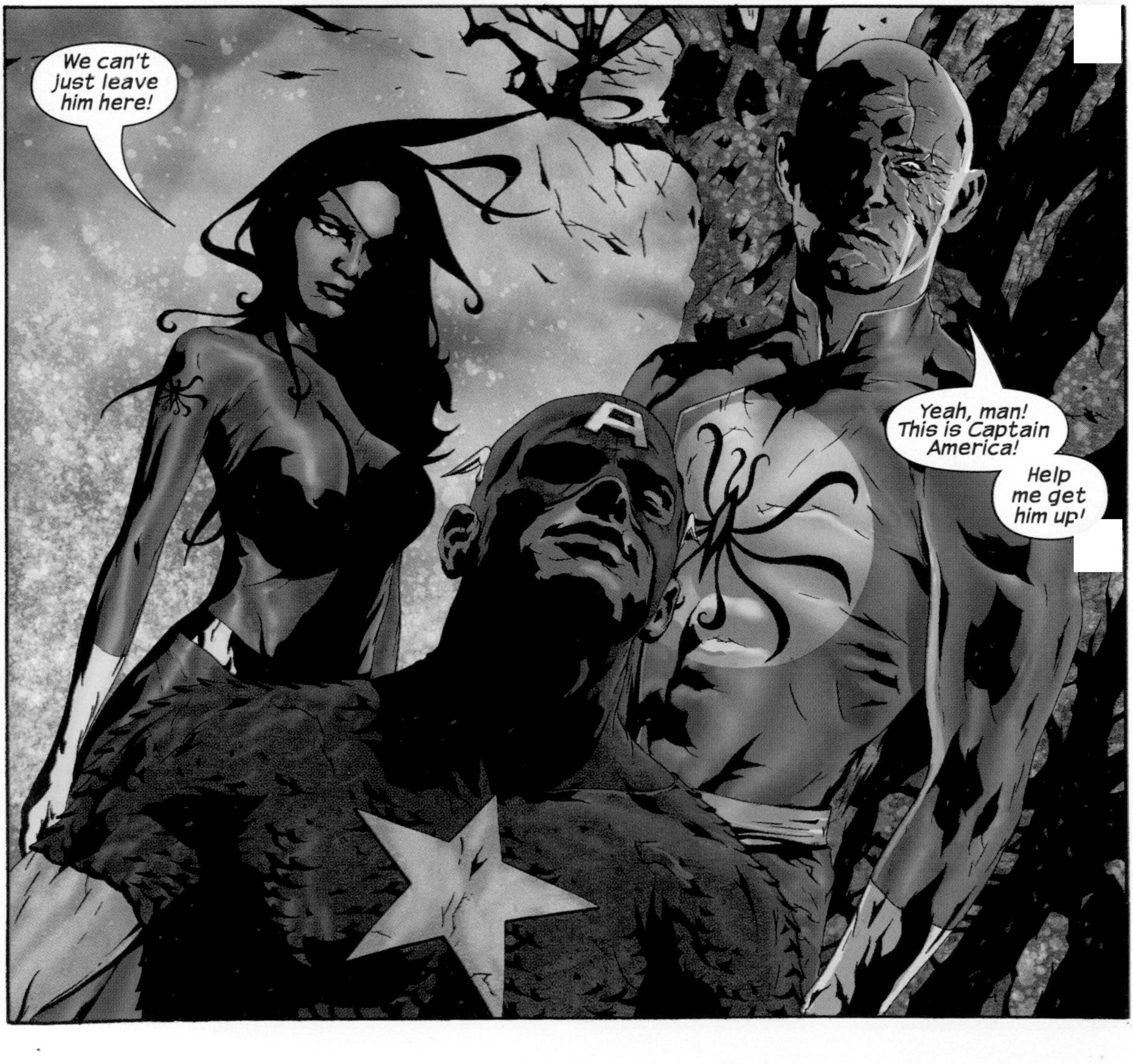
We can't just leave him here!
Yeah, man! This is Captain America!
Help me get him up!

I am the world's most efficient fighting machine.
And for the first time, that thought makes me sick.
I did what I've done a thousand times.
I did what I've *never* done in my life.
I may blame myself for what I did--
-- but Inali is the one who's going to pay.

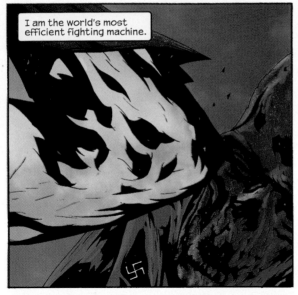

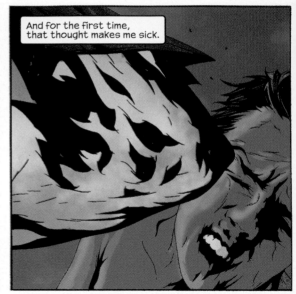

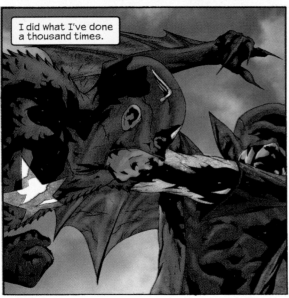

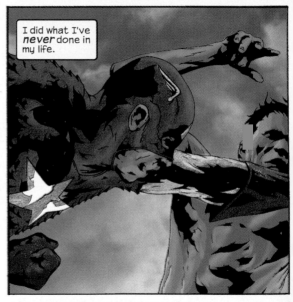

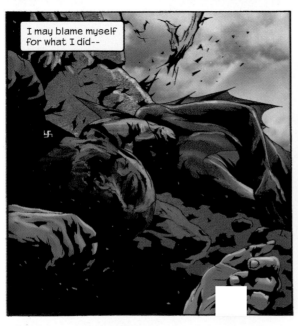

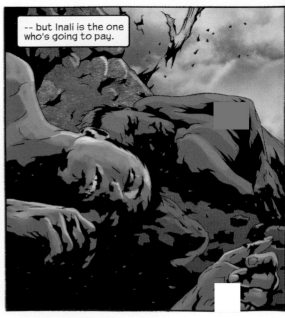

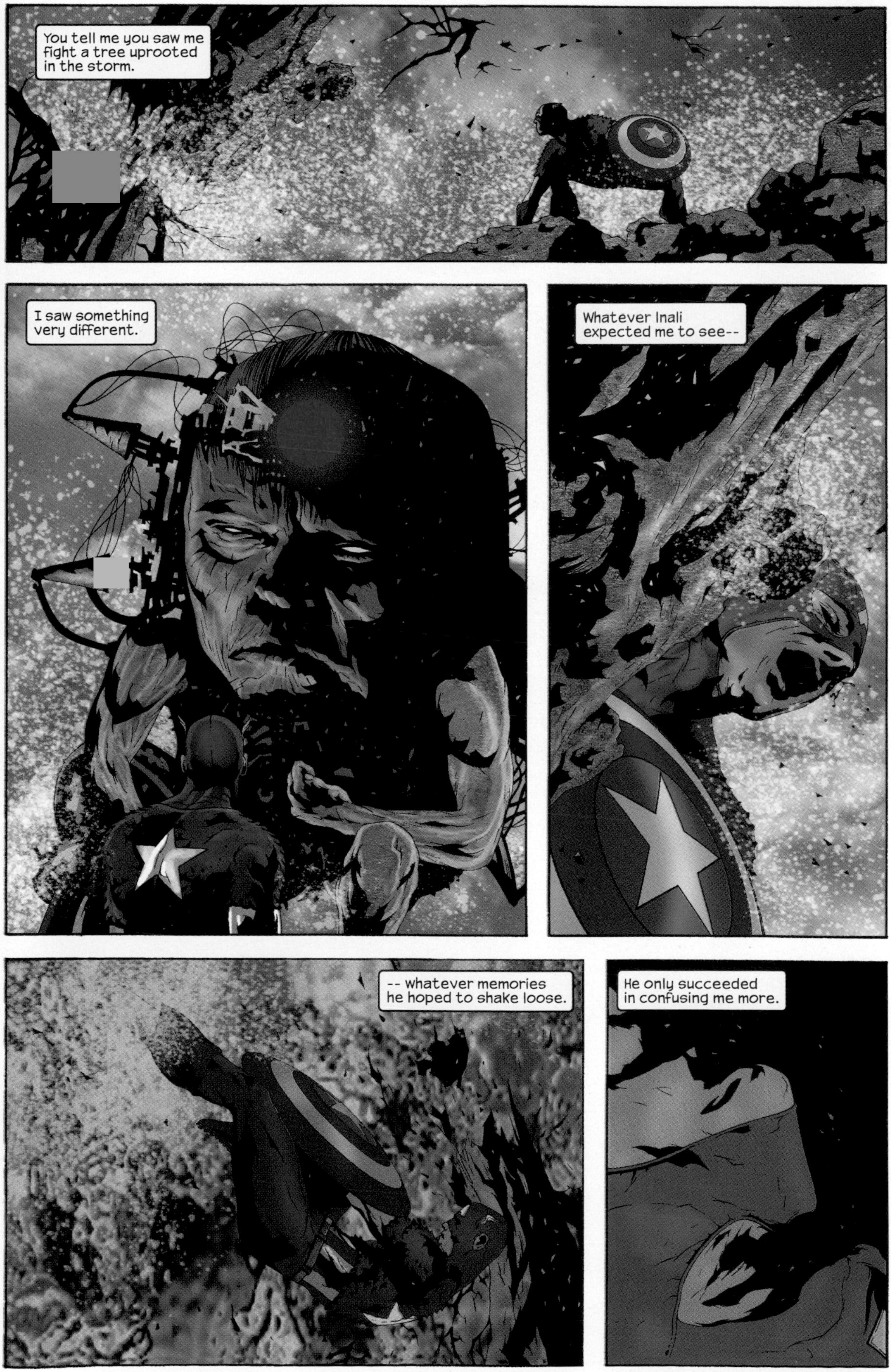
You tell me you saw me fight a tree uprooted in the storm.
I saw something very different.
Whatever Inali expected me to see--
-- whatever memories he hoped to shake loose.
He only succeeded in confusing me more.

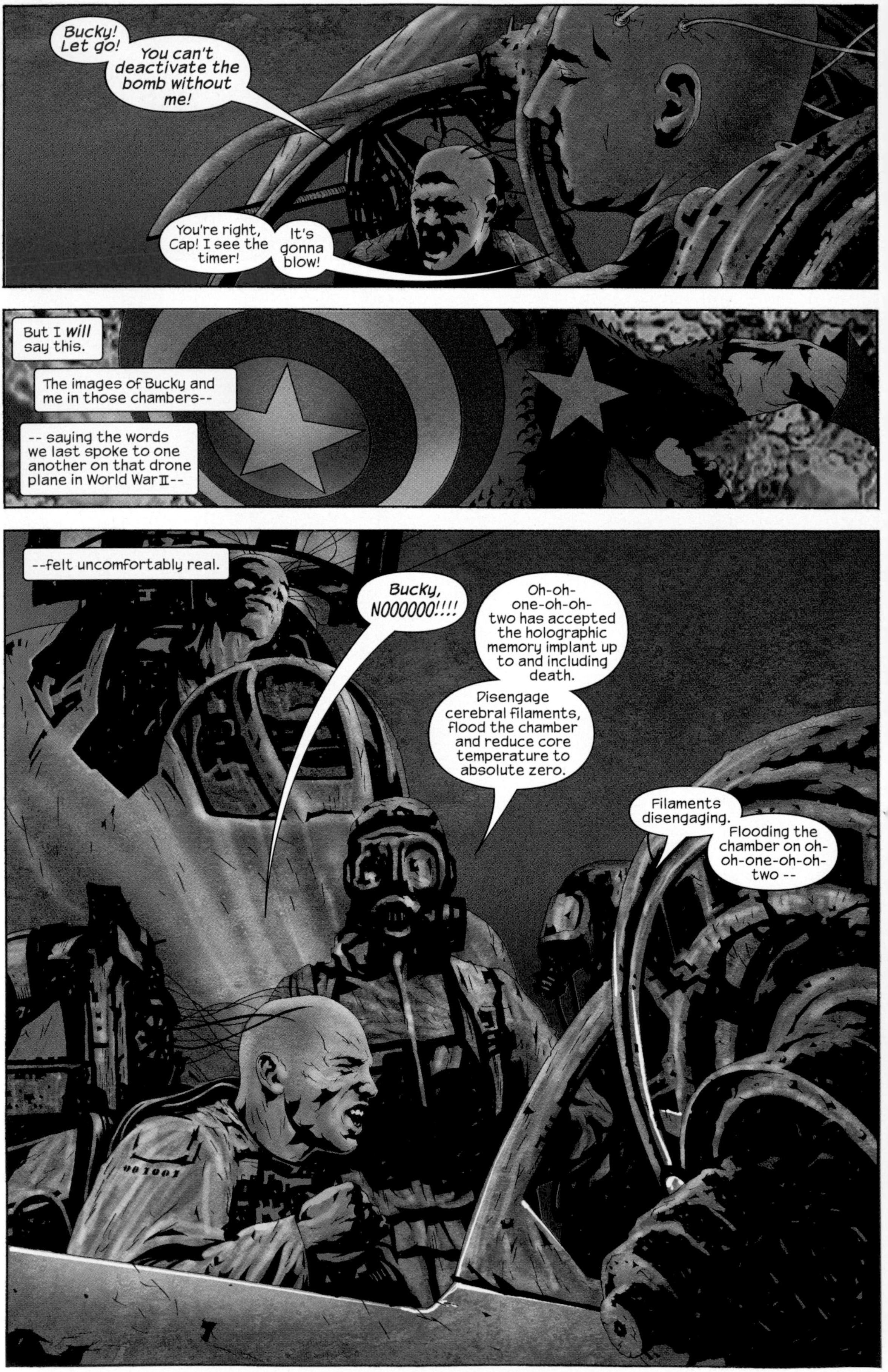
Bucky! Let go!
You can't deactivate the bomb without me!
You're right, Cap! I see the timer!
It's gonna blow!
But I will say this.
The images of Bucky and me in those chambers--
-- saying the words we last spoke to one another on that drone plane in World War II--
--felt uncomfortably real.
Bucky, NOOOOOO!!!!
Oh-oh-one-oh-oh-two has accepted the holographic memory implant up to and including death.
Disengage cerebral filaments, flood the chamber and reduce core temperature to absolute zero.
Filaments disengaging.
Flooding the chamber on oh-oh-one-oh-oh-two --

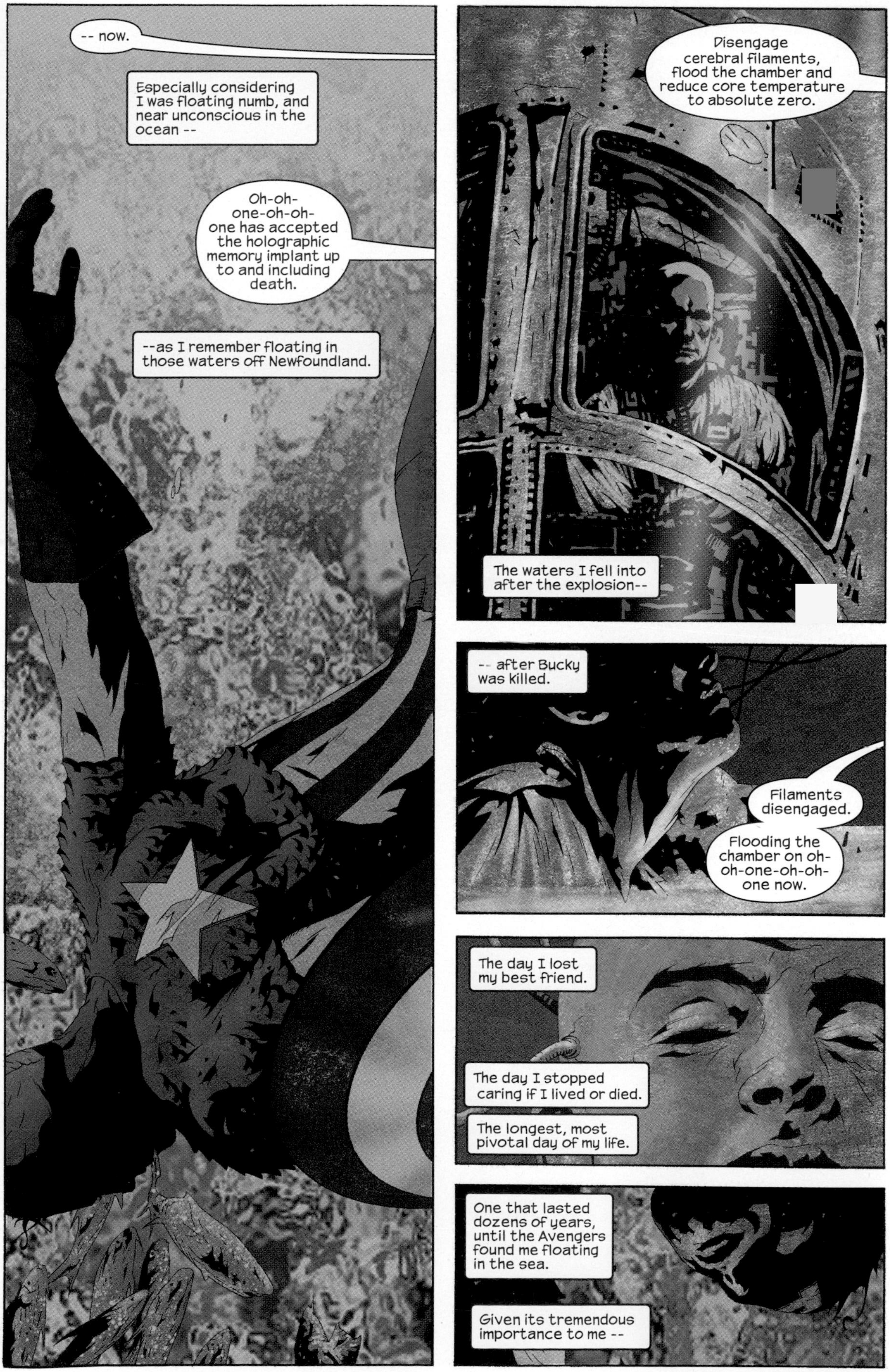
-- now.
Especially considering I was floating numb, and near unconscious in the ocean --
Oh-oh-one-oh-oh-one has accepted the holographic memory implant up to and including death.
--as I remember floating in those waters off Newfoundland.
Disengage cerebral filaments, flood the chamber and reduce core temperature to absolute zero.
The waters I fell into after the explosion--
-- after Bucky was killed.
Filaments disengaged.
Flooding the chamber on oh-oh-one-oh-oh-one now.
The day I lost my best friend.
The day I stopped caring if I lived or died.
The longest, most pivotal day of my life.
One that lasted dozens of years, until the Avengers found me floating in the sea.
Given its tremendous importance to me --

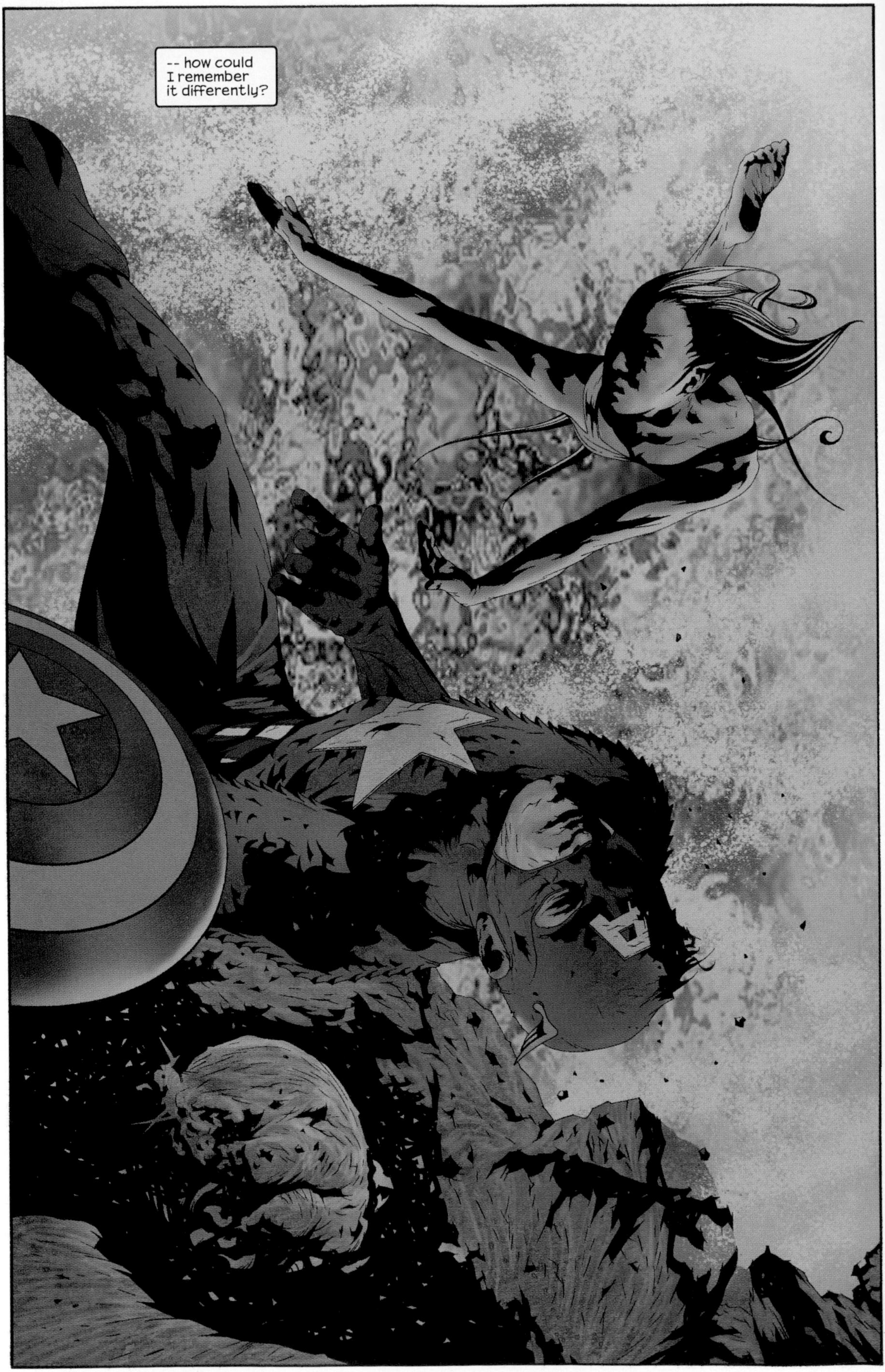
-- how could I remember it differently?

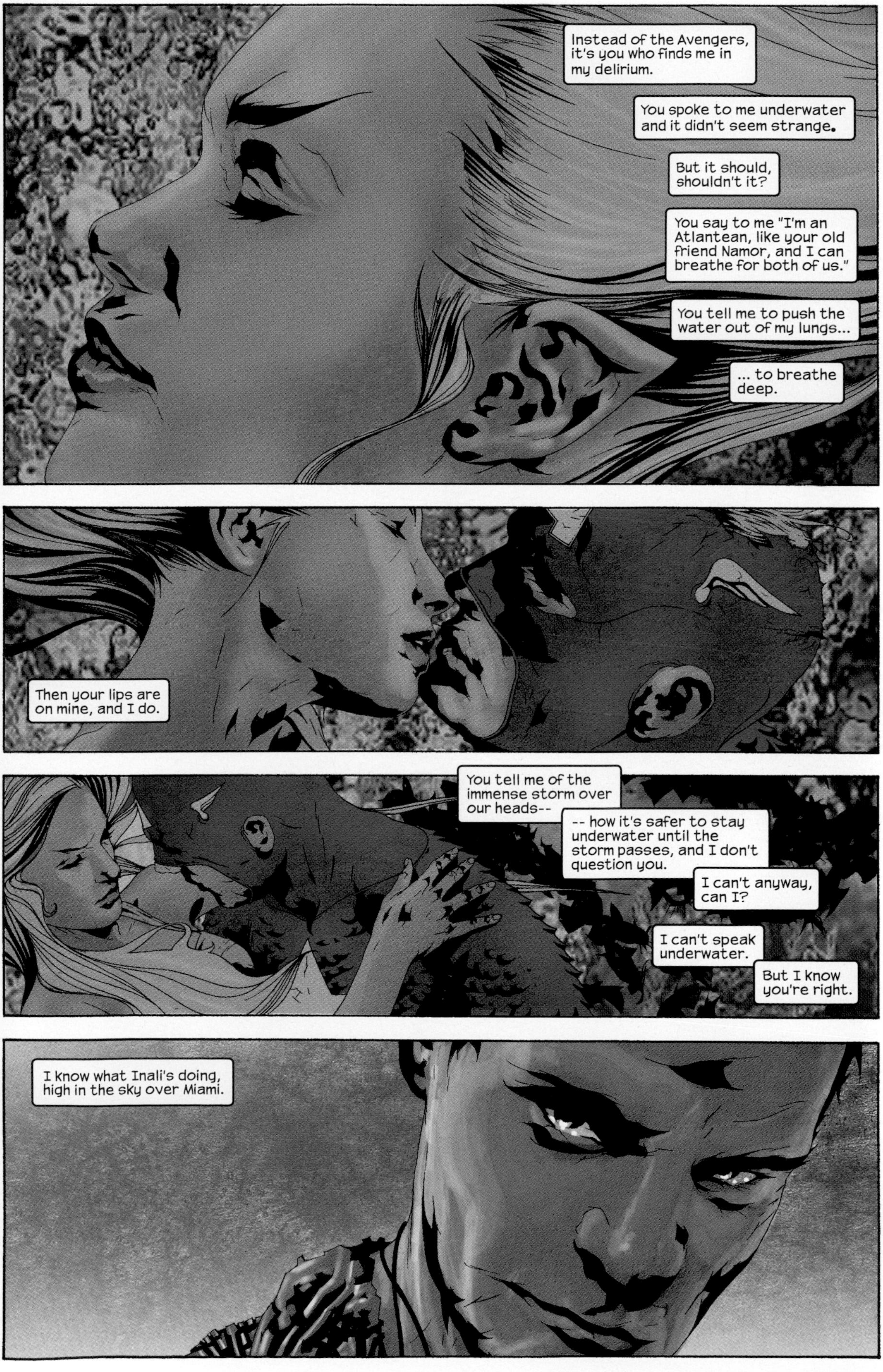
Instead of the Avengers, it's you who finds me in my delirium.
You spoke to me underwater and it didn't seem strange.
But it should, shouldn't it?
You say to me "I'm an Atlantean, like your old friend Namor, and I can breathe for both of us."
You tell me to push the water out of my lungs...
... to breathe deep.
Then your lips are on mine, and I do.
You tell me of the immense storm over our heads--
-- how it's safer to stay underwater until the storm passes, and I don't question you.
I can't anyway, can I?
I can't speak underwater.
But I know you're right.
I know what Inali's doing, high in the sky over Miami.

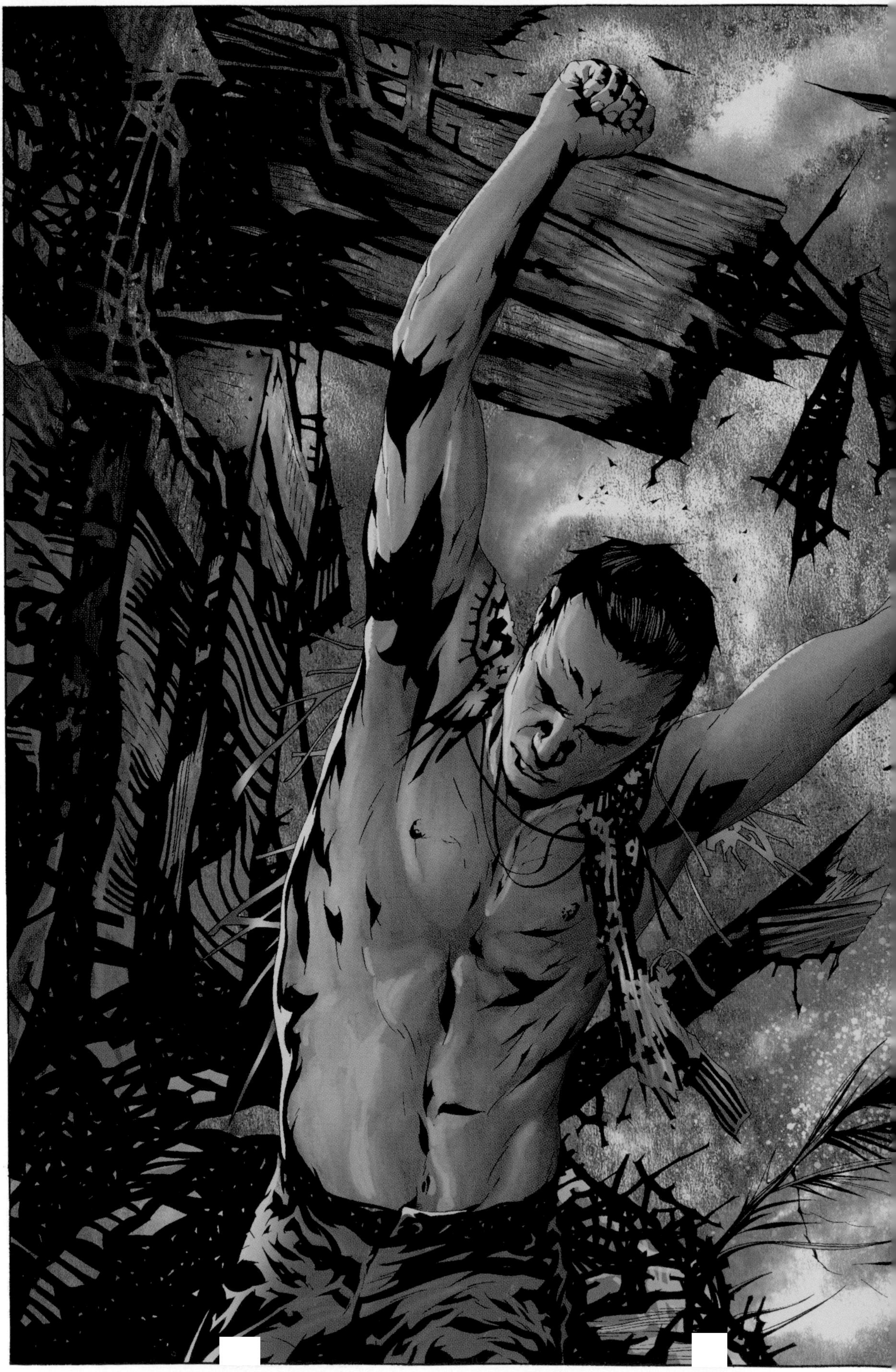

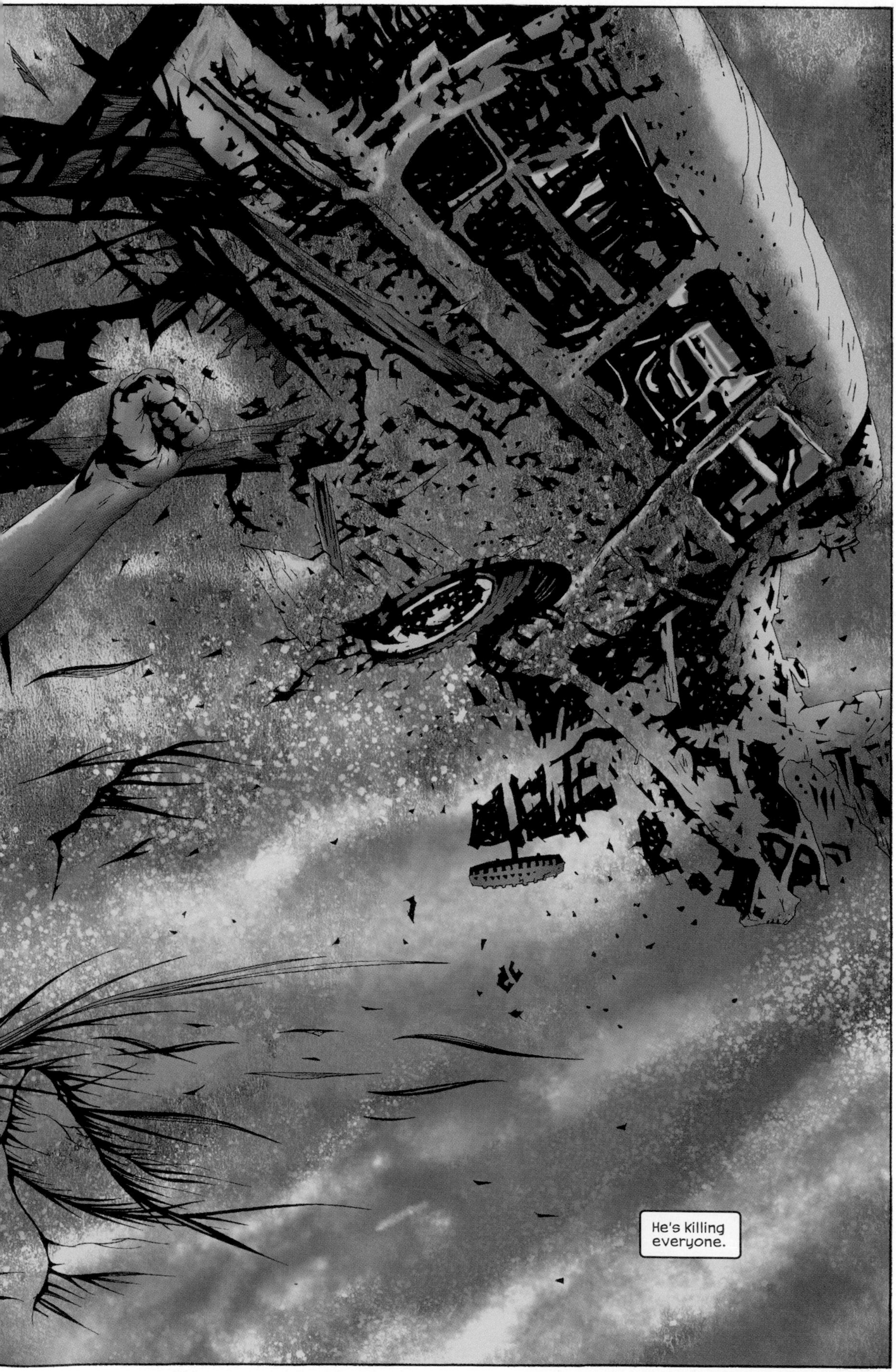
He's killing everyone.

He's waiting for me to see whatever it is he expects me to see.

To come to his side in this war he wages against innocent people who can't defend themselves --

-- against people who need me to stop him.

Because if I don't--

-- who will?

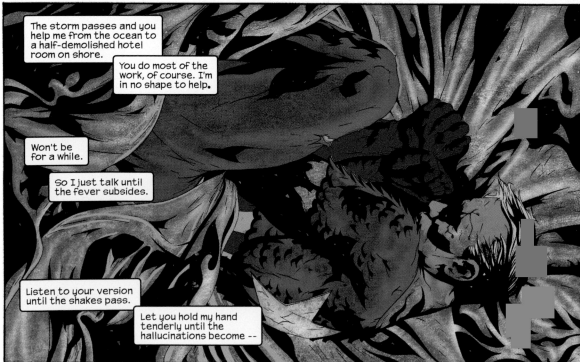

The storm passes and you help me from the ocean to a half-demolished hotel room on shore.

You do most of the work, of course. I'm in no shape to help.

Won't be for a while.

So I just talk until the fever subsides.

Listen to your version until the shakes pass.

Let you hold my hand tenderly until the hallucinations become --

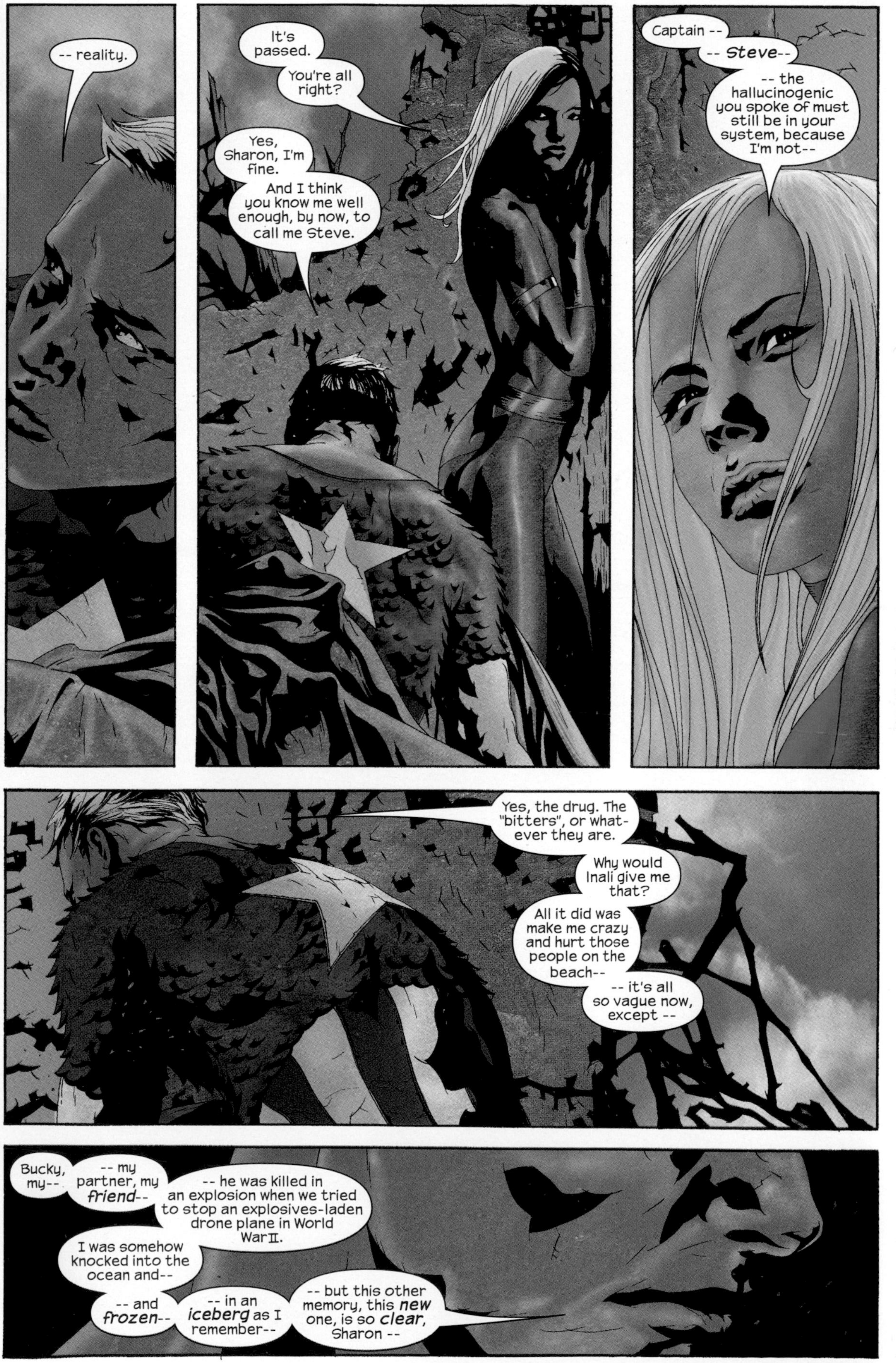
-- reality.
It's passed.
You're all right?
Yes, Sharon, I'm fine.
And I think you know me well enough, by now, to call me Steve.
Captain --
-- Steve--
-- the hallucinogenic you spoke of must still be in your system, because I'm not--
Yes, the drug. The "bitters", or whatever they are.
Why would Inali give me that?
All it did was make me crazy and hurt those people on the beach--
-- it's all so vague now, except --
Bucky, my--
-- my partner, my friend--
-- he was killed in an explosion when we tried to stop an explosives-laden drone plane in World War II.
I was somehow knocked into the ocean and--
-- and frozen--
-- in an iceberg as I remember--
-- but this other memory, this new one, is so clear, Sharon --

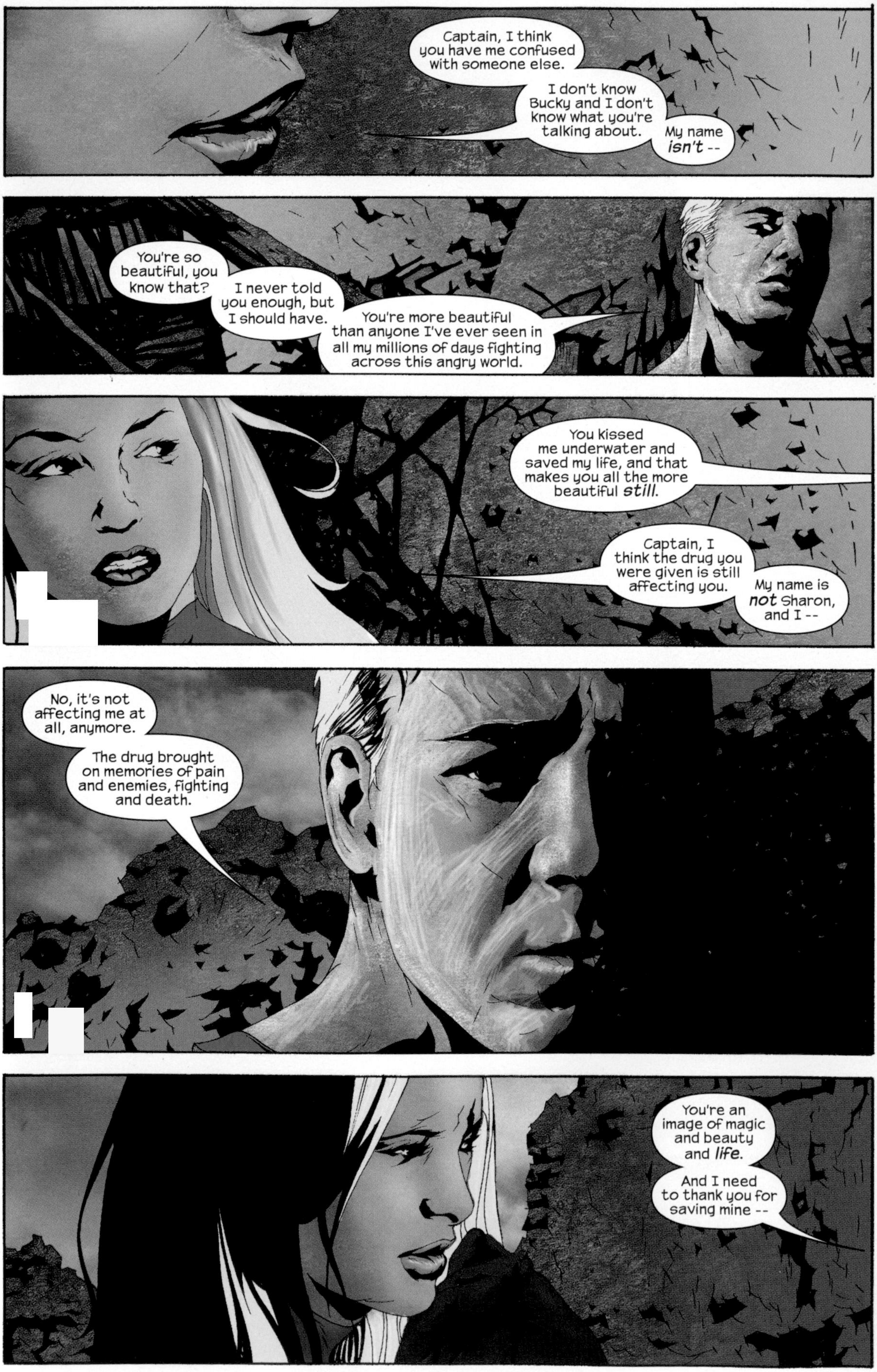
Captain, I think you have me confused with someone else.
I don't know Bucky and I don't know what you're talking about.
My name *isn't* --
You're so beautiful, you know that?
I never told you enough, but I should have.
You're more beautiful than anyone I've ever seen in all my millions of days fighting across this angry world.
You kissed me underwater and saved my life, and that makes you all the more beautiful *still*.
Captain, I think the drug you were given is still affecting you.
My name is *not* Sharon, and I --
No, it's not affecting me at all, anymore.
The drug brought on memories of pain and enemies, fighting and death.
You're an image of magic and beauty and *life*.
And I need to thank you for saving mine --

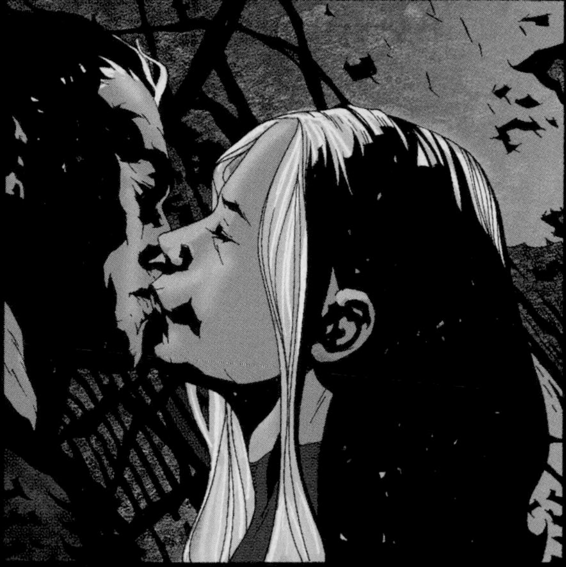
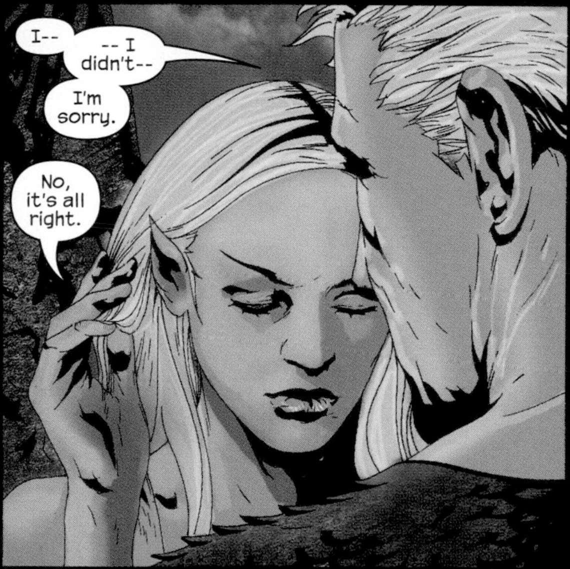
I--
-- I didn't--
I'm sorry.
No, it's all right.
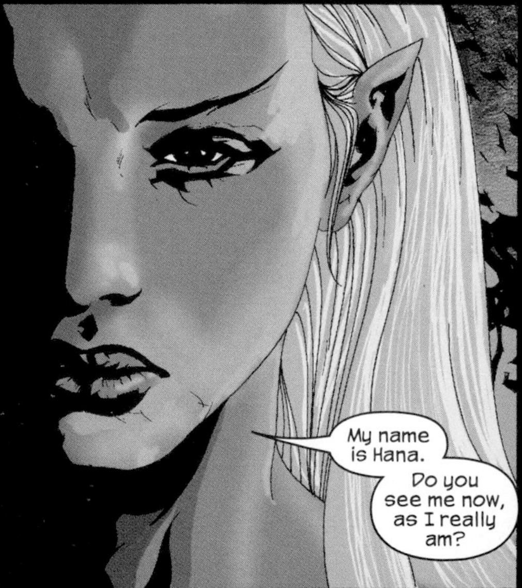
My name is Hana.
Do you see me now, as I really am?

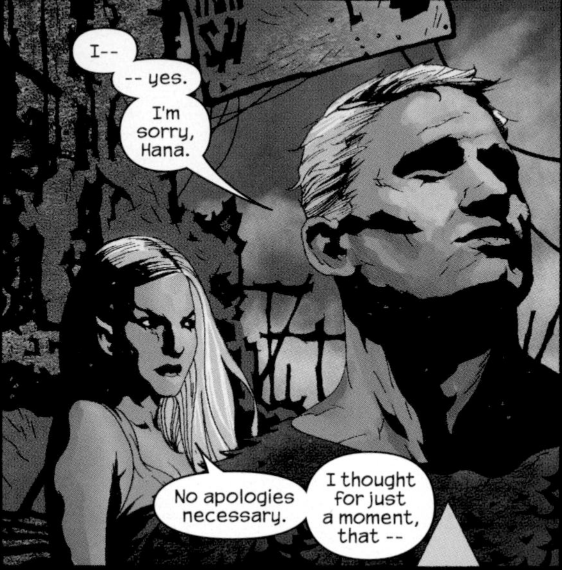
I--
-- yes.
I'm sorry, Hana.
No apologies necessary.
I thought for just a moment, that --

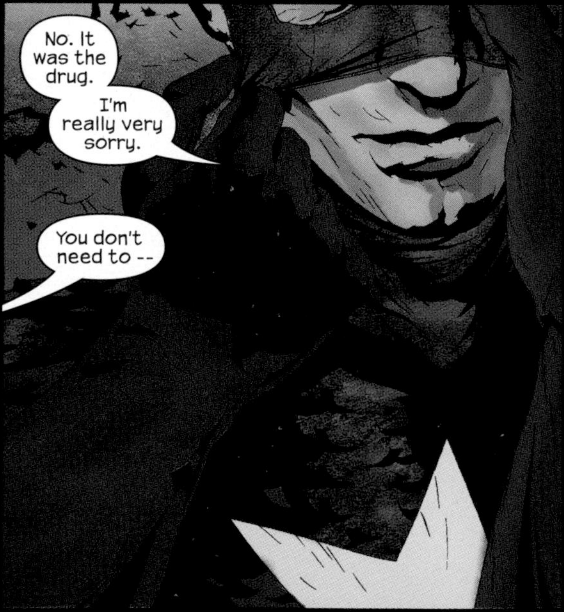
No. It was the drug.
I'm really very sorry.
You don't need to --

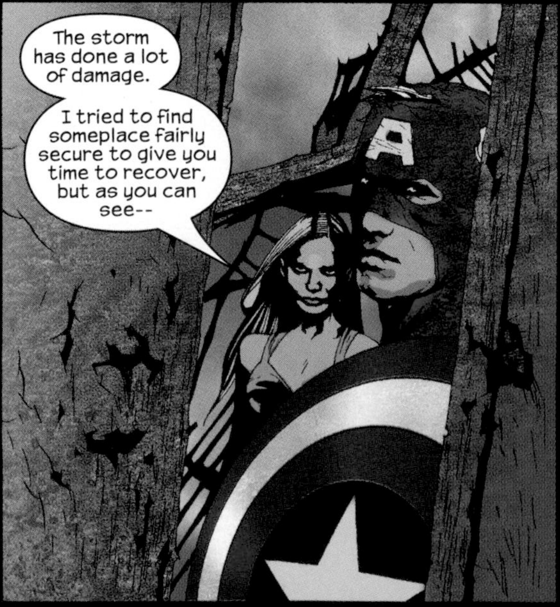
The storm has done a lot of damage.
I tried to find someplace fairly secure to give you time to recover, but as you can see--

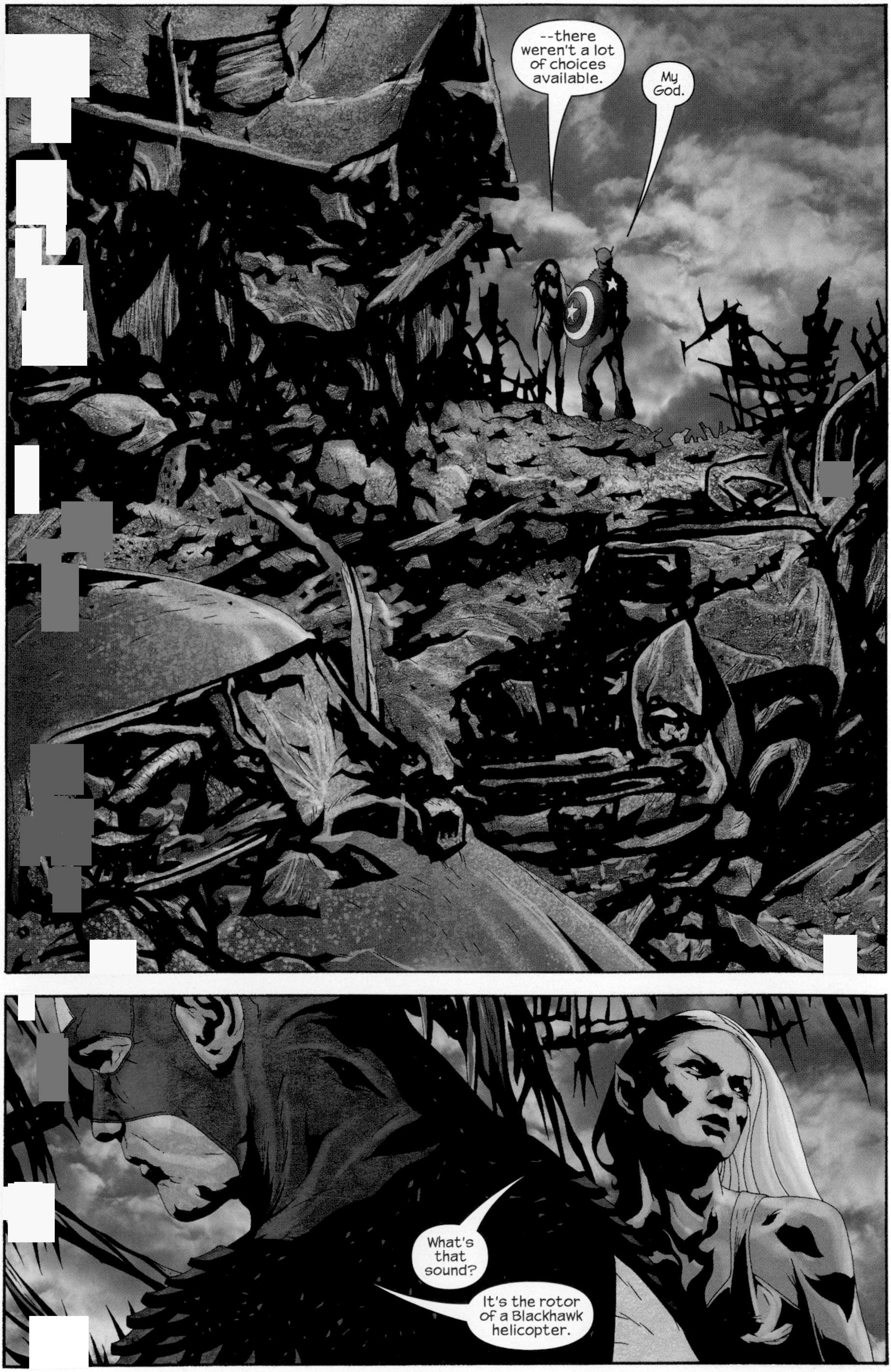
--there weren't a lot of choices available.
My God.
What's that sound?
It's the rotor of a Blackhawk helicopter.

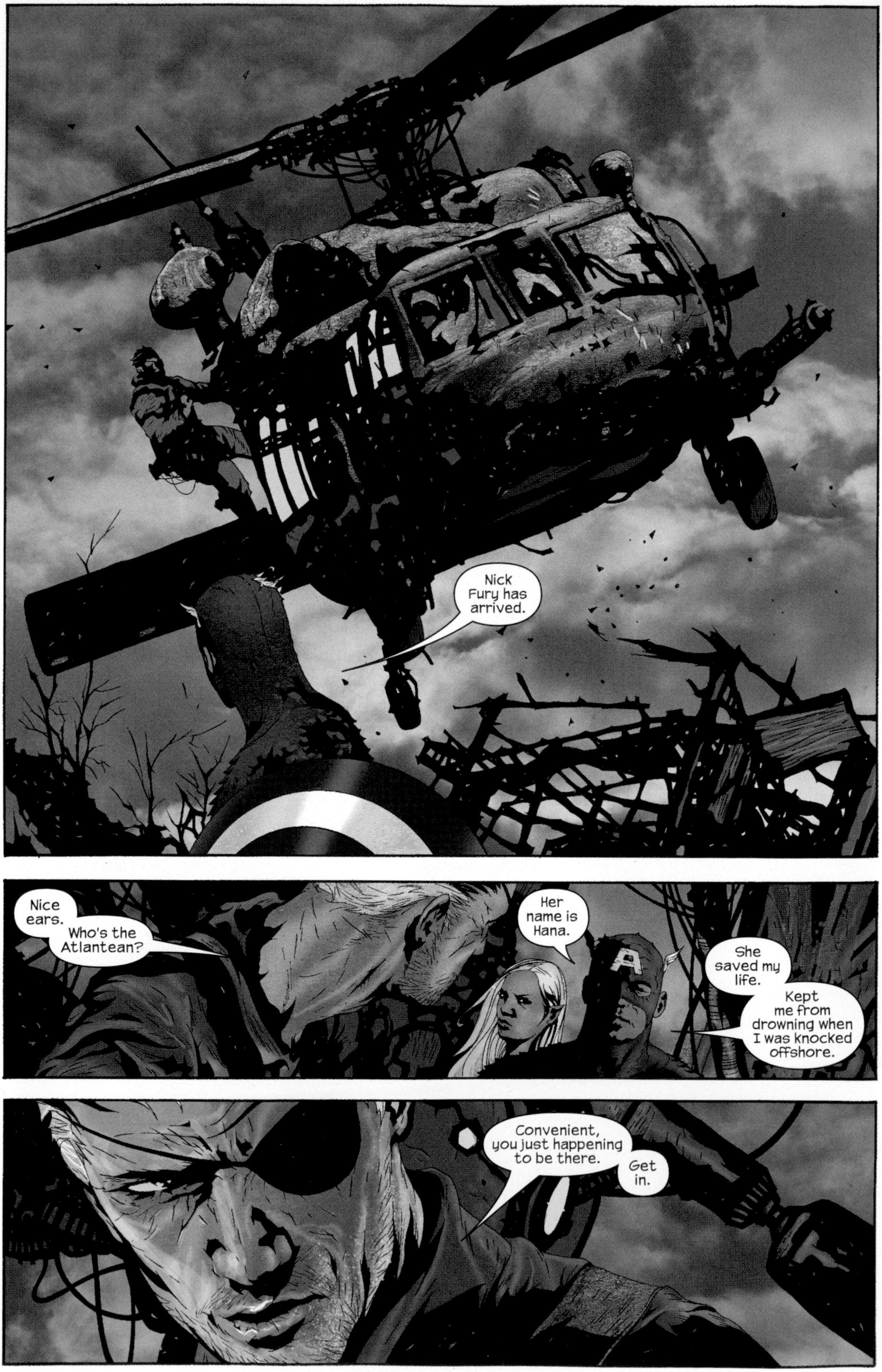

Nick Fury has arrived.
Nice ears.
Who's the Atlantean?
Her name is Hana.
She saved my life.
Kept me from drowning when I was knocked offshore.
Convenient, you just happening to be there.
Get in.

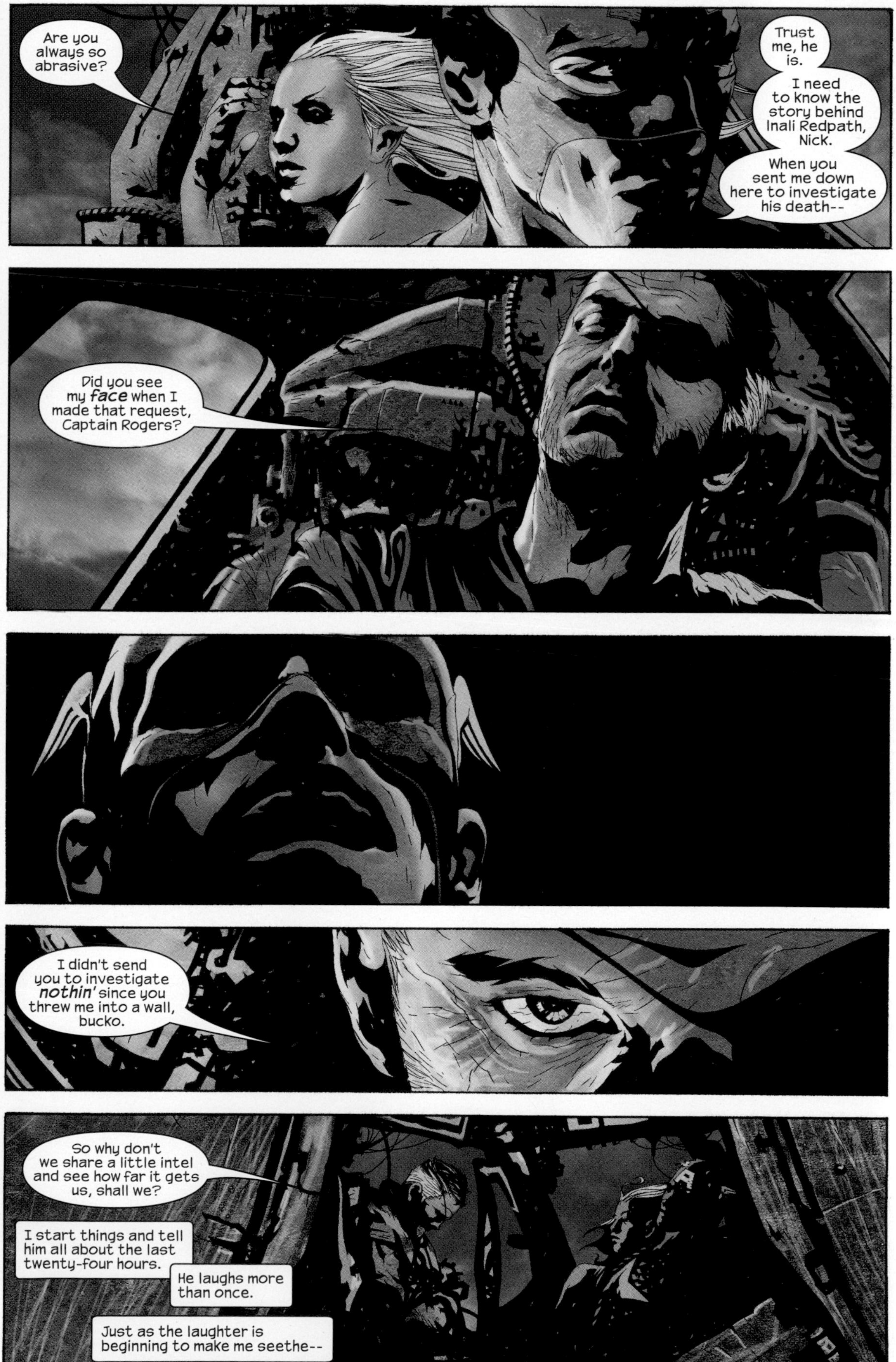
Are you always so abrasive?
Trust me, he is.
I need to know the story behind Inali Redpath, Nick.
When you sent me down here to investigate his death--
Did you see my *face* when I made that request, Captain Rogers?
I didn't send you to investigate *nothin'* since you threw me into a wall, bucko.
So why don't we share a little intel and see how far it gets us, shall we?
I start things and tell him all about the last twenty-four hours.
He laughs more than once.
Just as the laughter is beginning to make me seethe--

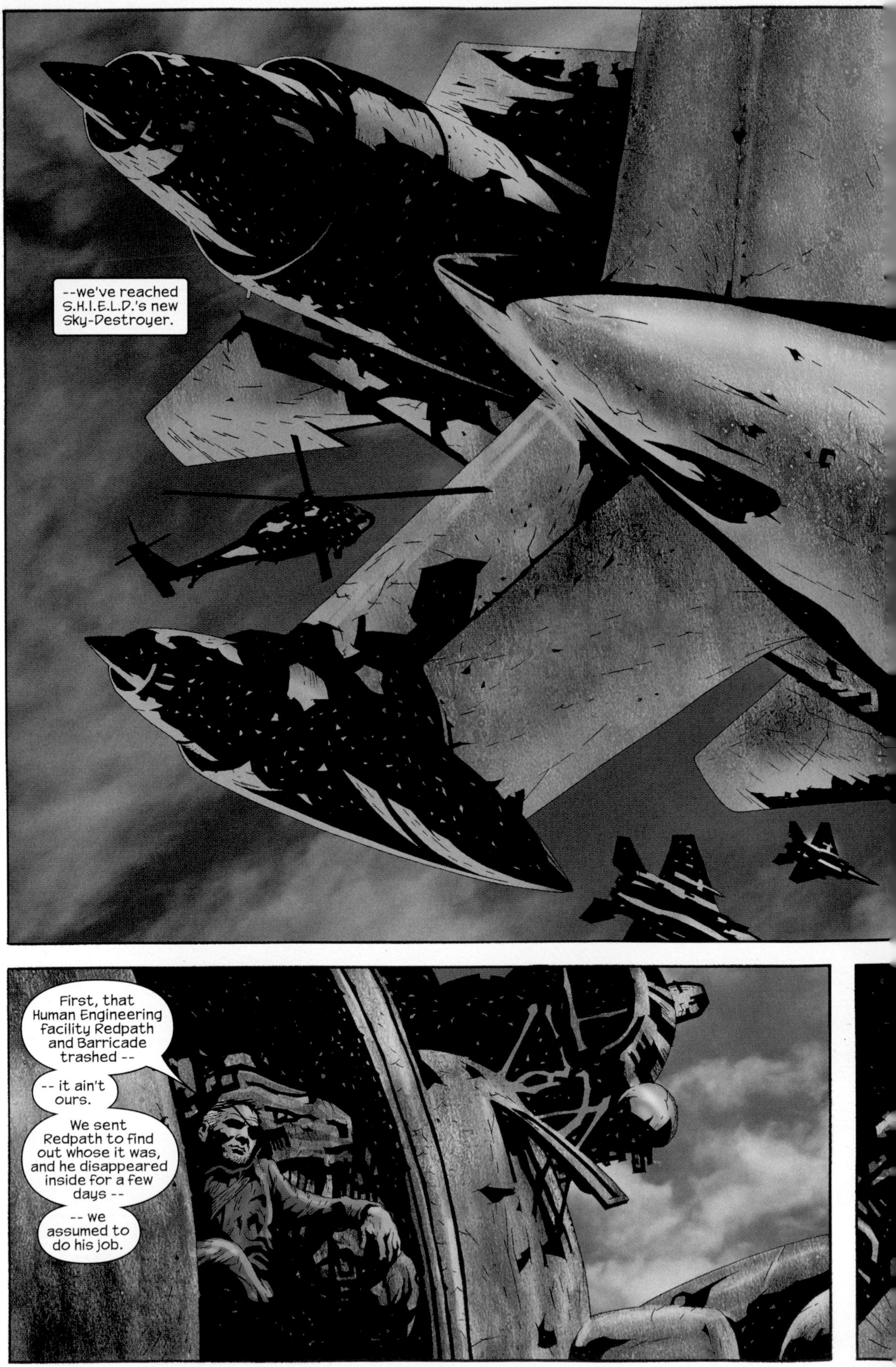
--we've reached S.H.I.E.L.D.'s new Sky-Destroyer.
First, that Human Engineering facility Redpath and Barricade trashed --
-- it ain't ours.
We sent Redpath to find out whose it was, and he disappeared inside for a few days --
-- we assumed to do his job.

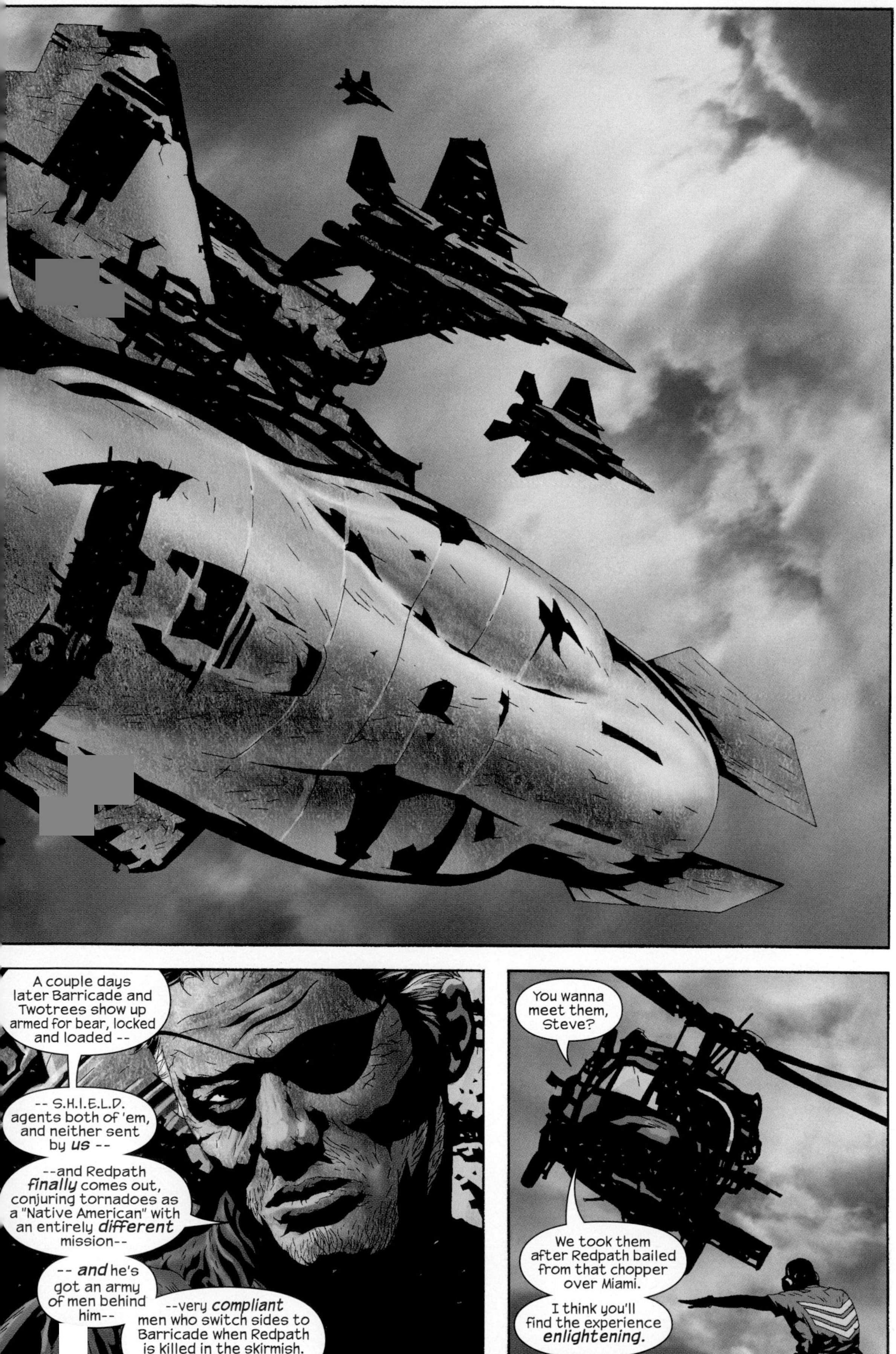
A couple days later Barricade and Twotrees show up armed for bear, locked and loaded --
-- S.H.I.E.L.D. agents both of 'em, and neither sent by *us* --
--and Redpath *finally* comes out, conjuring tornadoes as a "Native American" with an entirely *different* mission--
-- *and* he's got an army of men behind him--
--very *compliant* men who switch sides to Barricade when Redpath is killed in the skirmish.
You wanna meet them, Steve?
We took them after Redpath bailed from that chopper over Miami.
I think you'll find the experience *enlightening.*

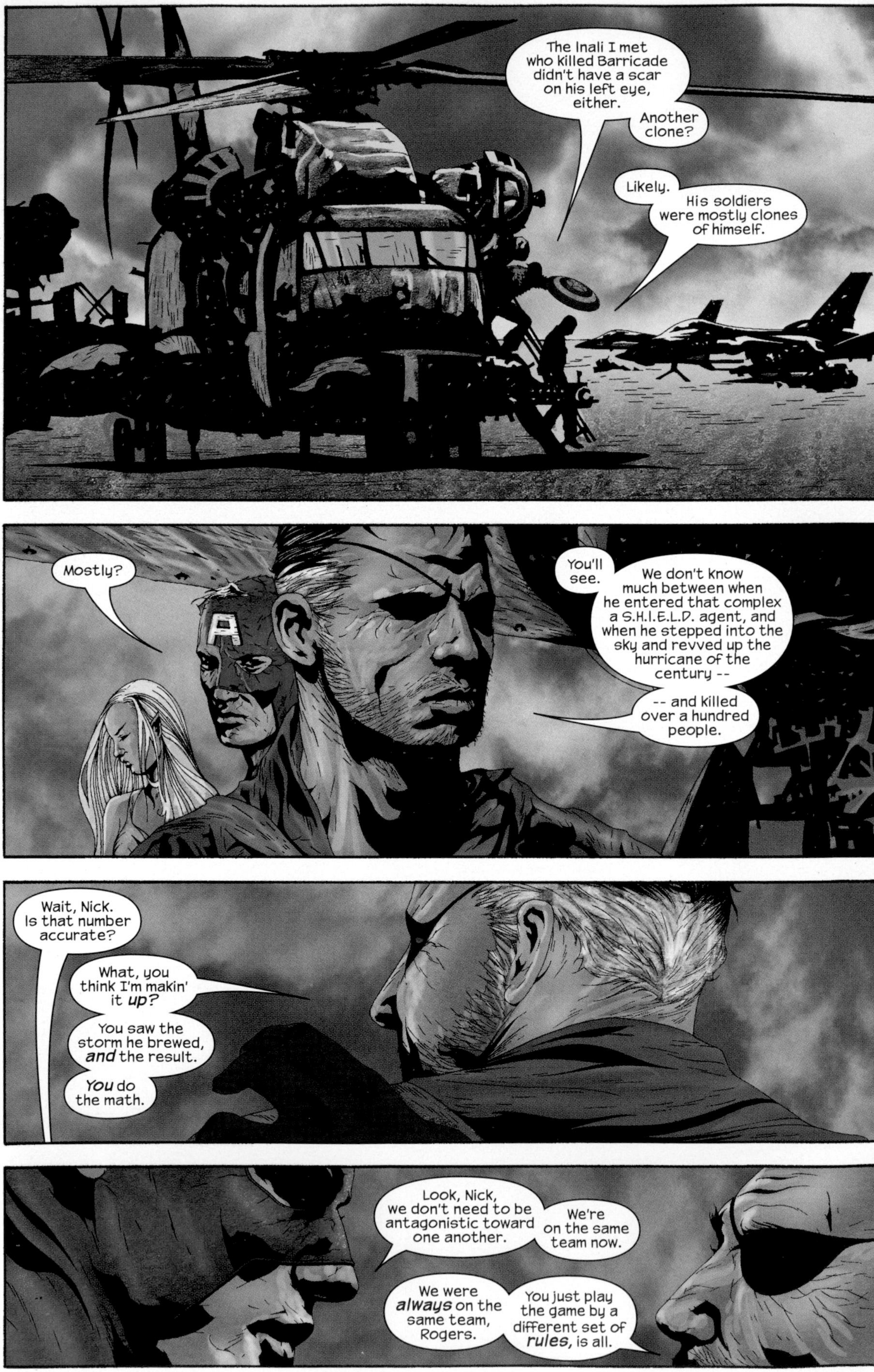
The Inali I met who killed Barricade didn't have a scar on his left eye, either.
Another clone?
Likely.
His soldiers were mostly clones of himself.
Mostly?
You'll see.
We don't know much between when he entered that complex a S.H.I.E.L.D. agent, and when he stepped into the sky and revved up the hurricane of the century --
-- and killed over a hundred people.
Wait, Nick. Is that number accurate?
What, you think I'm makin' it *up?*
You saw the storm he brewed, *and* the result.
You do the math.
Look, Nick, we don't need to be antagonistic toward one another.
We're on the same team now.
We were *always* on the same team, Rogers.
You just play the game by a different set of *rules,* is all.

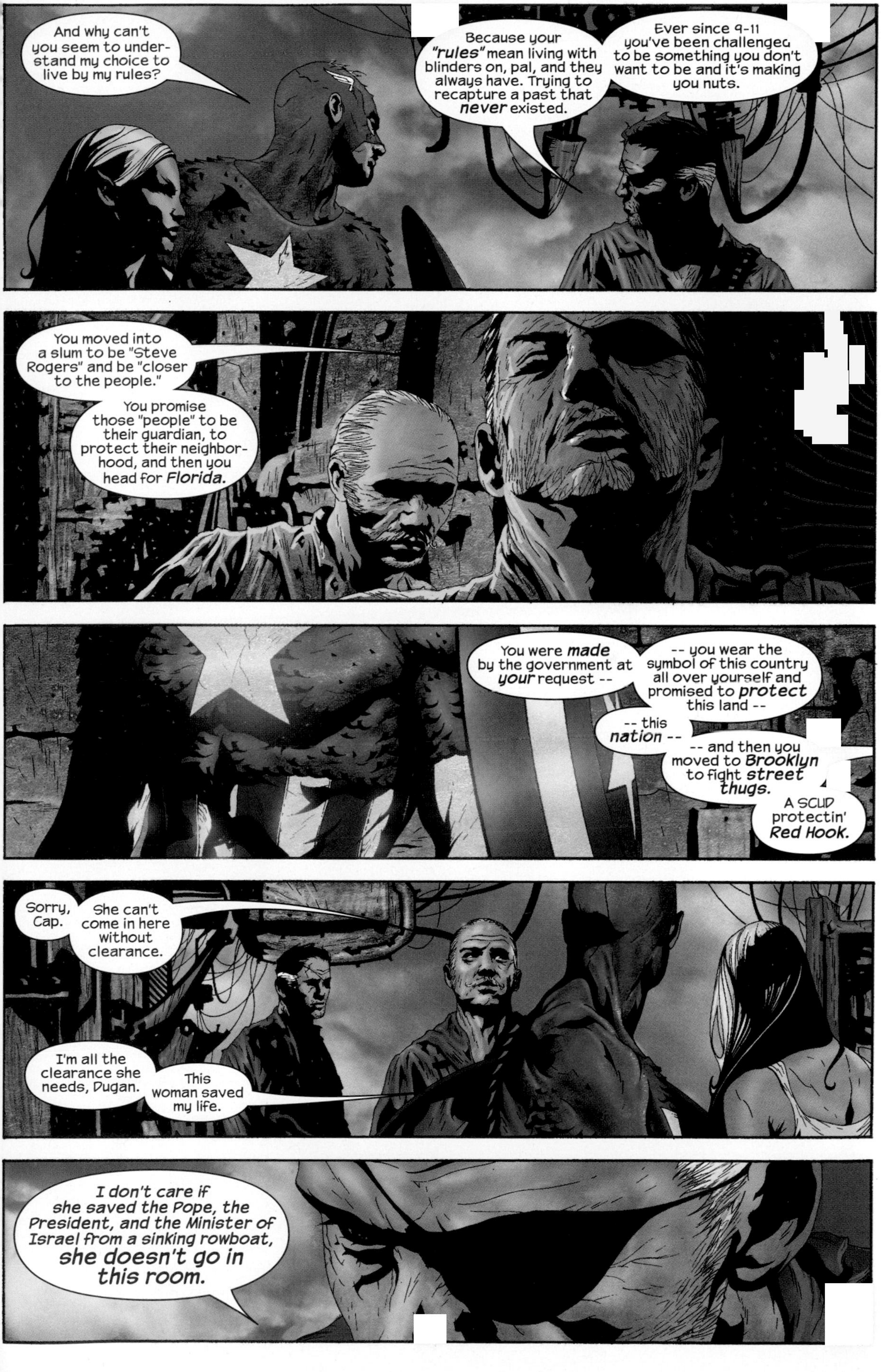

And why can't you seem to understand my choice to live by my rules?
Because your "rules" mean living with blinders on, pal, and they always have. Trying to recapture a past that never existed.
Ever since 9-11 you've been challenged to be something you don't want to be and it's making you nuts.
You moved into a slum to be "Steve Rogers" and be "closer to the people."
You promise those "people" to be their guardian, to protect their neighborhood, and then you head for Florida.
You were made by the government at your request --
-- you wear the symbol of this country all over yourself and promised to protect this land --
-- this nation --
-- and then you moved to Brooklyn to fight street thugs.
A SCUD protectin' Red Hook.
Sorry, Cap.
She can't come in here without clearance.
I'm all the clearance she needs, Dugan.
This woman saved my life.
I don't care if she saved the Pope, the President, and the Minister of Israel from a sinking rowboat, she doesn't go in this room.

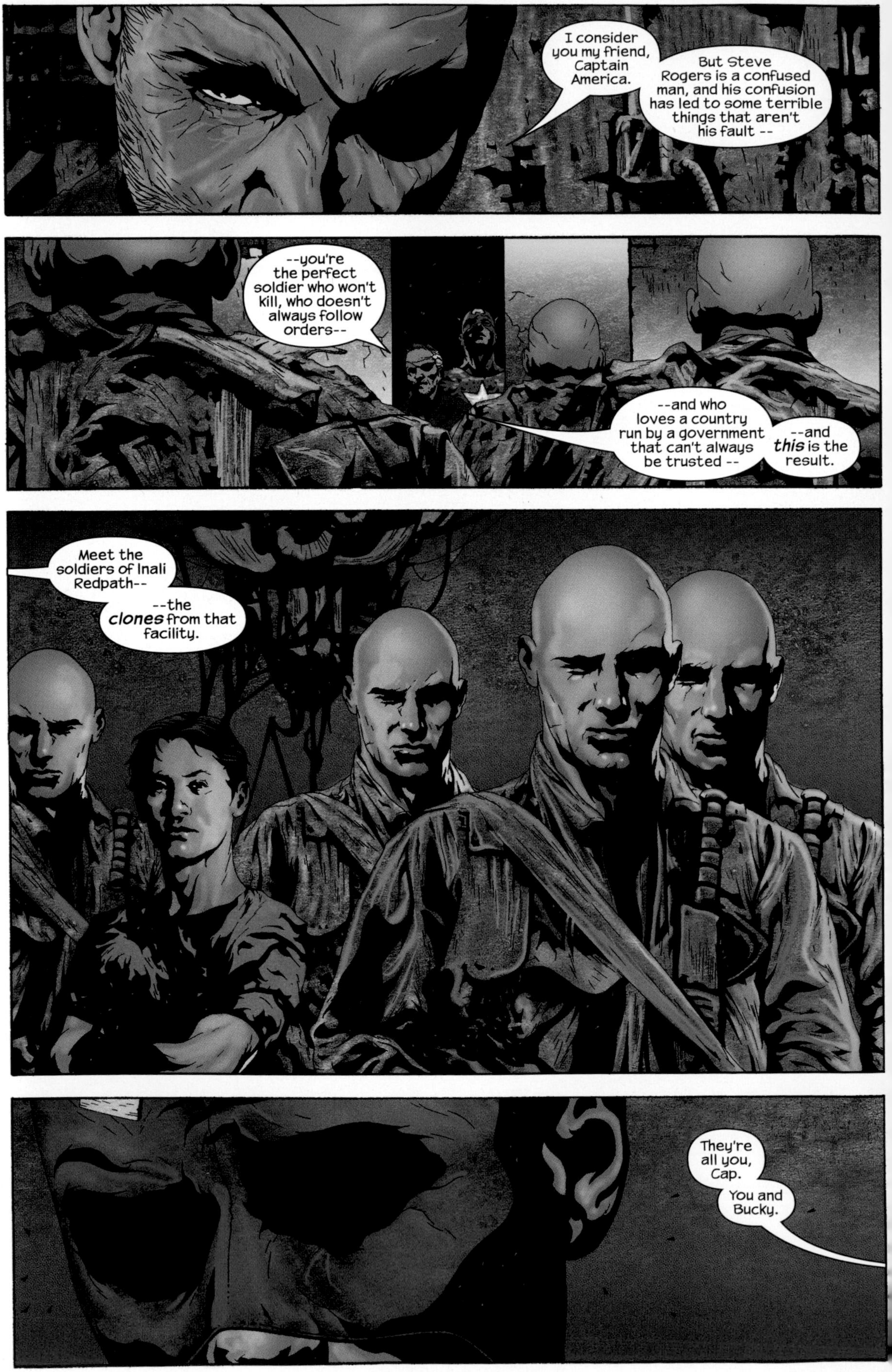

I consider you my friend, Captain America.
But Steve Rogers is a confused man, and his confusion has led to some terrible things that aren't his fault --
--you're the perfect soldier who won't kill, who doesn't always follow orders--
--and who loves a country run by a government that can't always be trusted --
--and *this* is the result.
Meet the soldiers of Inali Redpath--
--the *clones* from that facility.
They're all you, Cap.
You and Bucky.

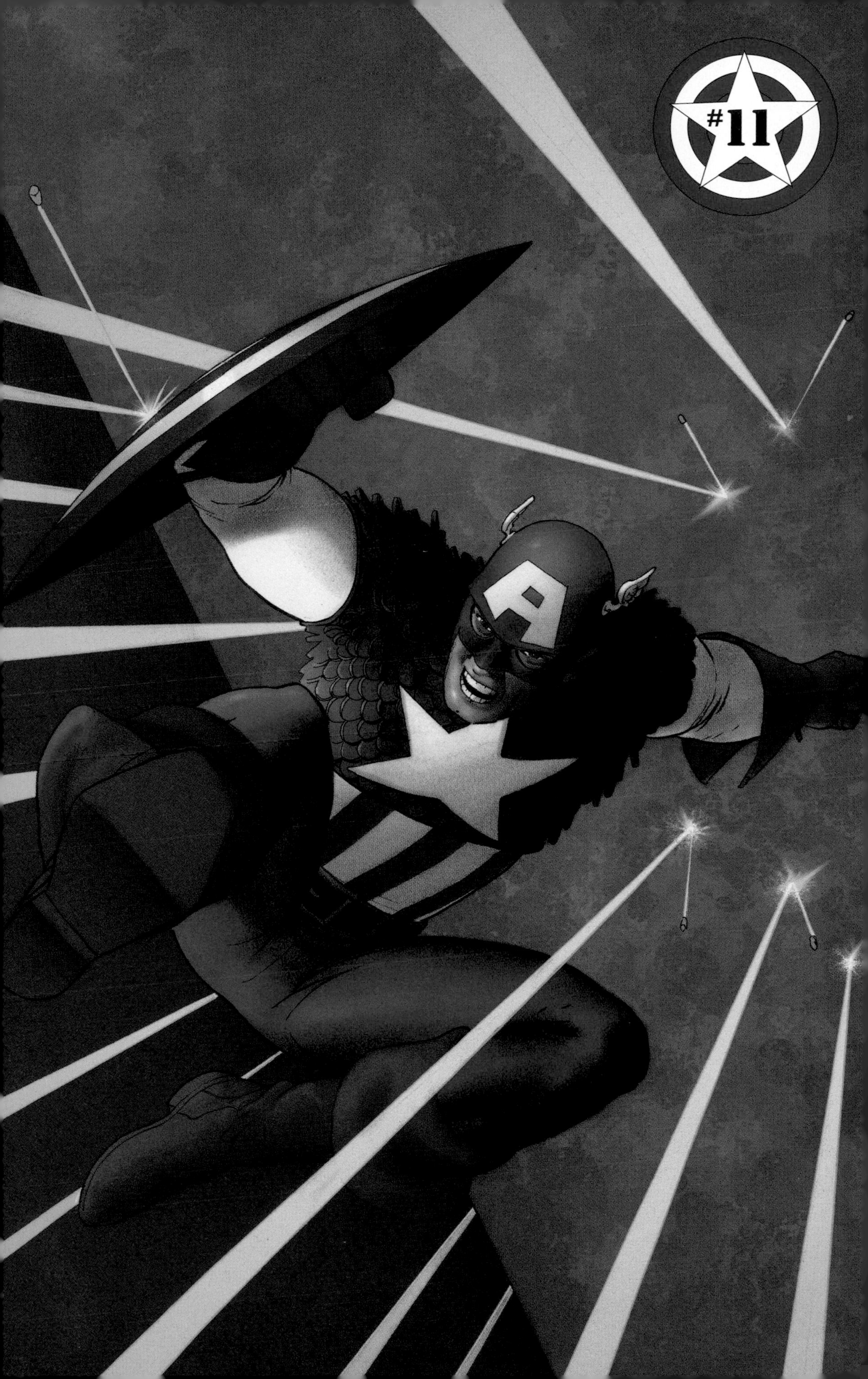
#11

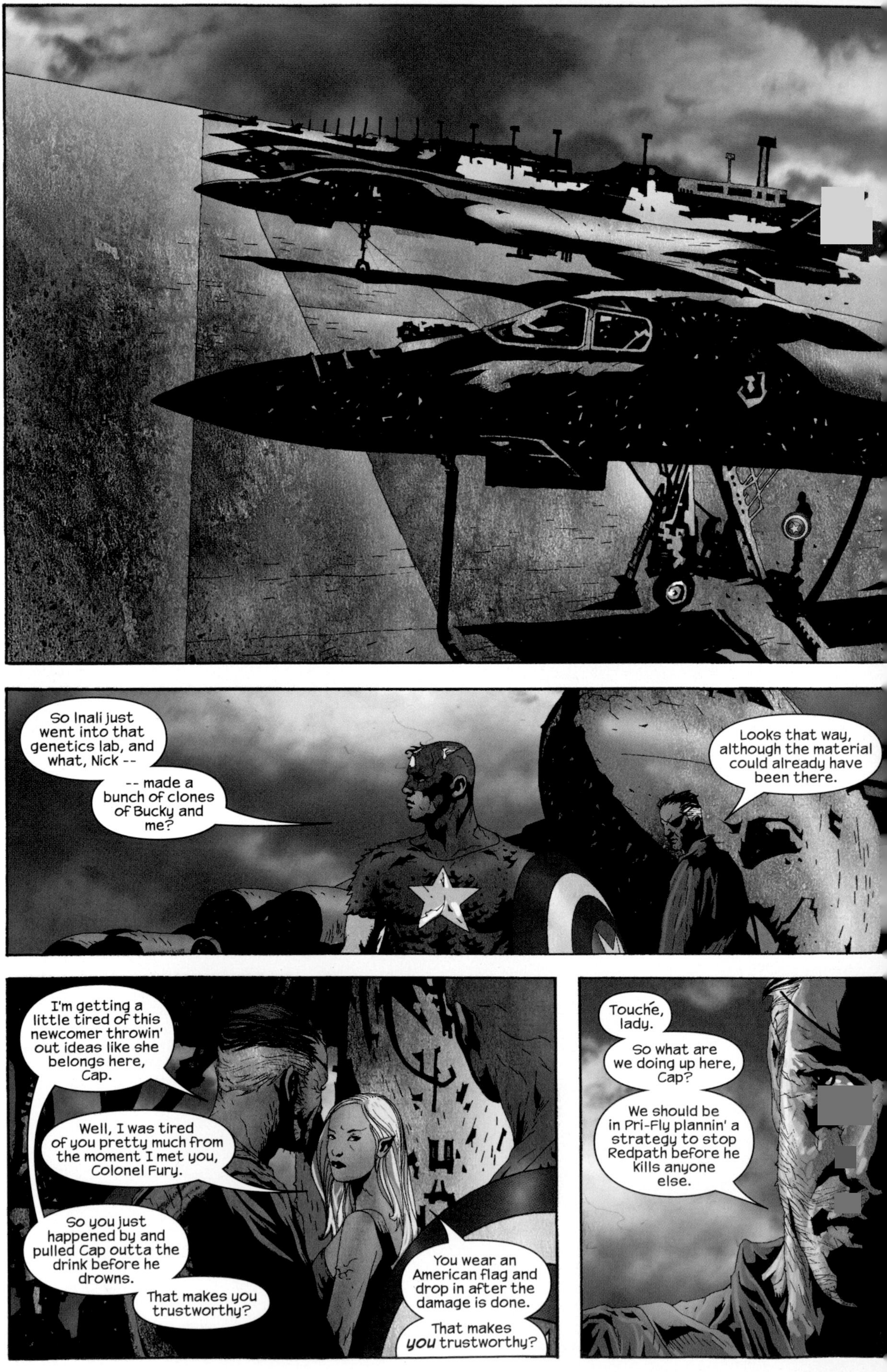
So Inali just went into that genetics lab, and what, Nick --
-- made a bunch of clones of Bucky and me?
Looks that way, although the material could already have been there.
I'm getting a little tired of this newcomer throwin' out ideas like she belongs here, Cap.
Well, I was tired of you pretty much from the moment I met you, Colonel Fury.
So you just happened by and pulled Cap outta the drink before he drowns.
That makes you trustworthy?
You wear an American flag and drop in after the damage is done.
That makes *you* trustworthy?
Touché, lady.
So what are we doing up here, Cap?
We should be in Pri-Fly plannin' a strategy to stop Redpath before he kills anyone else.

It's possible he could have found them there, already made.

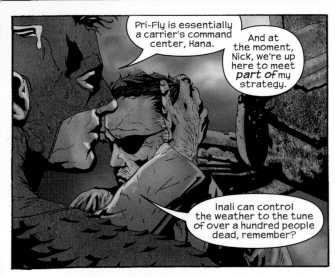

Pri-Fly is essentially a carrier's command center, Hana.

And at the moment, Nick, we're up here to meet *part of* my strategy.

Inali can control the weather to the tune of over a hundred people dead, remember?

So I've called in the big guns.

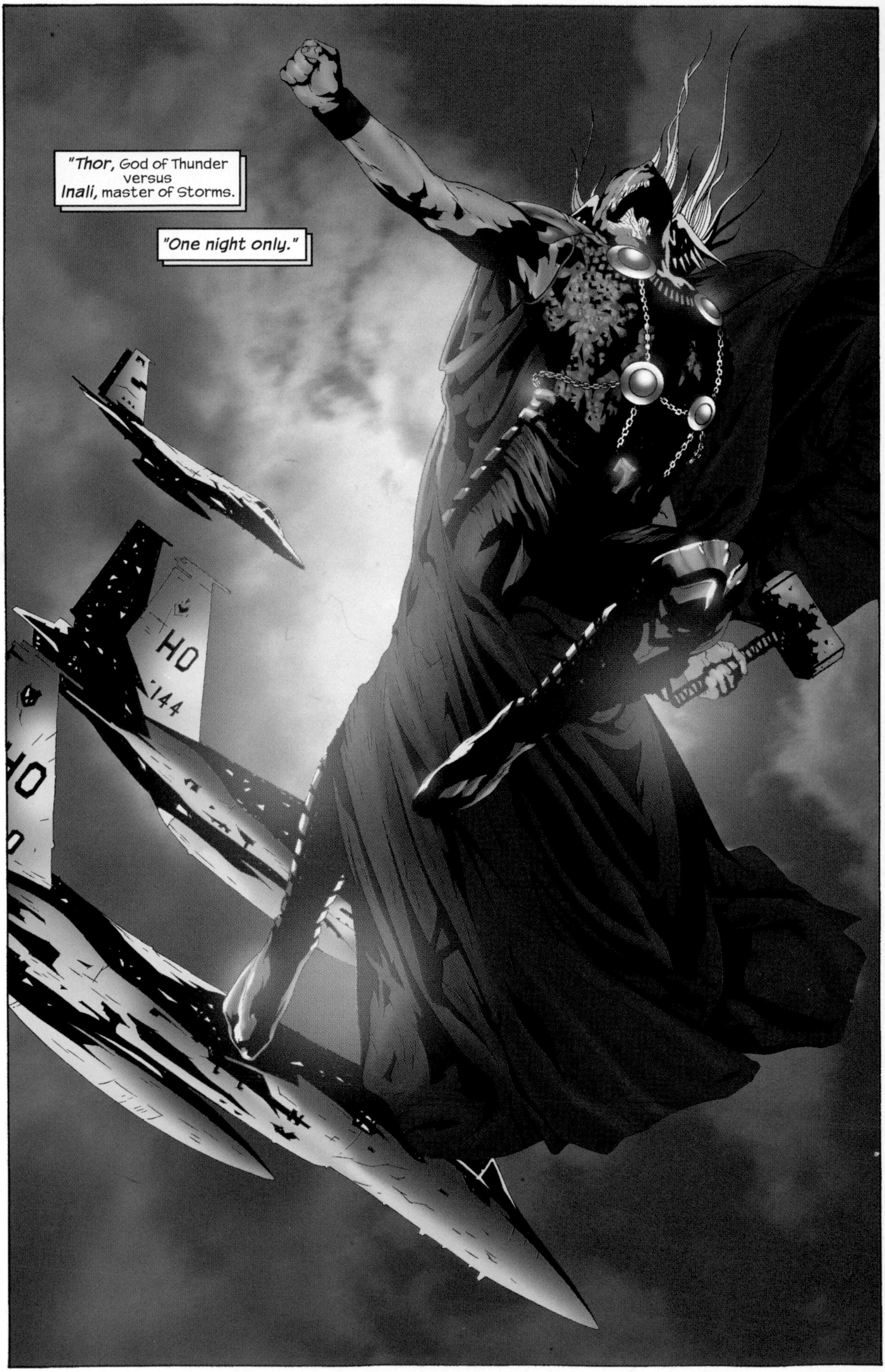
"Thor, God of Thunder versus Inali, master of Storms.
"One night only."
HO
144
HO

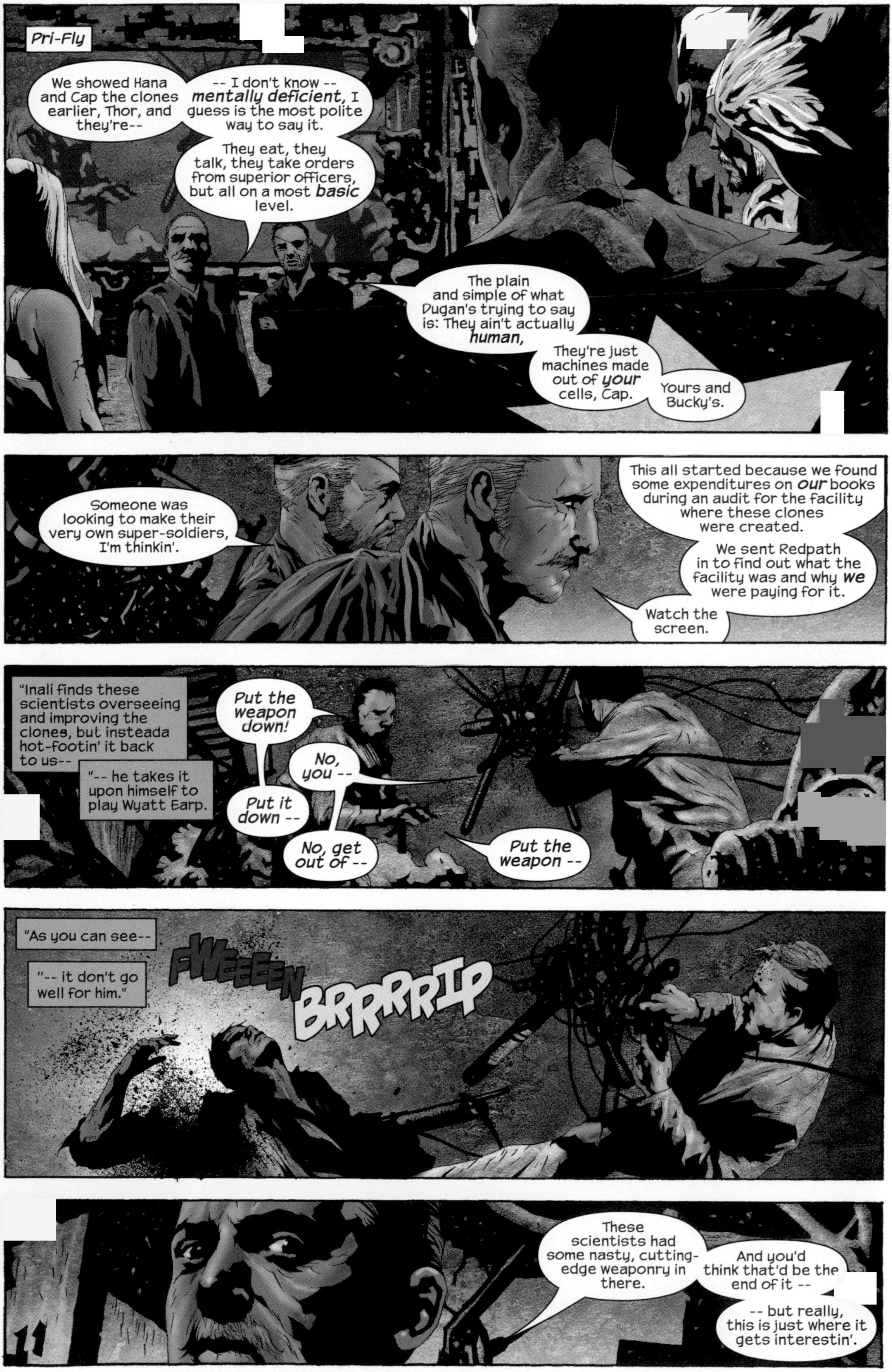

Pri-Fly
We showed Hana and Cap the clones earlier, Thor, and they're--
-- I don't know -- mentally deficient, I guess is the most polite way to say it.
They eat, they talk, they take orders from superior officers, but all on a most basic level.
The plain and simple of what Dugan's trying to say is: They ain't actually human,
They're just machines made out of your cells, Cap.
Yours and Bucky's.
Someone was looking to make their very own super-soldiers, I'm thinkin'.
This all started because we found some expenditures on our books during an audit for the facility where these clones were created.
We sent Redpath in to find out what the facility was and why we were paying for it.
Watch the screen.
"Inali finds these scientists overseeing and improving the clones, but insteada hot-footin' it back to us--
"-- he takes it upon himself to play Wyatt Earp.
Put the weapon down!
No, you --
Put it down --
No, get out of --
Put the weapon --
"As you can see--
"-- it don't go well for him."
FWEEEEN
BRRRRRIP
These scientists had some nasty, cutting-edge weaponry in there.
And you'd think that'd be the end of it --
-- but really, this is just where it gets interestin'.

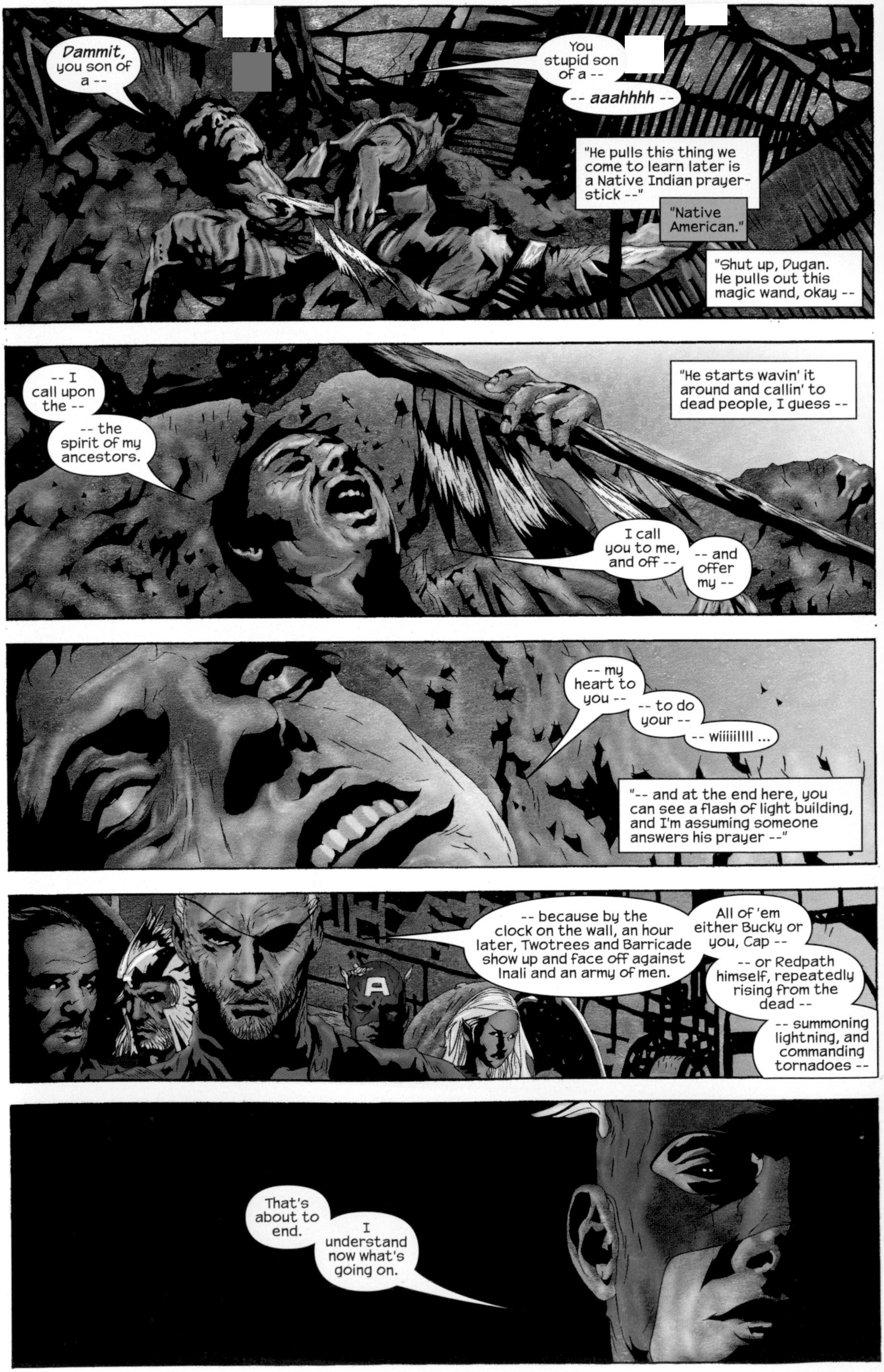

Dammit, you son of a --
You stupid son of a --
-- *aaahhhh* --
"He pulls this thing we come to learn later is a Native Indian prayer-stick --"
"Native American."
"Shut up, Dugan. He pulls out this magic wand, okay --
-- I call upon the --
-- the spirit of my ancestors.
"He starts wavin' it around and callin' to dead people, I guess --
I call you to me, and off --
-- and offer my --
-- my heart to you --
-- to do your --
-- wiiiiillll ...
"-- and at the end here, you can see a flash of light building, and I'm assuming someone answers his prayer --"
-- because by the clock on the wall, an hour later, Twotrees and Barricade show up and face off against Inali and an army of men.
All of 'em either Bucky or you, Cap --
-- or Redpath himself, repeatedly rising from the dead --
-- summoning lightning, and commanding tornadoes --
That's about to end.
I understand now what's going on.

I tell Nick my theory.

Fury tells me he intercepted conversations made from Repath's S.H.I.E.L.D. issue cel-phone.

One from Inali to S.H.I.E.L.D. HQ.

One from Inali to Twotrees.

The last from Inali to Barricade.

All calls were made from the Washington DC area.

He went immediately to the seat of government after his "death and rebirth" in Florida.

It doesn't take a genius to realize Inali most likely went *back* there, after the destruction in Miami.

It'll be two hours before the *Vengeance* --

-- S.H.I.E.L.D.'s new Sky Destroyer --

-- can get us there.

Stopping Inali is going to be a difficult, coordinated effort.

Before long, my brain is mush considering and reconsidering all the options and possibilities.

I need to clear my head before the battle --

-- and Hana joins me in the onboard gym for some mind-clearing.

She's remarkably agile, and can almost keep up with me.

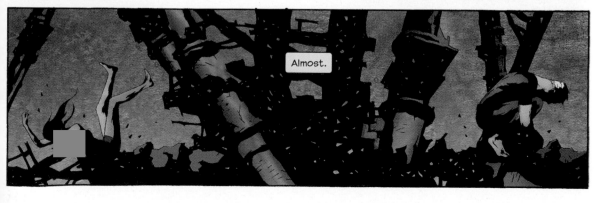

Almost.

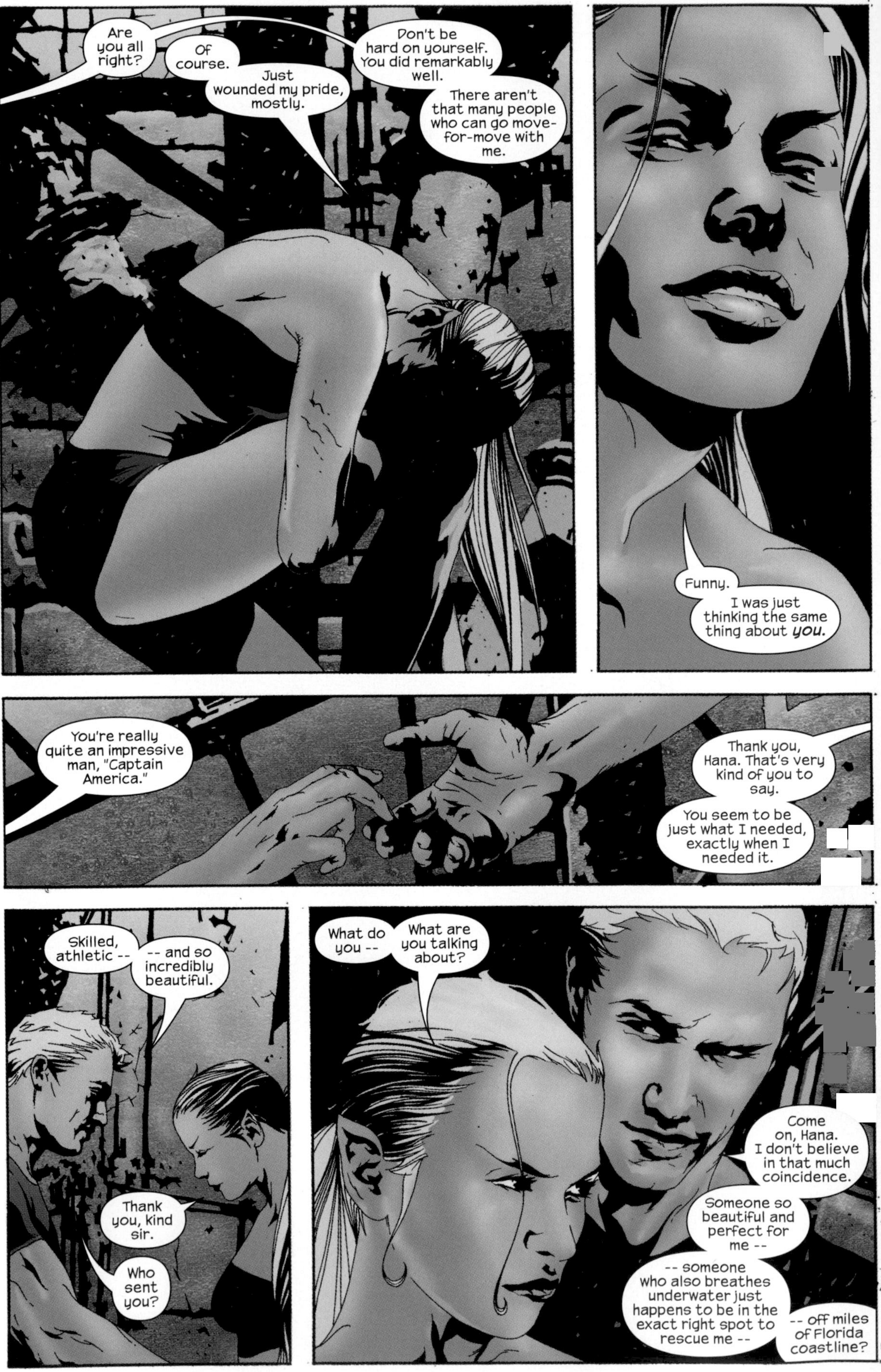
Are you all right?
Of course.
Just wounded my pride, mostly.
Don't be hard on yourself. You did remarkably well.
There aren't that many people who can go move-for-move with me.
Funny. I was just thinking the same thing about *you.*
You're really quite an impressive man, "Captain America."
Thank you, Hana. That's very kind of you to say.
You seem to be just what I needed, exactly when I needed it.
Skilled, athletic --
-- and so incredibly beautiful.
Thank you, kind sir.
Who sent you?
What do you --
What are you talking about?
Come on, Hana. I don't believe in that much coincidence.
Someone so beautiful and perfect for me --
-- someone who also breathes underwater just happens to be in the exact right spot to rescue me --
-- off miles of Florida coastline?

It's not so inconceivable, Steve.

Atlantis is not far from there.

But my level of credibility is.

The only reason I'm not pressing the point is because whoever sent you must have wanted me alive.

And as long as it stays that way, we'll be on good terms.

Have you awakened to the conspiracy around you, Steve?

This victory over Washington DC would not be so sweet without you here to be awed and pleased by it.

I pray your awakened memories have brought you to our side.

As I conjure a new storm, I pray you see the courage of my actions.

Actions motivated by your ideals. Your wisdom.

"The better American is the man who does what his heart tells him is right for the betterment of all mankind --

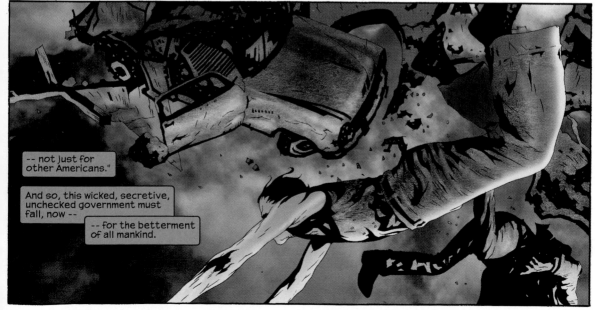

-- not just for other Americans."

And so, this wicked, secretive, unchecked government must fall, now --

-- for the betterment of all mankind.

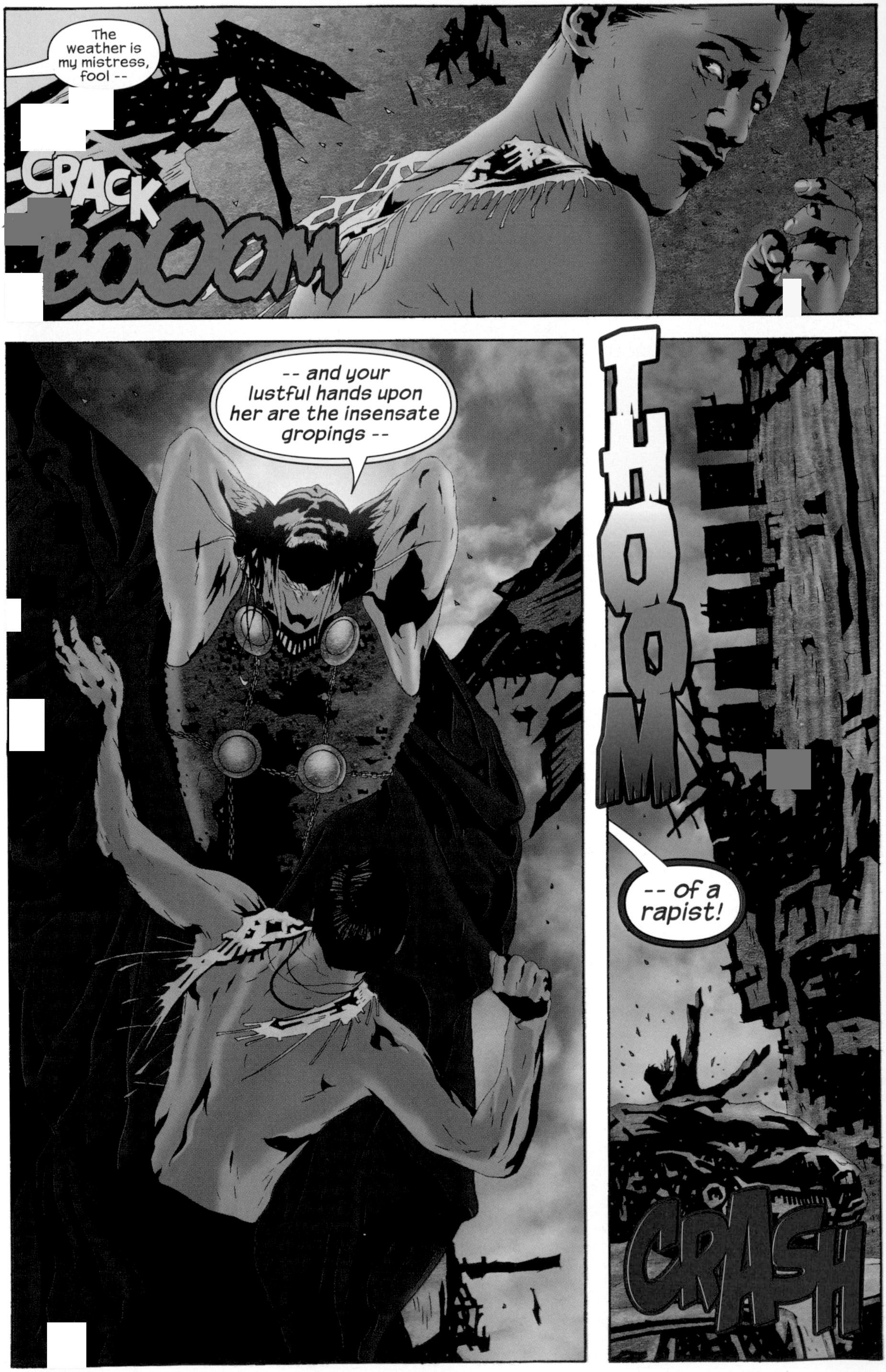
The weather is my mistress, fool --
CRACK
BOOOOM
-- and your lustful hands upon her are the insensate gropings --
THOOOM
-- of a rapist!
CRASH

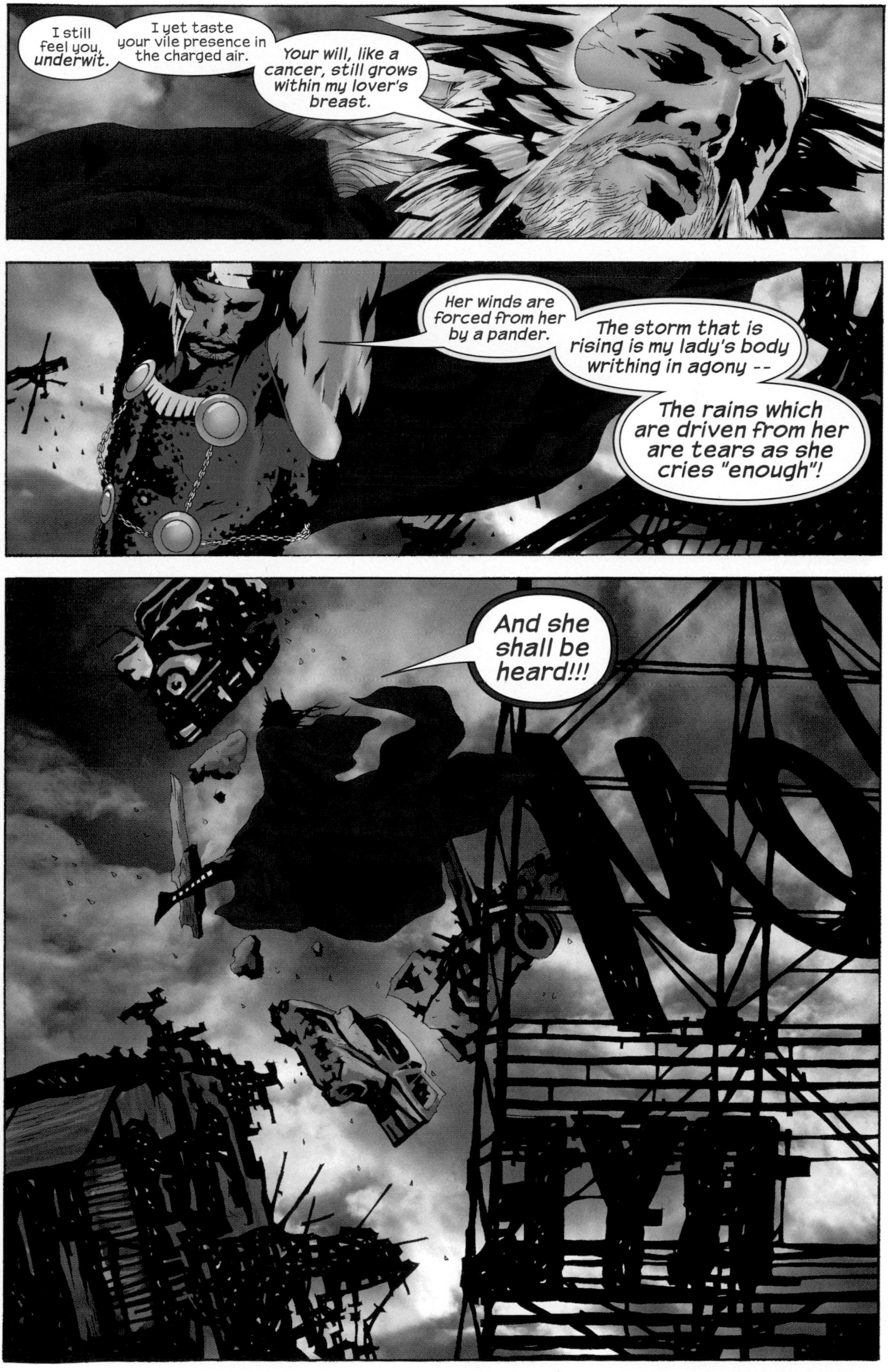
I still feel you, *underwit.*
I yet taste your vile presence in the charged air.
Your will, like a cancer, still grows within my lover's breast.
Her winds are forced from her by a pander.
The storm that is rising is my lady's body writhing in agony --
The rains which are driven from her are tears as she cries "enough"!
And she shall be heard!!!

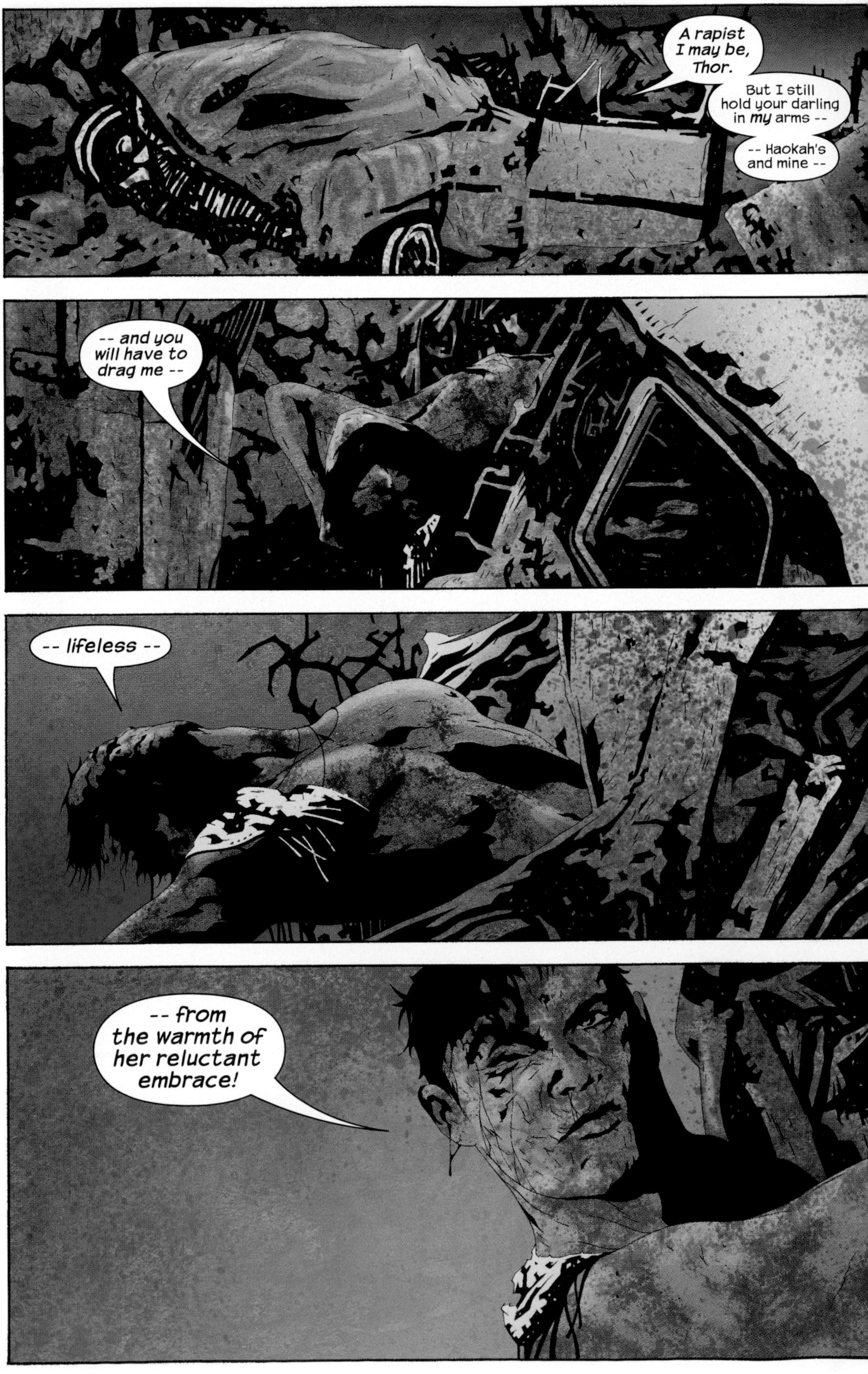
A rapist I may be, Thor.
But I still hold your darling in *my* arms --
-- Haokah's and mine --
-- and you will have to drag me --
-- lifeless --
-- from the warmth of her reluctant embrace!

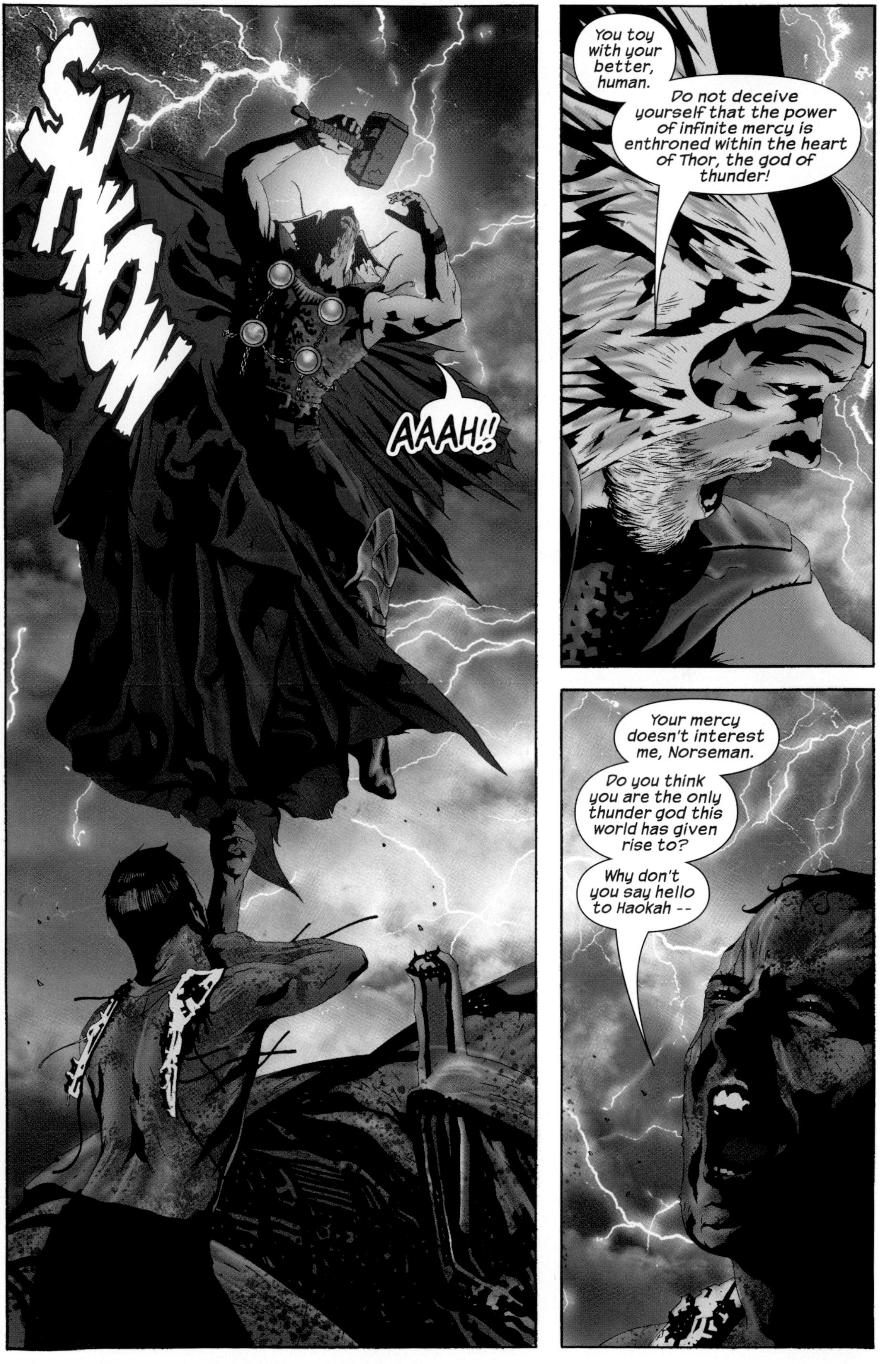
SHOOM
AAAH!!
You toy with your better, human.
Do not deceive yourself that the power of infinite mercy is enthroned within the heart of Thor, the god of thunder!
Your mercy doesn't interest me, Norseman.
Do you think you are the only thunder god this world has given rise to?
Why don't you say hello to Haokah --

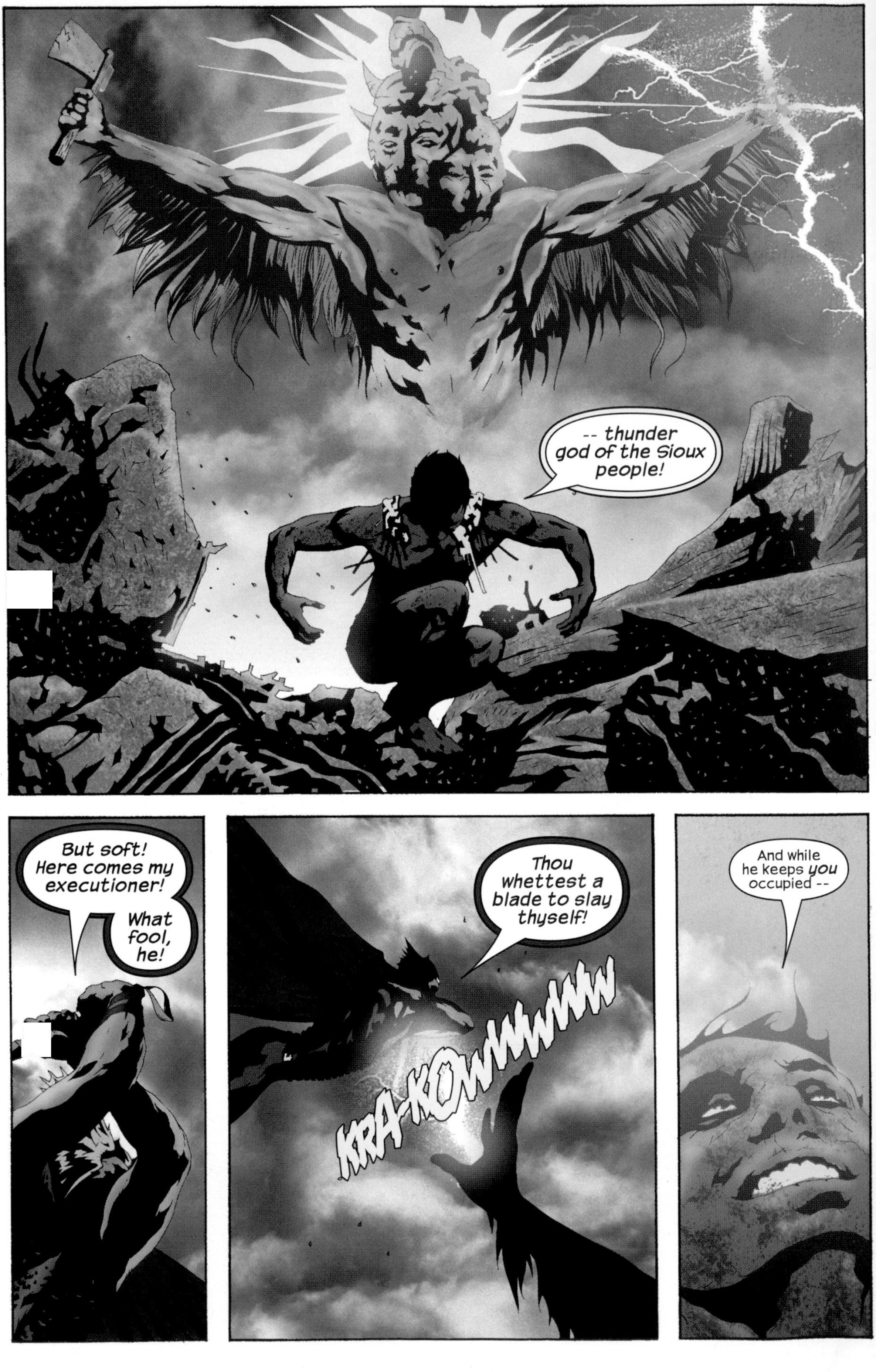
-- thunder god of the Sioux people!
But soft! Here comes my executioner!
What fool, he!
Thou whettest a blade to slay thyself!
KRA-KOWWWWW
And while he keeps you occupied --

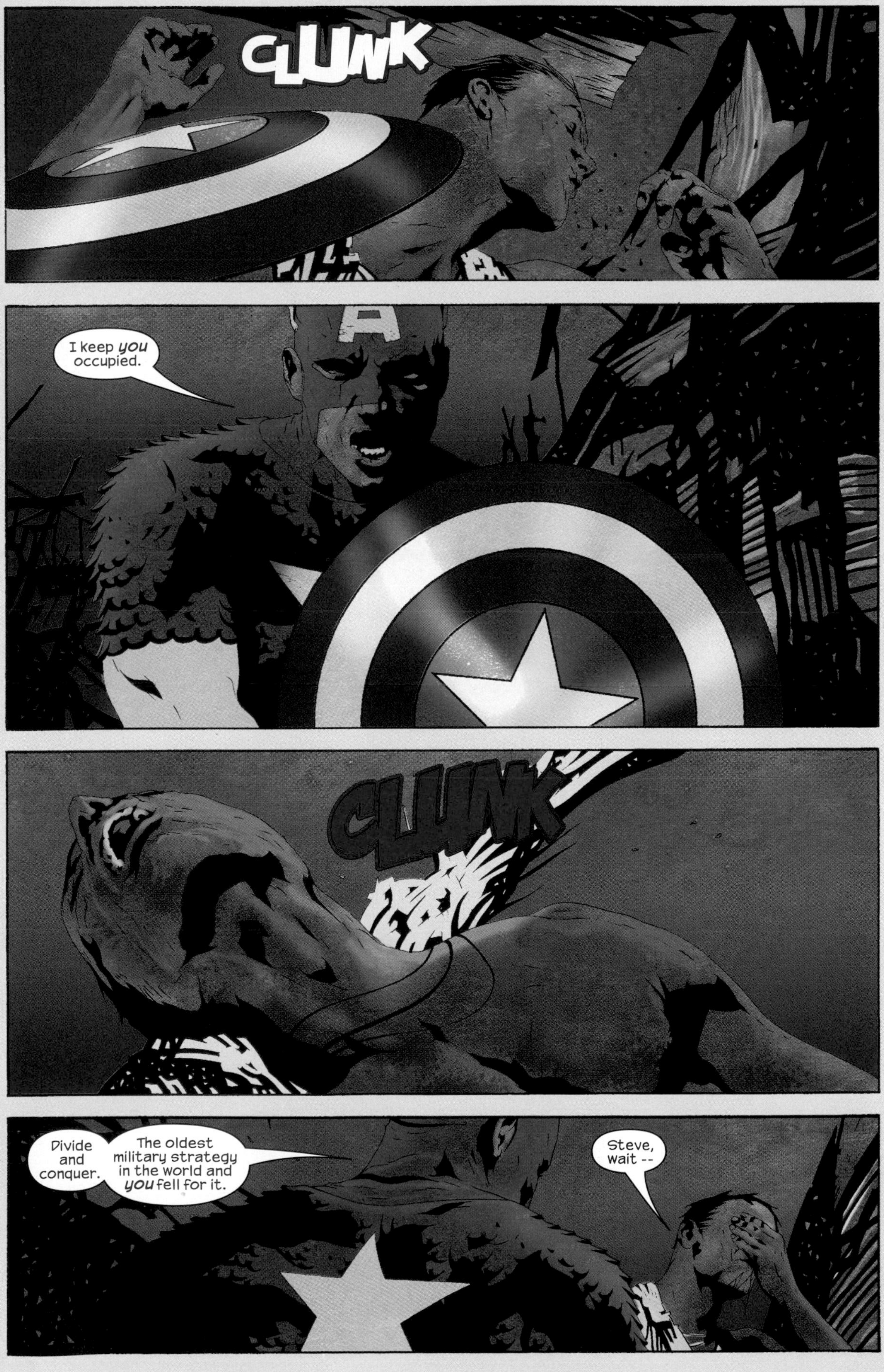
CLUNK
I keep *you* occupied.
CLUNK
Divide and conquer.
The oldest military strategy in the world and *you* fell for it.
Steve, wait --

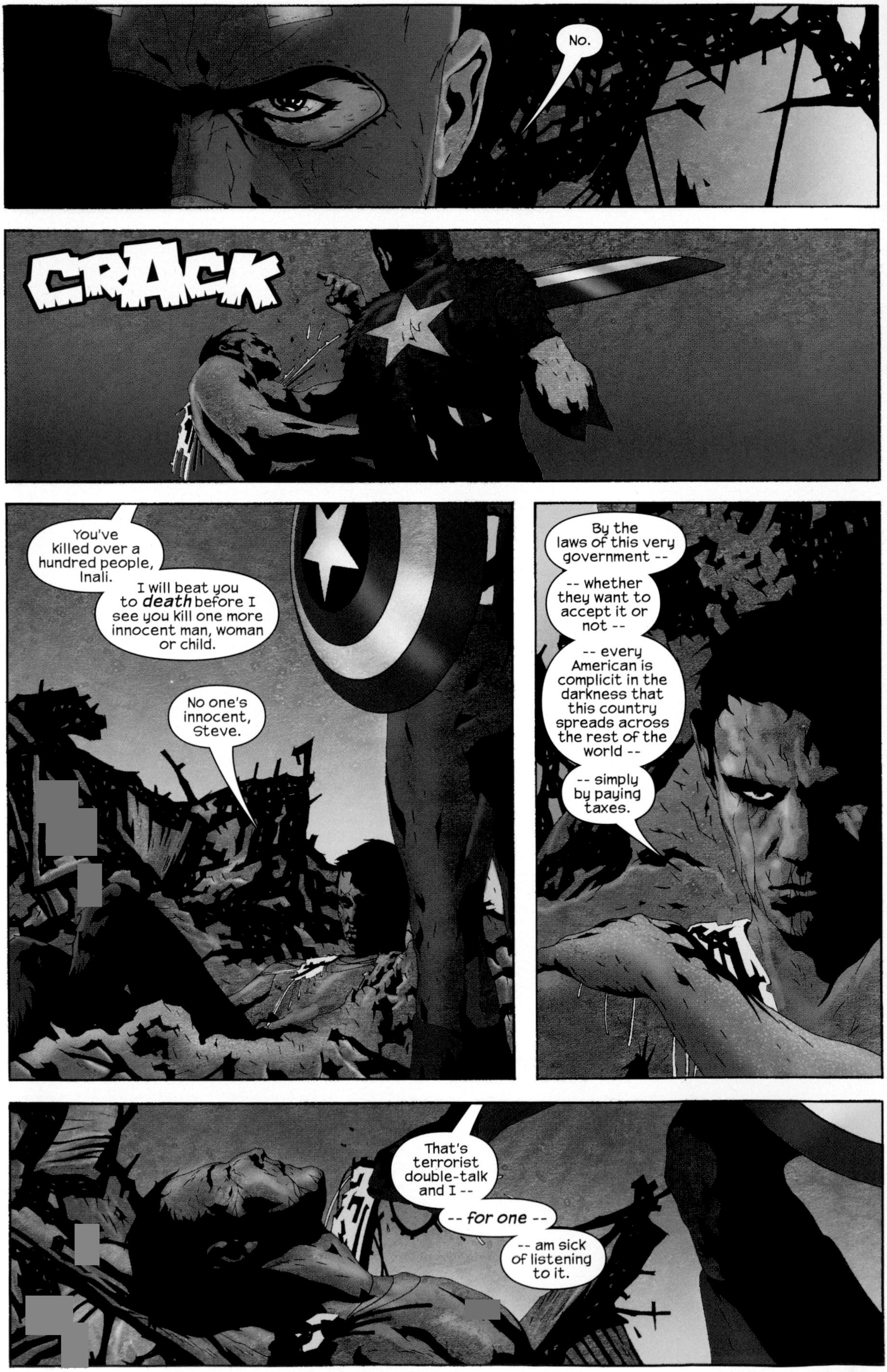
No.
CRACK
You've killed over a hundred people, Inali.
I will beat you to *death* before I see you kill one more innocent man, woman or child.
No one's innocent, Steve.
By the laws of this very government --
-- whether they want to accept it or not --
-- every American is complicit in the darkness that this country spreads across the rest of the world --
-- simply by paying taxes.
That's terrorist double-talk and I --
-- *for one* --
-- am sick of listening to it.

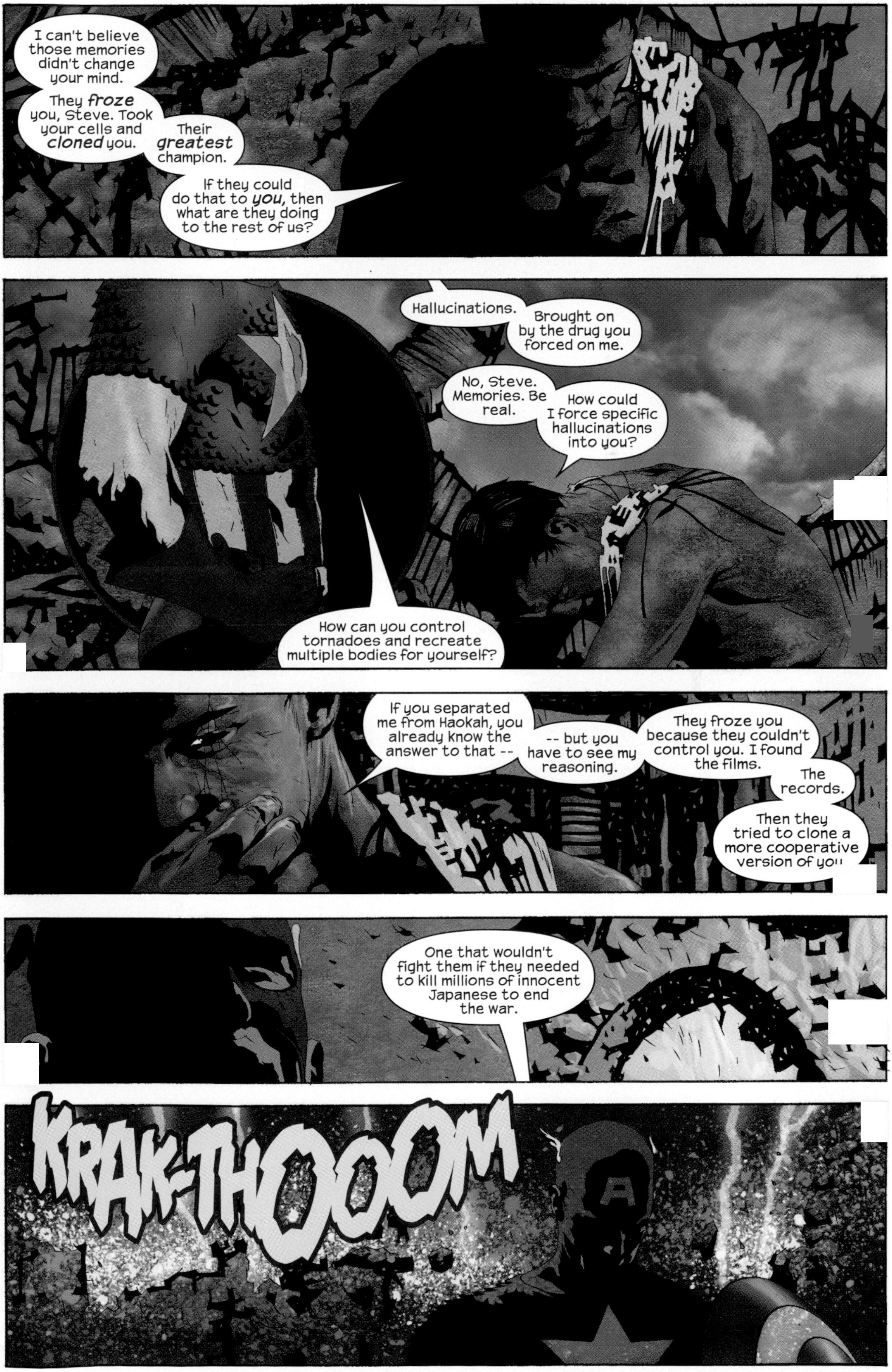

I can't believe those memories didn't change your mind.
They *froze* you, Steve. Took your cells and *cloned* you.
Their *greatest* champion.
If they could do that to *you*, then what are they doing to the rest of us?
Hallucinations.
Brought on by the drug you forced on me.
No, Steve. Memories. Be real.
How could I force specific hallucinations into you?
How can you control tornadoes and recreate multiple bodies for yourself?
If you separated me from Haokah, you already know the answer to that --
-- but you have to see my reasoning.
They froze you because they couldn't control you. I found the films.
The records.
Then they tried to clone a more cooperative version of you.
One that wouldn't fight them if they needed to kill millions of innocent Japanese to end the war.
KRAK-THOOOM

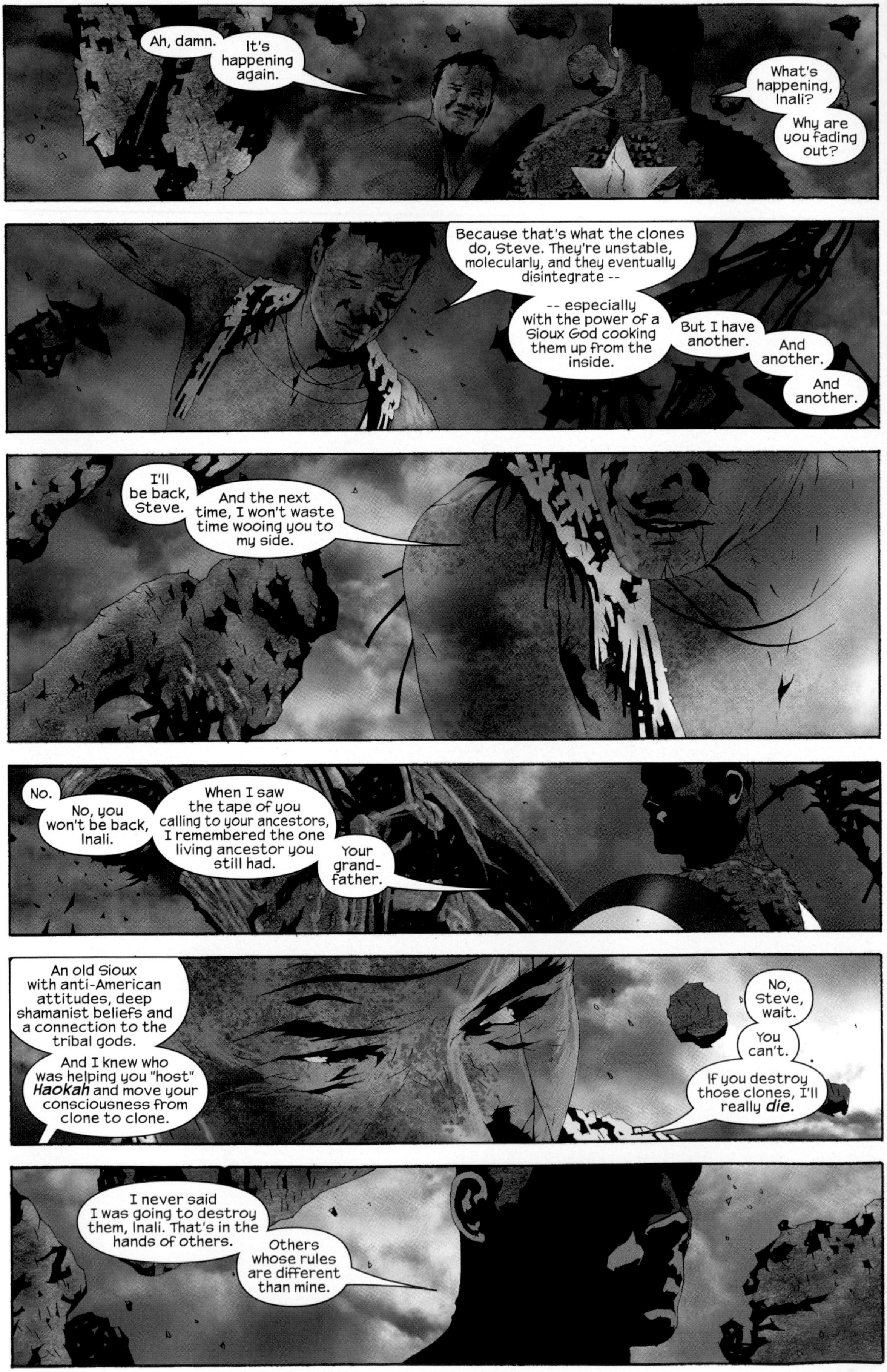
Ah, damn.
It's happening again.
What's happening, Inali?
Why are you fading out?
Because that's what the clones do, Steve. They're unstable, molecularly, and they eventually disintegrate --
-- especially with the power of a Sioux God cooking them up from the inside.
But I have another.
And another.
And another.
I'll be back, Steve.
And the next time, I won't waste time wooing you to my side.
No.
No, you won't be back, Inali.
When I saw the tape of you calling to your ancestors, I remembered the one living ancestor you still had.
Your grand-father.
An old Sioux with anti-American attitudes, deep shamanist beliefs and a connection to the tribal gods.
And I knew who was helping you "host" *Haokah* and move your consciousness from clone to clone.
No, Steve, wait.
You can't.
If you destroy those clones, I'll really *die.*
I never said I was going to destroy them, Inali. That's in the hands of others.
Others whose rules are different than mine.

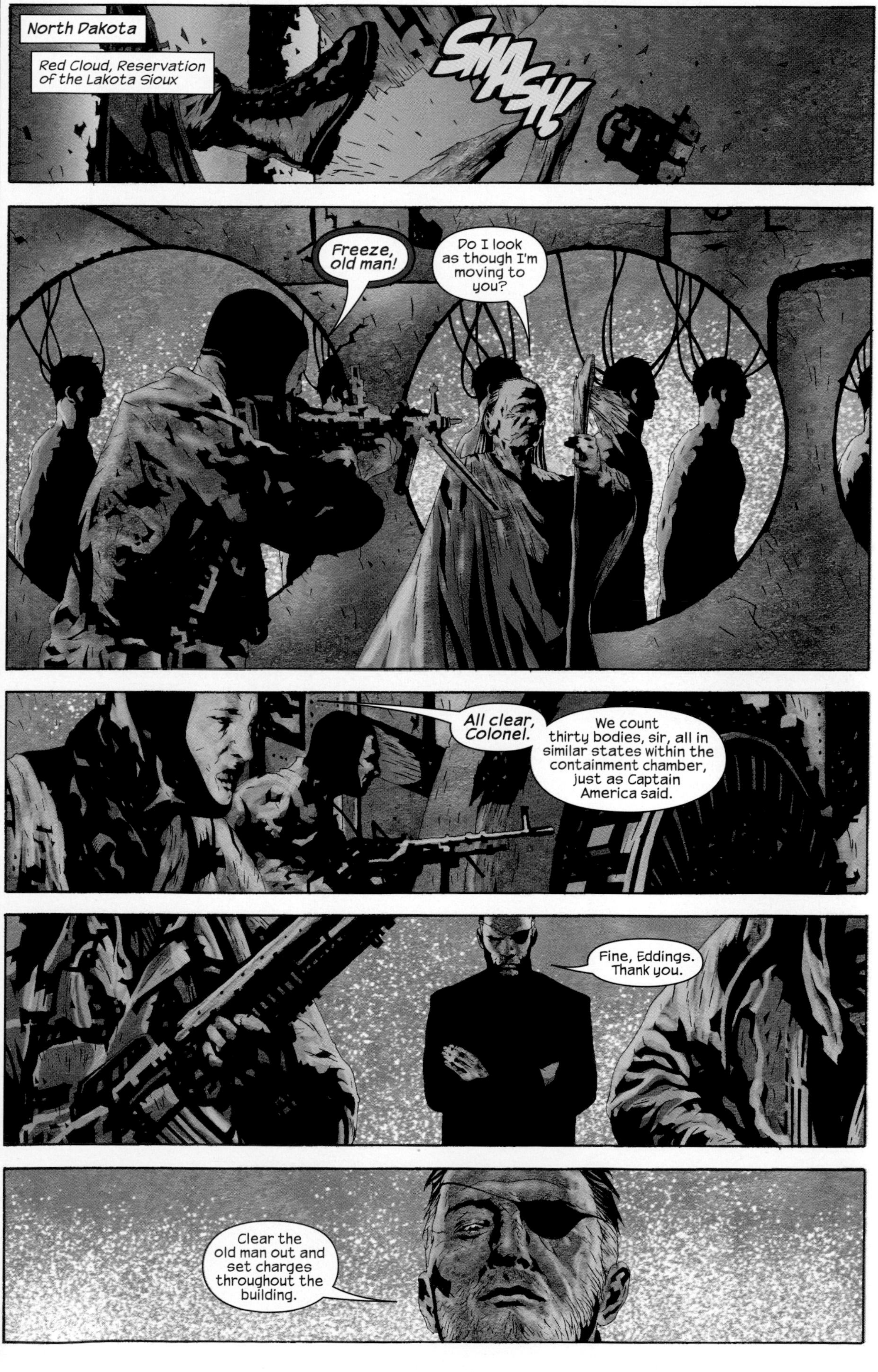
North Dakota
Red Cloud, Reservation of the Lakota Sioux
SMASH!
Freeze, old man!
Do I look as though I'm moving to you?
All clear, Colonel.
We count thirty bodies, sir, all in similar states within the containment chamber, just as Captain America said.
Fine, Eddings. Thank you.
Clear the old man out and set charges throughout the building.

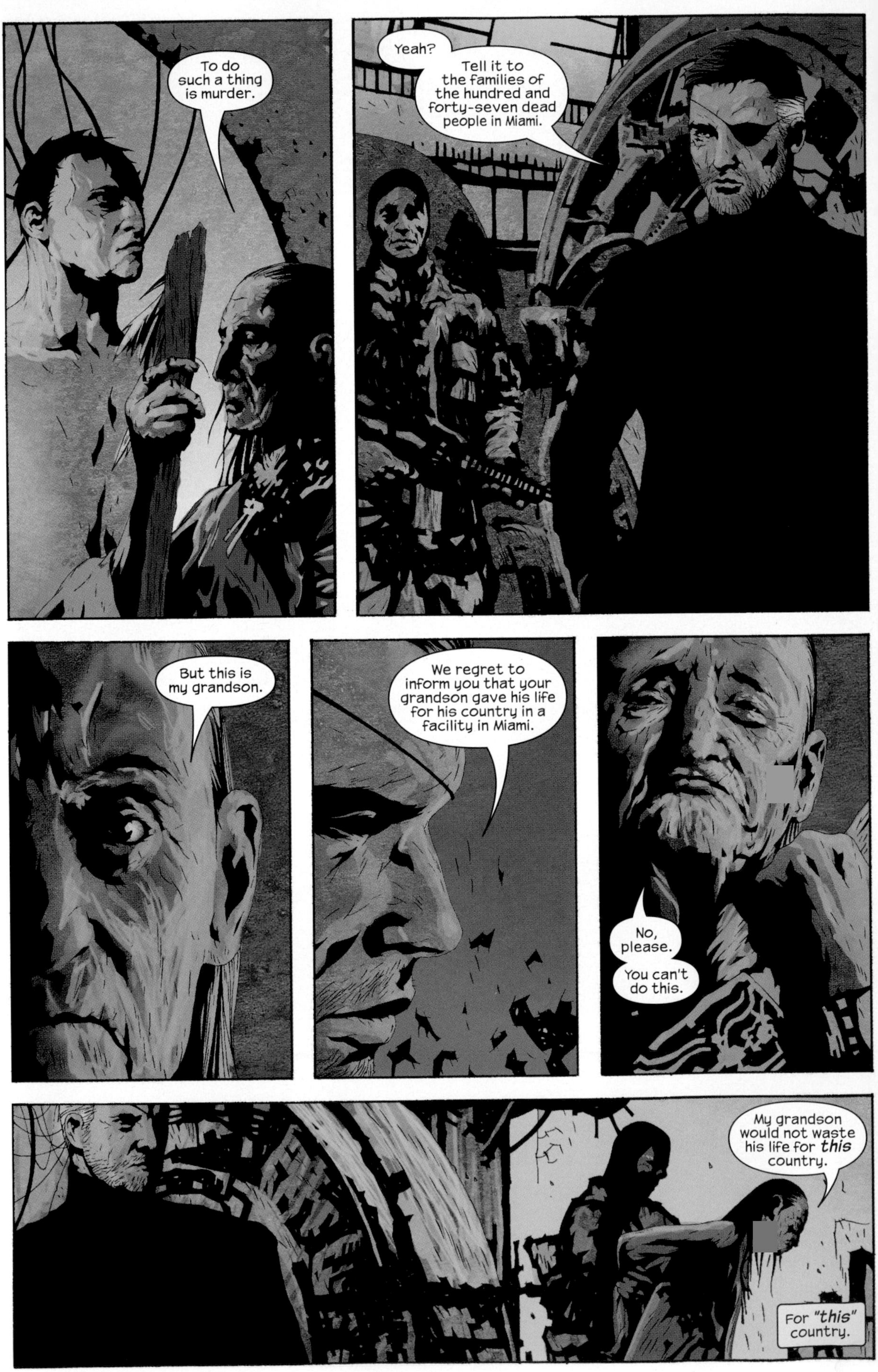

To do such a thing is murder.
Yeah?
Tell it to the families of the hundred and forty-seven dead people in Miami.
But this is my grandson.
We regret to inform you that your grandson gave his life for his country in a facility in Miami.
No, please.
You can't do this.
My grandson would not waste his life for *this* country.
For "*this*" country.

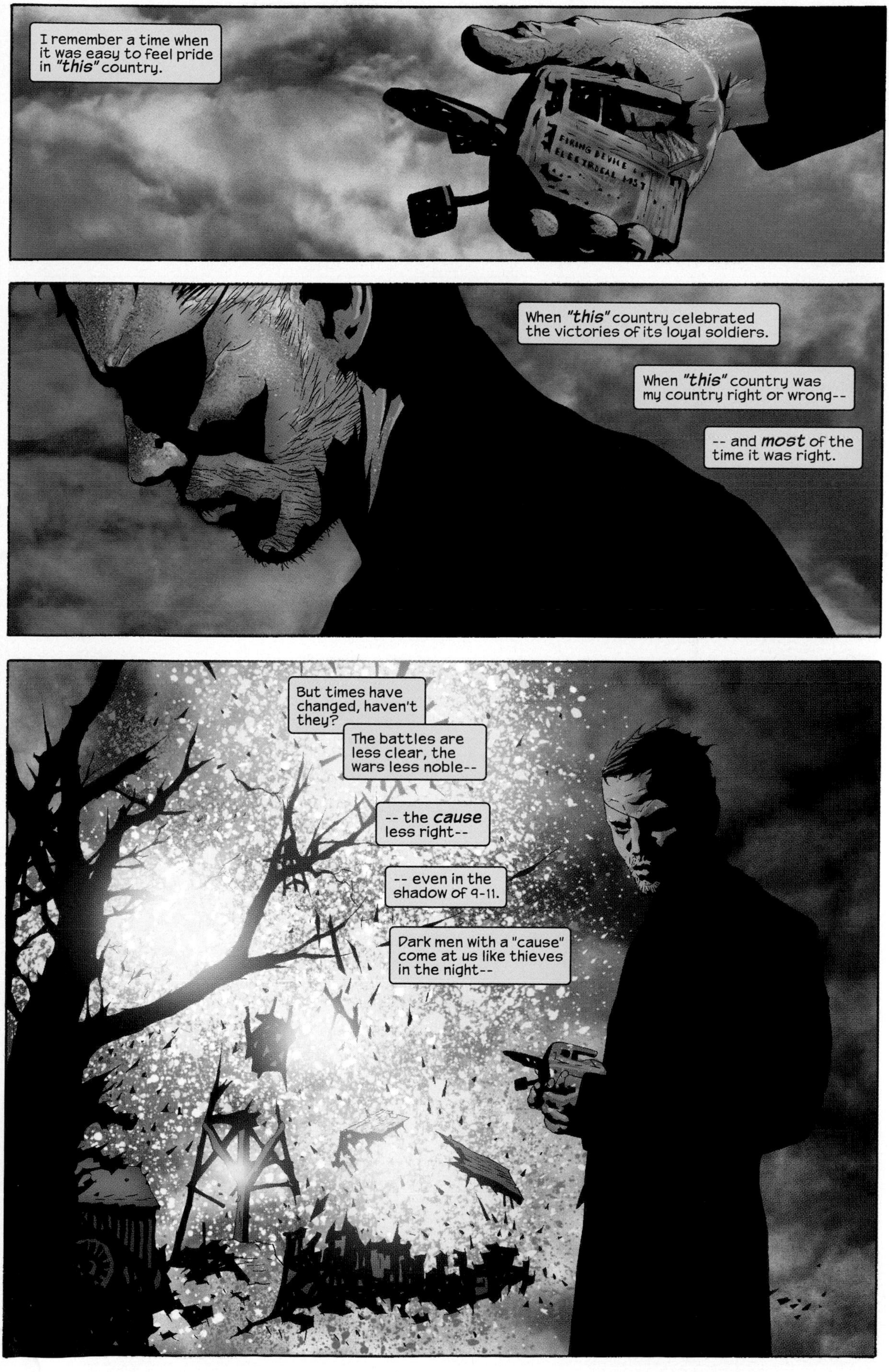
I remember a time when it was easy to feel pride in *"this"* country.
When *"this"* country celebrated the victories of its loyal soldiers.
When *"this"* country was my country right or wrong--
-- and ***most*** of the time it was right.
But times have changed, haven't they?
The battles are less clear, the wars less noble--
-- the ***cause*** less right--
-- even in the shadow of 9-11.
Dark men with a "cause" come at us like thieves in the night--

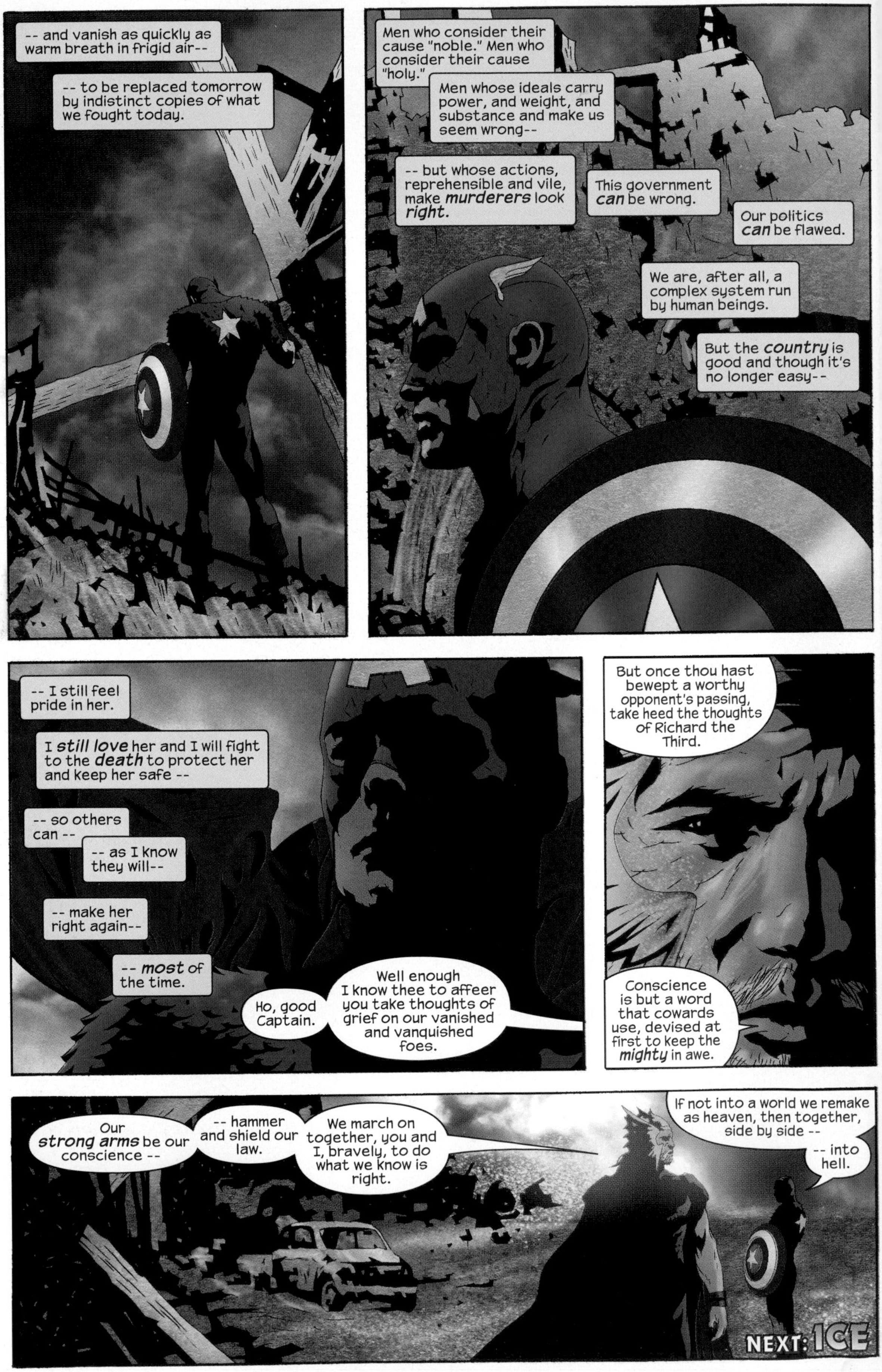

-- and vanish as quickly as warm breath in frigid air--
-- to be replaced tomorrow by indistinct copies of what we fought today.
Men who consider their cause "noble." Men who consider their cause "holy."
Men whose ideals carry power, and weight, and substance and make us seem wrong--
-- but whose actions, reprehensible and vile, make *murderers* look *right.*
This government *can* be wrong.
Our politics *can* be flawed.
We are, after all, a complex system run by human beings.
But the *country* is good and though it's no longer easy--
-- I still feel pride in her.
I *still love* her and I will fight to the *death* to protect her and keep her safe --
-- so others can --
-- as I know they will--
-- make her right again--
-- *most* of the time.
Ho, good Captain.
Well enough I know thee to affeer you take thoughts of grief on our vanished and vanquished foes.
But once thou hast bewept a worthy opponent's passing, take heed the thoughts of Richard the Third.
Conscience is but a word that cowards use, devised at first to keep the *mighty* in awe.
Our *strong arms* be our conscience --
-- hammer and shield our law.
We march on together, you and I, bravely, to do what we know is right.
If not into a world we remake as heaven, then together, side by side --
-- into hell.
NEXT: ICE